# Before He Wakes

# BEFORE
# HE WAKES

A True Story of Money,
Marriage, Sex and Murder

## Jerry Bledsoe

A DUTTON BOOK

DUTTON
Published by the Penguin Group
Penguin Books USA Inc., 375 Hudson Street,
New York, New York 10014, U.S.A.
Penguin Books Ltd, 27 Wrights Lane, London W8 5TZ, England
Penguin Books Australia Ltd, Ringwood, Victoria, Australia
Penguin Books Canada Ltd, 10 Alcorn Avenue,
Toronto, Ontario, Canada M4V 3B2
Penguin Books (N.Z.) Ltd, 182–190 Wairau Road, Auckland 10, New Zealand

Penguin Books Ltd, Registered Offices: Harmondsworth, Middlesex, England

First published by Dutton, an imprint of Dutton Signet,
a division of Penguin Books USA Inc.
Distributed in Canada by McClelland & Stewart Inc.

First Printing, August, 1994

10  9  8  7  6  5  4  3  2  1

 REGISTERED TRADEMARK—MARCA REGISTRADA

Library of Congress Cataloging-in-Publication Data:
Bledsoe, Jerry.
  Before he wakes : a true story of money, marriage, sex, and murder / Jerry Bledsoe.
    p.    cm.
  ISBN 0-525-93826-5
  1. Murder—North Carolina—Case studies. 2. Husbands—Crimes against—Case
studies. I. Title.
HV6533.N8B53   1994
364.1′523′09756563—dc20                                              94–1782
                                                                       CIP

Printed in the United States of America
Set in Garamond Light

*For The Spring Break Brunch—Karl Hill, Jim Jenkins,
Bill Lee, Stan Swofford, Nat Walker, Ernie Wyatt,
and to the memory of Jim McAllister*

# Acknowledgments

This book evolved from a series of articles that appeared in the *Greensboro* (N.C.) *News & Record.* Libby Lewis and I worked together on that series, which was edited by Cole Campbell. Ned Cline allowed that series to run at length and scrounged extra space for it at the last minute when it ran even longer than expected. The *News & Record* not only granted me permission to use material and photographs from that series in this book, it gave me leave to work on it, and while I have not been employed at the newspaper for several years now, my heart is still there. The title of this book was the title of one segment of that series. It was suggested by Diane Luber. Many people contributed to this book and I am grateful to all. I owe particular thanks to Doris and Henry Ford, Doris Stager, Jo Lynn Snow, Rick Buchanan, Bill Cotter, Eric Evenson and Ron Stephens. Dot Shoaf of the Durham County District Attorney's office was especially helpful, and my friend Joe John of the North Carolina Court of Appeals was always willing to answer my legal questions. John Paine's suggestions made this a better book. Some names in this book have been changed to protect privacy. They are marked with an asterisk on first use.

# Contents

*The heart is deceitful above all things,
and desperately wicked. Who can know it?*

—JEREMIAH 17:9

# PART ONE

# An Incident on Fox Drive

# Chapter One

The hour before dawn was always the quietest. Criminals had retired for the night, and most decent citizens were not yet up to crash their cars, start fires, get into squabbles, have heart attacks or find other ways to create havoc. This was the time for police officers to take a break, catch up on report writing or stop for coffee and early breakfasts.

The city of Durham, North Carolina, was just beginning to stir to a new work week on this Monday morning. High-intensity lights still cast an orange glow over nearly deserted downtown streets. The sweet, pungent aroma that always hovered in the air of the second-biggest cigarette-making city in a tobacco state was even stronger than usual this morning, held close to the ground by low-lying clouds. Dawn would come gray and damp, unusually warm for a day so deep in winter.

In the basement of the Durham Police Department headquarters, the five dispatchers who received all of Durham County's emergency calls had no hint of the weather outside. Isolated in the glass-enclosed radio room, they were nearing the end of their twelve-hour shift, wondering if six-thirty would ever come. Radio traffic had all but died, and there had been no telephone calls for more than an hour. The dispatchers were beginning to unwind. Normally they would have been chatting about the events of the night, but this had been a quieter night than usual, leaving them nothing to discuss. To fill the void, Terry Russell started to tell a joke he'd heard the day before. He was interrupted by a light that began flashing on every console, accompanied by the irritating buzz of the 911 emergency line.

Barbara Parson was first to reach to stop the noise by punching the flashing button. "Durham County nine-eleven," she said.

"Can you send an ambulance to twenty-eight-thirty-three Fox Drive?" asked a frightened and plaintive voice so high-pitched that Parson thought she was talking to a young girl.

"What's the problem?" she asked, reaching for an ambulance dispatch card. She could tell that the child was terribly upset, and as a mother she felt the little clutch at her throat that always arose when a child in trouble called.

"My father had a gun and it went off."

"Where is he shot, ma'am?" Parson asked, at the same time inserting the card into the time clock that recorded the date and time of the call: February 1, 1988, 6:08 A.M.

"I'm not sure, but just do it, please!"

"Is he conscious?" Parson pressed. She had to have information for the emergency medical technicians so that they would know what to expect. It could mean the difference between life and death.

"I don't know. My mom told me to call."

Durham County had not yet turned to computers for its dispatch room, and as Parson had been talking into her headset, she was wheeling her chair toward one of the two big circular files in the center of the room. The files contained the locations of every street and road in the county. She quickly thumbed up Fox Drive, only to discover that there were two in the county, and she had to question the child about nearby streets so the emergency vehicles wouldn't go to the wrong location.

Turning to another console, she activated electronic tones alerting the Lebanon Volunteer Fire Department and Durham County Hospital Ambulance Service to an emergency. Before she hung up, her motherly concern caused her to ask one more question of the child.

"Are you all right?"

"Yes," said the child, "just hurry."

Parson disconnected the line and called the Durham County Sheriff's dispatch room just a block away in the courthouse to tell them about the shooting in one of Durham's most prosperous northern suburbs.

\* \* \*

A shrill, piercing beep stirred Doug Griffin from sleep. He reached instinctively for the pager in its bedside charger to keep it from waking his wife and two children.

An architect, Griffin felt a strong duty to community. That was why he had joined the Lebanon Volunteer Fire Department four years earlier and become a first responder. First responders were trained in basic emergency medical care. Scattered throughout the county, they could reach victims long before an ambulance arrived, giving first aid that greatly increased chances for survival. Helping to save lives gave Griffin deep satisfaction.

"Subject shot," he heard Barbara Parson's matter-of-fact voice as he climbed out of bed. "Twenty-eight-thirty-three Fox Drive." That was only a few blocks from Griffin's house.

A short, dark-haired man with a neatly trimmed full beard, Griffin pulled on a blue jumpsuit that he kept on a nearby chair for nighttime emergencies, slipped on jogging shoes and hurried outside into the misty predawn darkness. He climbed into his white Volvo, and as he was leaving his driveway, he picked up a red light from the seat beside him, plugged it into the cigarette lighter, placed it on the dashboard and accelerated into the empty morning streets.

The house on Fox Drive was set back from the road, hidden by a stand of trees and thick undergrowth, its presence marked only by a black mailbox at the foot of a long concrete drive, and Griffin drove by it at first. He realized his mistake and turned around in the next driveway. As he headed up the drive, he saw a modern house, one section of the front pointed like the prow of a ship, with huge angled picture windows set in a facade of brown and gray stone.

A boy barely in his teens stood just inside the open doors of the double garage at the back of the house. He looked as if he had dressed quickly and incompletely, and he was scared and bewildered, almost in shock.

"Who's shot?" Griffin asked as he jumped from the car, but the boy said nothing.

Griffin asked again after fetching his hard plastic blue first aid case from the trunk of his car and heading for the garage.

"He's in the last bedroom," the boy finally said. "Go left, then right, down the hall."

"You stay here and direct the others," Griffin told him. Already he'd seen his department's assistant chief, James Wingate, pull up at the foot of the drive.

Griffin had one cardinal purpose: reaching the patient and helping him. But as he entered the house through the kitchen, he was overcome by a feeling he later described as "spooky." He had no idea who had been shot, how or by whom. Could somebody with a cocked and loaded gun be lurking there in wait?

The thought unnerved him, but he continued on, turning into a dark hallway, pounding the wall with his fist to announce his presence.

"Lebanon Fire Department," he called. "Anyone here? Did you call an ambulance?"

As he neared the door at the end of the hallway, Griffin noticed that it was open a few inches. Suddenly a light came on in the room, the door opened and a disheveled and distraught woman in owlish glasses appeared before him. She was short and blond, maybe in her late thirties, wearing only a large red and green plaid flannel shirt that drooped from her narrow shoulders and reached well below her waist.

"Is someone hurt?" Griffin asked.

The woman gestured toward a king-size bed with a brass headboard, where a stocky, muscular man lay on his left side under a flowered bedcover.

The man was snoring loudly, and Griffin's first impulse was to try to shake him awake, but as he rounded the end of the bed, he saw a bloodstain spreading darkly across the back of the pillow under the man's head.

While the woman stood watching from the opposite side of the bed, Griffin felt for a pulse and found it racing wildly. The left side of the man's head was buried in the pillow, his left eye obscured, and Griffin rotated his head slightly to get his nose and mouth out of the pillow and to check for breathing restrictions. Blood and mucus were choking the man, the blood oozing from his mouth and nostrils and running down the side of his face. Simply moving the man's head caused his breathing to come easier, though, and Griffin reached into his kit for a blood pressure gauge.

James Wingate, a contractor and captain in the Lebanon Volunteer Fire Department, had left his pickup truck on the street with emergency lights flashing to mark the site for other rescuers.

A rotund, balding neighbor of Griffin's, he hurried into the room carrying his trauma box, an oxygen bottle, squeeze airbag and radio.

"What've we got?" he asked.

"Gunshot," Griffin said. "Looks like it's to the head."

The man was unconscious, his eyes rolled back and dilated, his face ashen gray, but his body was warm and dry, with normal color. Wingate took out a clipboard and began recording vital statistics as Griffin called them out. Blood pressure was 170/120. The man was breathing at twenty breaths per minute. Wingate radioed the information to Barbara Parson so that she could relay it to the ambulance crew, which was on its way.

Wingate readied an oxygen mask, but it couldn't be applied because of the bleeding from the mouth and nose, and he placed it on the pillow by the man's head. Both men donned rubber gloves to search the man's blood-matted hair for a wound so that they could control the bleeding, but they found only what at first appeared to be an abrasion behind the left ear. As they looked, the woman, who was now sitting on the foot of the bed, began crying, asking, "Why does he keep those things in here?"

"What happened?" Wingate asked her.

She told him that she had been pulling a gun out from under her husband's pillow when it discharged. Her husband had been hearing sounds outside the house recently and was concerned about burglars, she said. The gun was for protection. He had put it under his pillow the night before. This morning, when she heard her son get up and go to the bathroom, she reached to remove the pistol in case her husband woke up and thought somebody was in the house. It just went off, she said.

Bob Hunt, another first responder, was the third emergency worker to enter the room. He immediately recognized the woman talking with Wingate. He knew the man in the bed, too. He was Russ Stager, forty years old, a member of his church and a popular coach at Durham High School.

Hunt was shocked. His wife, Brenda, had been friends since childhood with Russ's wife, Barbara. But Barbara showed no sign of recognizing him.

As Griffin and Wingate turned Russ's head to begin suctioning the blood and mucus from his air passages, the pillow shifted, and Griffin saw a pistol.

It was a small black .25-caliber semiautomatic Beretta with plastic grips, lying between the two pillows, the barrel aimed at his patient's head. A spent shell lay only a few inches away.

Griffin saw that the pistol was cocked, a potential danger. He automatically reached for it, then caught himself. He had been drilled not to touch anything that might be evidence.

"That's okay," the woman said, noticing his hesitation. "I've already moved it."

Still, Griffin's training wouldn't allow him to touch it. A Durham County Sheriff's deputy, Clark Green, now entered the room. He had been on his way into town to refuel after a night of patrolling county roads when he heard the Fox Drive call. He had been concerned because he had friends who lived on the street. Racing to answer the call, he was relieved to discover that the emergency was next door to his friends' house.

"What happened?" he asked.

"An accidental shooting," one of the first responders told him.

The ambulance arrived, and with it Tom Scott, a paramedic. The first responders yielded to his greater experience, and he began to administer to the man in the bed, whose blood pressure had started falling quickly, his pulse racing. At 6:18 his blood pressure was 170/110, four minutes later 140/102. During the same period, his pulse went from 120 beats per minute to 130. This was known as the Cushing reflex, and it was typical of patients with head injuries who were bleeding. Since Russ was not bleeding externally, Scott knew that his cranium was filling with blood, and if it could not be stopped and his condition stabilized, the increasing pressure on his brain would soon kill him.

As worried as they were about their patient, the rescue workers also had another concern: the cocked pistol still lying on the bed. If it had gone off so easily once, might it not do so again? Clark Green was unfamiliar with .25 semiautomatics, though, and was reluctant to handle it. Another deputy, Paul Hornbuckle, had arrived and he picked it up by inserting a ballpoint pen into the trigger guard. He was carrying it into the hallway to disarm it when Kevin Wilson rushed into the house. A tall, thin man with glasses and a thick mustache, Wilson saw the gun pointing in his direction as he entered the hallway and called out to let the officer know that he was there, causing Hornbuckle to swing the pistol barrel away from him.

Not only was Wilson a captain in the Lebanon Fire Department, he also was in charge of emergency medical training in the county and was by far the most experienced medical technician at the scene. Seeing Tom Scott working on the man in the bed, he asked, "What can I do?"

"He's got a lot of blood in the oropharynx," Scott said.

Wilson climbed onto the bed to assist him. The man's face was now covered with blood, and Wilson had no idea who he was. As he donned a stethoscope to listen to the patient's heart and lungs, he was distracted by a woman's voice saying, "My God, I'm scared of these guns. I wish he wouldn't keep them there." He looked up and realized that he knew the woman. She was Barbara Stager. While the first responders had been working on Russ, she had slipped into the bathroom and changed clothes, emerging in blue jeans, a gray and blue sweatshirt and sneakers.

"You ever have the feeling that your heart has dropped to your stomach and what hasn't dropped is up in your throat?" he later asked. If that was Barbara, he knew, this had to be Russ. "I thought, 'My God, it can't be!' "

Wilson had been in Sunday school classes with Russ. They had socialized at church and attended boat shows together. Russ's sister, Cindy, was a close friend of his wife's. Russ's father, Al, served with him as a deacon at Grey Stone Baptist Church near downtown Durham. Wilson's years of training forced him to block out emotion and concentrate on his patient, but Barbara was talking so loudly that he couldn't hear what the other rescuers were saying.

"My God," she kept repeating, "I'm scared of these guns. I wish he didn't have these guns. I wish he wouldn't keep them under the pillow. Guns are not safe. There are kids in the house."

"Somebody get her out of here," Wilson said, and Green and Hornbuckle led her from the room and into the kitchen, where they attempted to quiet her so that they could ask routine questions for their reports.

Wilson and Scott suctioned the blood from Russ's mouth and throat and inserted a breathing tube. They slipped a needle into his arm and started an IV. They put a neck immobilizer on him and called for a backboard. Not only would the board protect Russ's spine from being further damaged by any bullet, it also would provide a hard surface for administering chest compressions if his heart and breathing stopped.

Meanwhile, Green and Hornbuckle were questioning Barbara in the kitchen, where her thirteen-year-old son, Jason, had been waiting anxiously.

"I kept telling him about those damn guns," she said, repeating herself several times. Russ, a National Guardsman, had "stages" in which he became enamored with guns, she said. She turned to her son. "Tell him, Jason, about him having these stages about guns," she urged, and her son agreed.

"He carries guns in cars, leaves them under the pillow," Barbara went on. "He is scared about somebody coming into the house, but it's just the dogs barking."

At one point Green asked, "Have you had any marital problems?"

"No," she quickly responded.

Kevin Wilson emerged from the bedroom, where others now were putting Russ on the backboard, and asked Barbara to which hospital she wanted Russ to be taken. Regulations required the rescue workers to take critically injured patients to the nearest facility, but since they were equidistant from Durham County General Hospital and the Duke University Medical Center, Wilson decided to leave the decision to Barbara.

"Duke," she said without hesitation. She worked there as a staff assistant. Her mother, father and brother also worked at the medical center.

It was 6:43 when the ambulance pulled away from the house, the siren rending the morning calm of the peaceful suburb.

Wilson saw the ambulance off, then returned to the kitchen to see what he could do for Barbara. He knew that Russ's father had had heart surgery some years earlier, and he thought perhaps he and their minister, Malbert Smith, should go to the house to tell him what had happened. If Al should have an attack of some sort, he would be there to administer aid.

"Can I help in any way?" he asked. "I would be happy to go to Al and Doris to get them. Or get Malbert."

At the suggestion Barbara thrust out both hands, as if to push him away. "No," she said sharply. "Don't call anybody. Don't call Malbert and don't call Al. I don't want you to do anything."

Wilson was taken aback. For long moments he looked at her,

uncertain of what to do. "Fine," he finally said. "I'm sorry. I was just trying to help."

Green said that he would take Barbara to the hospital, and Wilson turned and went outside, where Doug Griffin was putting his emergency first aid case back into his Volvo.

"Before you do anything else," Wilson told Griffin, "I want you to sit down and document everything you saw and heard so we can attach it to the regular report."

Wilson had known Barbara from the time she had married Russ, but he had heard nothing about her that had led him to believe that she was anything other than a devoted mother, a loving wife, an upstanding employee, a dedicated Christian. Like many others who knew her, he soon would be shocked as reports began to circulate about a far different side of her character. Then he would be glad that he had made certain that a careful accounting of the morning's events had been set down.

# Chapter Two

**D**oris Stager did not hear the wailing siren of the ambulance that roared by on Cole Mill Road just a few hundred yards from her shaded brick house on Rivermont Drive. She awoke at seven as usual and went about getting ready for work, unaware that her only son lay gravely wounded with a bullet in his head.

By eight, Doris was at her secretarial job at Bull City Oil Company, ready for another day's work, expecting nothing out of the ordinary. Not until forty-five minutes later did her phone ring and she hear the voice of Marva Terry, her son's mother-in-law.

Marva rarely called her and never at work, and Doris was surprised. Barbara's mother had always been aloof and disdainful to Doris, and the two women were not close. She could tell from Marva's voice that something was wrong, and without preliminaries Marva told her what it was:

"Russ is in emergency at Duke."

"What is the matter?" Doris asked anxiously, but Marva didn't answer.

"What is the matter?" Doris demanded.

"Barbara wants you out here," Marva told her, but would say no more. Doris should just come to the hospital, she insisted.

Clearly, something terrible had happened to her son. A heart attack? A car accident? Russ should have been at work by now. He was a driver's education instructor at school. Had some nervous student driver made a horrible mistake at the wheel? A swirl of fears raced in her mind.

A tiny, intense woman, Doris normally took charge of any situation, but she found herself so upset that she couldn't even remember how to get to Duke Medical Center, only a few miles away. Coworkers tried to calm her and gave her directions. She drove as fast as she dared, her mind tumultuous with uncertainty and a dreadful sense of foreboding.

Doris practically ran into the emergency room, frantic with worry. When she asked about her son, she was immediately shown into a small room off the emergency room waiting area, a room reserved, she knew, for families receiving the direst of news.

Barbara was standing in a corner, sobbing softly, her son, Jason, crying at her feet. Barbara's parents were there as well, looking grave, as was her minister, Larry Harper. Against one wall leaned a man Doris had never seen, whom she soon would discover to be a hospital chaplain.

"I'm sorry," Barbara cried out as soon as she saw Doris. "I didn't mean to do it. Forgive me." She kept saying it over and over, Doris later would remember, yet she offered no explanation of what had happened to Russ, the only thing that Doris wanted to know.

She was desperate for the truth that all in the room seemed reluctant to share with her, and finally Marva stepped forward to tell her. Doris heard the awful words but later she wouldn't be able to remember a thing that Marva had said. Her mind simply couldn't accept that her son had been shot in the head. Her concern was only for Russ. What was his condition? What was being done for him? When could she see him?

"Where are the doctors?" she asked. "What do the doctors say?"

The questions kept tumbling from her lips. "Why aren't they here? When are they coming? When can we talk to them?"

Nobody had answers, and Doris couldn't accept the uncertainty. She had to escape the confines of that room, these grave faces without answers. She could not remain still. She wheeled and burst out of the small room, uncertain where she was going or what she intended to do.

Walk. She had to walk. Nervousness always made her walk. The chaplain followed, hoping to comfort, stopping her just outside the door.

Only then did the enormity of the situation strike Doris with full force. "No, God!" she cried, putting her head in her hands.

Awed by her grief and helpless to relieve it, the chaplain stood close, saying nothing.

Al! Doris suddenly realized that her husband didn't know yet. Retired because of his medical disability, he was at home. She had to tell him, had to get to a telephone. There was a phone in the family room, the chaplain told her, and she went back inside and dialed her own number. Later, she wouldn't remember what she told Al or how he responded. She could only recall emphasizing to him to be careful driving to the hospital. She tried to sit after talking with Al but found it impossible.

Only walking could relieve her explosive anxiety.

"If you have to walk, why don't you go to the outside corridor?" the chaplain suggested, and she did, walking back and forth as hard as she could, all alone, talking with God, crying, pleading for her son's sake, not caring who might see or hear her, or what they might think.

Finally, Marva came out to the corridor, but before she could say anything, Doris looked up and saw her husband hurrying past the glass doors of the emergency room. Marva turned to leave.

"There's no need for you to go," Doris said to Marva. "Here comes Al."

But Marva went back to the waiting room, leaving them to comfort each other. Doris rushed into her husband's arms, and then they both started walking the corridor, back and forth, crying together, praying, telling themselves that Russ wouldn't want to become a vegetable locked in a coma, hooked to machines; he loved life too much.

Three doctors arrived in white smocks and marched in rank into the family waiting room. When Doris saw them and tried to follow, one of them, not knowing who she was, raised a hand to stop her. As he closed the door on her, Doris heard Barbara saying, "Oh, no, you're going to tell us that you've got to perform surgery."

Doris was so distraught that she just stood with her forehead against the door, unable to move, cut off not only from her son but from those who held his fate in their hands.

The doctors quickly got to the point. The bullet had passed

through Russ's brain and lodged in the front of his skull. The situation was hopeless. He was brain-dead. Extreme measures could prolong the life in his body, but he would never again be a functioning human being. Did Barbara want them to use these measures?

She looked at them quizzically.

One of the doctors explained that "extreme measures" meant hooking Russ to life-support equipment. "That's a decision you'll have to make," he said. "We can't decide that."

Barbara turned to Jason with a look of distress.

"Daddy wouldn't want that," Jason said, and Barbara agreed.

The doctors offered their condolences.

When they opened the waiting room door to leave, Doris was standing there with a look of helplessness on her face.

"Please," she said. "I'm his mother."

"There's nothing we can do," one of the doctors told her.

"Can't you perform surgery?" she pleaded. "Can't you do something?"

"I'm sorry. The damage has been done. It's just a matter of time."

Doris would not allow herself to collapse. Things had to be done. People had to be notified. The telephone numbers of people she needed to call were all at home, and she told Al to stay at the hospital while she drove there to make calls. She was concerned foremost about her daughter, Cindy, who lived in Chattanooga, Tennessee. Although she was much younger than Russ, Cindy was very close to her brother. A speech pathologist in the public schools, Cindy moved from school to school and would be difficult to find. Doris called Cindy's husband, David, at work, to have him take care of Cindy and arrange an immediate flight to Durham. She called her preacher, Malbert Smith, who had known Russ since he was a child. Al, she knew, would need him. She called a sister in Durham and asked her to pick up Cindy and David when they arrived at the airport.

After Doris had left for home, Marva had suggested that Barbara take a break from the ordeal of waiting and go home for a rest, but Barbara protested that she didn't want to leave Russ. The doctors had not yet granted permission for family to see him, though, and a short time later, Barbara decided that she should go home to shower and change clothes before going to him. Seeing that she was in no condition to drive, Larry Harper offered to take her. As they were leaving, Marva suggested that Barbara ought to clean up the bedroom while she was there.

Doris hurried back to the hospital but couldn't find a parking place. Her son was dying, and she couldn't get to him because she couldn't park her car. She was becoming frantic with frustration when a car stopped alongside hers. Barbara was inside with her minister. She said there'd been no change in Russ's condition, and she was going home to shower.

"I can't find a parking place," Doris said in an exasperated plea.

"Park across the street," Barbara told her, "because if you stay over here, your car will be towed."

Doris parked there, ran back to the emergency room and found Al waiting alone. Russ had been taken to a room, he told her.

"Malbert is coming," he said. "He'll be here in a minute."

"Al, Russ is up in that room by himself, and I am not waiting for anybody," Doris said, heading for the elevator, her husband following.

As they stepped off the elevator at the intensive care ward, Malbert Smith appeared with Wally Fowler, a church member. Together they went to Russ's room. Wally went inside with Doris while Al remained outside. Wally stood back quietly as Doris went to her son's side. She gently took his hand and began rubbing his arm, crying softly and telling him over and over that she loved him. She knew that he knew that, because they told each other regularly. Still, she couldn't tell him enough.

"Can he hear me?" she asked a nurse.

"I don't know."

His Adam's apple bobbed, and she thought it meant that he must be hearing her, that that was his way of letting her know, and she kept telling him over and over, rubbing his arm all the while.

She didn't know how long she stayed at his side, but when she went to check on Al, she found that Malbert had him stretched out in a recliner, putting cold compresses on his forehead. Al wanted to go to Russ, and she waited while Malbert took him inside.

Later, they traded places at their son's side, one of them always there, until nurses asked them to leave briefly. They walked around a corner of the corridor and saw Barbara and her family. Coworkers from the medical center were stopping by to express condolences to Barbara. Her parents were preparing to go back to work.

Doris and Al had been told several times that if Al didn't move his car from the emergency room parking lot where he had left it, it would be towed. Doris knew that if Russ died on this day, she and Al would want to ride home together. They wouldn't need both cars. Doris asked Barbara's brother, Steve, if he would follow her home in Al's car so that she could leave hers.

When they returned, everybody was gathered in a conference room in the intensive care ward. A nurse had asked them to leave Russ's room. Soon a doctor appeared, looking grim.

"I don't know any other way to tell you," he said. "He has expired."

Doris was looking at the clock behind his head as he spoke. It was a little after twelve-thirty. She exploded from her chair. She had to get to her son, but a nurse stopped her.

"Sit down," she said firmly. "You can't go now."

When Doris finally was allowed to go to him, she took his limp hand, surprisingly still warm, and rubbed his arm as if she were trying to rub life back into him, crying and telling him how much she loved him. Several times she left, but each time she was compelled back to his side. Nurses finally told her that she shouldn't go back, but when she pleaded to return just one more time for a final goodbye, they relented.

Afterward, while Barbara went in to see Russ with her minister, Doris and Al walked the hallway outside intensive care, back and forth, crying and asking why.

Bryan, their grandson adopted by Russ, came in. He was nineteen, a student at the University of North Carolina at Wilmington, a three-and-a-half-hour drive to the southeast.

"Will somebody please tell me what is going on?" he said.

Family members told him.

"Oh, no!" he cried, throwing up his arms and sinking to the floor against the hallway wall, where he sat sobbing, his Uncle Steve trying to console him.

Barbara stopped Doris and Al and said, "I want to have the

coaches as pallbearers and the baseball team as honorary pall-bearers."

"Fine," Doris said, and then she was riding home with Al, both of them stunned and unable to accept the harsh reality of the morning's events.

# Chapter Three

Sergeant Rick Buchanan was at his desk in the detective division of the Durham County Sheriff's Department, starting a new work week, when the telephone rang. Frank Honkanen, a young pathologist at Duke University Medical Center who served as the county's medical examiner, was on the line. Buchanan jotted down the time of the call: 10:35.

A previously healthy forty-year-old male was at the hospital, shot in the head, supposedly accidentally, Honkanen said. The man was brain-dead. Death was certain. The family wanted no extreme measures taken to keep him alive. He was an organ donor. Would organ removal interfere in any investigation? Would an autopsy be required?

Buchanan couldn't give an answer. He hadn't heard of the case. That was unusual, because as lead homicide investigator for the Durham County Sheriff's Department, he normally was alerted to any shooting in the county.

What was the name? Buchanan asked.

"Stager," Honkanen said. "A. Russell."

He'd have to look into it and get back to him, Buchanan told him.

When Buchanan located the incident report filed by the deputies, he realized that the shooting had happened before the shift change. Both deputies would be home asleep after their all-night shifts. The reports contained only the barest details of Barbara's version of events and gave no indication that the shooting was anything other than an accident, but Buchanan would have to talk with the deputies before determining whether any additional investigation would be required.

Before he was able to get in touch with the deputies, though, Buchanan received a call from the hospital saying that Russell Stager had died at 12:35. The possibility of an autopsy had kept doctors from taking his organs for transplant.

At midafternoon, Buchanan got into his unmarked silver-gray Plymouth cruiser and drove to Barbara's parents' house, a beige brick ranch-style house set deep in woods in the Willow Hill subdivision north of Durham. He was met in front of the house by Barbara's father, James Terry, who showed him the bloodied sheets and pillowcases from his daughter's bed and asked if he would need them. One of the investigating deputies had told him they wouldn't be needed, he said, since the shooting was an accident.

"No, we won't need them," Buchanan said. He just wanted to speak briefly with Barbara.

He met her in the dining room, and he was surprised that she was not as distraught as he had expected.

She told him about hearing the alarm going off in her son's room and reaching to remove the gun from beneath her husband's pillow. It went off as she raised it, she said. She described how she and Russ were lying in the bed, and when Buchanan asked if she would mind going with him to the house so that he could see the room and bed, she quickly agreed.

That surprised Buchanan, too. Somebody who'd undergone such a traumatic experience presumably would be reluctant to return so soon to the scene.

Yet another surprise was in store. Buchanan assumed that Barbara would be overcome with emotion upon entering the bedroom. The guilt of having caused such a horrible event, even though accidentally, surely would be overwhelming. But she showed no signs of distress as they walked in. Instead, she began calmly pointing out Russ's position on the bed and how she had been lying next to him.

The bed had been made. The room was immaculate, as if no tragedy had occurred there just hours earlier. Buchanan took note of a pump shotgun standing in one corner, and as he nosed about the room, setting the scene in his mind, Barbara picked up Russ's wallet from a dresser top and thumbed through it.

After returning Barbara to her parents' house, Buchanan wasn't sure what to think. "Most cases, you get a feel of them," he said later. "This one, I couldn't get a feel of it. Somehow it just didn't feel right."

He returned to his office and called the medical examiner to find out more about the wound. It had been a close shot to the back of the head, said Honkanen, who had questioned Barbara before she left the hospital. The bullet was still in Russ's brain.

Both men agreed that Barbara's story had sounded plausible enough. No autopsy would be necessary. The body would be released to the funeral home.

When Buchanan wrote up his reports about the shooting before going home, he added, "Based on the current information as was provided, the death was being declared accidental."

Still, something nagged him about it, and that night after he got home, he called Deputy Clark Green to question him about the position of the gun on the bed and the location of the cartridge. Nothing Green told him led him to think the shooting could have been anything other than an accident. Yet something about this incident still didn't feel quite right.


Russ Stager's first wife, Jo Lynn, had just arrived home from work Monday night when her parents appeared unexpectedly at the door of her house in north Raleigh. She could tell from their expressions that something was wrong.

"We have some bad news," her mother said without preliminaries. "Russ is dead."

Jo Lynn was shocked. "A car wreck?" she asked. Russ had narrowly escaped being killed in an accident just a year before.

"No, he was killed accidentally with a gun."

"How?" Jo Lynn asked. "Who shot him?"

"Barbara."

Jo Lynn was stunned. It had happened! When Russ had told her, it had seemed inconceivable, yet it actually had happened. She reacted instinctively. She went straight to the telephone and called the Durham police, only to learn that the department hadn't investigated the shooting. Try the Sheriff's Department, she was told. She called and asked to speak to the person investigating the Stager shooting, only to be told that he was gone for the day.

"You have to get a message to him," she said. "I have to talk to this person."

Twice more she called, but the return call never came. She was too agitated and upset to go to bed, and she sat up all night, her mind churning with memories and regrets. Early Tuesday morning she began calling again. After several tries, she finally reached Rick Buchanan. She identified herself as Russ Stager's former wife and said that she had to talk to him immediately. Could she come over?

Buchanan agreed to meet her at his office in the courthouse in downtown Durham at ten.

To organize her thoughts and make certain that she didn't forget anything that she intended to say, Jo Lynn sat down and wrote a letter of introduction before leaving.

As Jo Lynn drove into town, she was unaware that Durham's morning newspaper had spread the story about Russ's death across the top of the obituary page: " DURHAM HIGH BASEBALL COACH ACCIDENTALLY SHOT TO DEATH." The article quoted Buchanan and recounted the version of events that Barbara had told the officers. "There was no evidence of a struggle or foul play," it said.

Jo Lynn, though, was on her way to try to get somebody to think differently.

She got a bad impression of Buchanan when he remained seated at his desk as she introduced herself and offered the letter she had brought. He seemed utterly disinterested, she thought, and it irked her. Russ was dead and he didn't seem to care.

She took the chair that Buchanan offered and waited impatiently as he opened the letter and began to read.

Dear Officer Buchanan,

Thank you very much for agreeing to meet with me today regarding the death of A. Russell Stager III. In order to establish some credibility for myself, I would like to tell you the following. I am a 1975 graduate of Meredith College in Raleigh, N.C. I taught school briefly. I am currently office manager for a very large, successful residential builder in Raleigh. My employer is currently president of the Home Builders Association. Russell and I were married for approximately five years and after the usual distance a divorce brings, we became very close friends and confidants. That is why I can share the following information with you.

Russell feared for his safety with his wife, Barbara. Russell no longer believed that her first husband's wound was accidental.

Buchanan's interest suddenly picked up. First husband's wound?

He, too, died from a gunshot wound and Barbara was the only person with him. Russell always said that if anything suspicious happened to him that he would want me to remember his telling me that.

Barbara Stager had had another husband who died from an accidental gunshot wound in her presence? What were the odds of that?

Buchanan did not betray his surprise, though. He never wanted anybody to be able to guess what he was thinking or anticipate what he might do.

Russell thought Barbara did not have a firm grasp on reality. Supposedly she was writing about her first husband's death in a book entitled *Untimely Death*. She told him a publisher wanted to publish the book and showed him a letter from the publisher. He later found where she had written for information from the publisher, cut the letterhead from the response and made up her own stationery to write herself letters from the publisher.

Russ found huge sums of money missing and she would not account for it. He insisted she get a job so he could monitor her whereabouts during the day. He also thought she was having an affair and followed her one weekend morning to a parking lot where she parked her car, got out and got into a man's car and immediately began heavy petting.

Barbara received a huge insurance settlement from the accidental shooting death of her first husband.

Russell completed army basic training in the late 1960s, and I believe he has been in the army's reserves for at least 10 years, maybe more. He received the best training this country had to offer in the use and proper storage of the handgun. Russell had a gun during our marriage, but I only saw it on maybe two occasions. It was kept safely in a drawer unloaded. Russ had a very healthy respect for guns, and I remember his comments about accidental shootings and how they would never happen if people handled their guns with respect. He would never have slept with a loaded gun under his pillow. I pray that God's will be done in this tragedy.

Money problems. An affair. Bizarre behavior. Insurance. Nobody had to tell Buchanan that all of that could add up to murder. Nor did anybody have to tell him that murder could be difficult to prove.

"Well," he said, looking up at this woman who suddenly had changed everything, "the evidence is consistent with her story."

But he knew now that he would have to find out whether Barbara Stager could be believed. And to do that he would have to find out who Barbara Stager really was.

# PART TWO

# Paths Not Taken

# Chapter Four

People who had known Barbara Stager from childhood could not believe what they would hear about her in the wake of her second husband's death. It was as if they were being told about a total stranger. That this woman they knew as a loving mother, a doting wife, a devoted Christian and church leader, a respected and rising employee at one of America's most prestigious medical centers could be a woman obsessed with sex, possessed by spending money, a pathological liar willing to do anything to cover herself, was simply inconceivable.

"She was raised in church, and she just knew those things were wrong," said a lifelong friend who could not bring herself to believe that Barbara could do such things.

Although Barbara and her family would closely guard the details of their lives, Barbara's childhood and the events that led her to become seemingly two entirely different persons can be pieced together through records and the remembrances and observations of family, friends and acquaintances.

Her parents, James and Marva Terry, were country people, hard-working, churchgoing, with rock-solid values, "as fine a people as ever walked the earth," as some of their closest friends described them. Both grew up in large families on farms in Durham County, but after they married they settled in Durham, where the tobacco empire built by James Buchanan Duke had created a strong economic base upon which they would build their own lives. James got a job with Duke Power Company, where he would make a career beginning as a meter reader and rising to better positions. Marva went to work as a secretary at Duke University Medical Center, where her mother was employed and where she, too, would eventually make a career, rising to the position of staff assistant to the director.

Later, people who knew them had little doubt about who was dominant in their relationship. Marva was clearly stronger and more ambitious than her husband. James was quiet, easygoing, amiable, liked by almost everybody. "As good as gold," one friend described him. "He would do anything for you." Although Marva was talkative and could be warm and friendly to people she knew, she presented a different face to the world. She was reserved, cool, poised, precise, rigid, a person much concerned about appearances. Some thought of her as aloof, even smug. "Marva operated in a vacuum," one former coworker said, "the kind of person who would walk by and you would almost feel a chilly breeze."

As Marva rose to positions of greater authority at work, she began to associate with doctors, administrators and other important people in the community. These people, whose education, income and social standing were much greater than her own, she admired and wanted to impress. Some would come to think that the life she had made for herself did not live up to her dreams, and later they couldn't help but wonder if she had not transferred those expectations to her daughter.

When Barbara, her first child, was born at Watts Hospital in Durham on October 30, 1948, Marva was twenty, James twenty-two. Only a year later, a second child was born, a son, Alton. Both children were fair-haired and hazel-eyed, and people sometimes mistook them for twins.

Perhaps because she was the firstborn, perhaps because she was a daughter, Barbara was expected to be a perfect child, and she was. From the beginning she was shy, reserved and instinctively obedient, always striving to please. Her mother was closely protective of her and quick to reprimand her if she made a misstep. Some close to the family would recall that her mother continued to correct her even into adulthood, often saying, "Barbara, stand up straight."

Part of this drive to be perfect stemmed from Barbara's awareness even at an early age that physically she was not. She suffered an astigmatism that left her nearsighted and caused her to wear thick glasses even before she started school, and she did not grow as quickly as her brother, always remaining smaller than others her age. The awkwardness she felt may have been the reason that her favorite doll was big, freckled and considered ugly by some of her family and friends.

In other ways, though, Barbara was a parent's dream. Quiet and studious, she proved to be an outstanding student at Hillandale Elementary School. Teachers commented not only about her industry, but on her good conduct and proper manners. Her high grades did not come easily, however. Her eighth-grade teacher noted on her report card that she had to work exceptionally hard to maintain them, and that she remained immature emotionally.

Barbara's rapt attention and good behavior also were noted at Rose of Sharon Baptist Church, the church in which her father had grown up and in which he and Marva were among the most active members. Barbara was baptized there at the age of ten, and she not only attended Sunday school and Sunday services regularly but was always present with her family at prayer meetings, gospel singings, revivals and homecomings as well. Every summer she attended vacation Bible school with her brother. The family left the church soon after Barbara was baptized, however, because of controversy over the church's pastor. They moved to Ridgecrest Baptist, where Barbara joined the Baptist Training Union and became one of the church's most faithful young members.

Several years later, the family changed residence as well. James Terry helped his father and other family members raise tobacco every summer, and he wanted to be out in the country again, where he could have a big garden and be free of city strictures. Just before Barbara was to enter ninth grade, he built a four-bedroom brick house—trimmed in white, with a bay window in the living room—on seven acres carved from his father's farm north of Durham in a thickly wooded, sparsely settled area.

Barbara started the ninth grade amid strangers at nearby Northern High School and continued on the path her mother had set for her. In her first year she was selected as a member of the Knights and Ladies, an honorary society that recognized academic achievement. She also joined the Future Teachers of America. She liked children, she said, and hoped to become an elementary school teacher.

In the summer after Barbara's freshman year, her mother gave birth to a third child, another son, Steve. The Terrys always had been a tightly knit family, but the baby provided a new focus that brought them even closer. Barbara doted over her new baby brother and would become as fiercely protective of him as she always had been of Alton.

She and Alton were extremely close, often doing things together, and that fall Alton joined Barbara at Northern High and, like her, became a member of the band. Barbara, who looked tiny and lost in the heavy navy blue and gold uniform when she marched in parades and the halftime shows at football games, played clarinet, an instrument she had learned in grade school. Alton was a bass drummer, tall and stiffly erect. Several years later, Barbara would recall for a friend an incident on the band bus that year when an older boy picked on Alton. She rushed to his aid and later admonished him for not standing up for himself. "If he ever does that again, you kick him in the crotch," she said. As she told the story later, she seemed to relish the thought of such retaliation.

If Barbara harbored secret resentment toward boys, it may have been only because her desires were so strong. Few seemed even to notice her. She worried about her popularity and thought herself unattractive. She was slender, like her mother, but not nearly as tall, only five feet four inches. Her shoulders were narrow and tapered, her hips too big. Her chin was weak, her lips too fat, her mouth too wide. The toothiness of her smile made her look like a cartoon character. Her shoulder-length hair was mousy brown, and she still peered through unflattering heavy-framed glasses.

"We were shy," her childhood friend Brenda Hunt, recalled years later. "We were brought up in a Christian atmosphere. We were told always to act like ladies, and that's what we tried to do. We were not outgoing and what I would call provocative, because that was not the way we were brought up."

Her church taught that sex outside marriage was hell-sent. Even thoughts of sex were to be repressed, for fantasy was considered as sinful as the act itself. Although Barbara's was not one of them, some Baptist families did not even allow their daughters to go swimming for fear that all of that exposed skin might provoke sexual thoughts. While a good-night kiss between young couples might be tolerated by liberal Baptist families, a roving hand always was taboo, and a young woman who allowed such transgression was expected to pray for forgiveness. Such teachings created tremendous burdens of guilt when young libidos began to bud. Barbara's later affairs indicate that sexual fantasies not only budded in her teenage years but were kept under unnaturally rigid control. There were no secrets from God, as she well knew.

For the time being, however, it was enough for Barbara to keep such thoughts from her parents. In a time when almost all parents were strict, Barbara told friends that her parents were stricter than others, especially her mother. And although later she would suggest that she felt overprotected and resented her restrictions, people outside the family never knew her to challenge them. She was always home at whatever curfew her parents set, never complained when she was told that she couldn't go somewhere or do something. "She never talked back to her parents," one of her mother's friends recalled.

She didn't drink, smoke, use foul language or sneak out. She was just as polite, responsible and serious-minded as a perfect daughter should be. In her sophomore year, Barbara got her driver's license and her parents bought her an old blue Rambler to drive to school. When other students were cruising with dates, Barbara and her brother were seen riding together in the Rambler. That spring, Barbara took a part-time job at Duke University Medical Center as a clerk in the collections division of the bookkeeping office, a job she would keep until she went away to college. Her job, regular home chores, helping with her baby brother, church, school, band practice and homework left Barbara little free time. Still, she kept up her grades, and every year she was selected for Knights and Ladies. Somehow, too, she managed to find time for other school activities and to help family members or friends whenever they needed it.

Barbara graduated from Northern High in 1967, thirty-third in her class of 233. It was a given that she would attend college, and although her Scholastic Aptitude Test scores were barely average (395 verbal, 450 math), she had a choice of schools. She was accepted at North Carolina State University in Raleigh, not far from home. But Appalachian State Teachers College at Boone in the mountains of western North Carolina, nearly two hundred miles from Durham, offered her a modest scholarship, one of many presented to prospective teachers, and that decided her choice.

That summer, Barbara worked full-time at Duke University Medical Center, saving money to see her through her first year of college. Friends saw that she clearly was excited about the prospect of getting out on her own, away from the restrictions of home. But they did not know the depth of her longings, the strength of her resentments, and they could not foresee the nearly explosive urges that were stirring within her.

Barbara received her dorm assignment and the name and address of her roommate several weeks before she left for Boone. Her roommate was to be Laura Campbell,* an English major. She and Laura corresponded several times before they arrived on campus, planning who would bring what for their room.

They were to discover that they had much in common. Both were from families of modest means. Both had been brought up Baptist. Both were quiet and studious, serious about getting an education. Neither was a drinker or partygoer. Both were neat, good housekeepers, although Barbara was by far the more meticulous of the two. Both were early risers and usually were in bed by ten.

In some ways, though, they were very different. Laura, who was from a small mountain town near Asheville, was tall and strikingly beautiful. In August she had won the title of Miss Asheville and would be competing the following summer in the Miss North Carolina pageant. Next to her, Barbara seemed even shorter and plainer than she thought herself to be. Laura sensed an insecurity in Barbara about her looks, but that didn't interfere with their relationship. They struck up a quick friendship. "Like two little sisters together in this big place," Laura would recall years later.

Appalachian, which was in the process of becoming a university that year, enforced strict regulations, especially for female students, who were not allowed to wear shorts or slacks on campus or to be outside their dorm rooms after ten o'clock on weeknights. Closed study was required for two hours every night. Barbara and Laura found themselves together a lot and enjoyed each other's company. They chatted about school and classes, and Barbara talked a lot about her family, delighting in relating stories about her little brother Stevie. She talked often as well about Alton, with whom she corresponded regularly. She rarely mentioned her father but spoke proudly of her mother. Laura got the impression that her mother was the guiding force in her life.

Mostly, though, the two talked about "girl stuff," as Laura termed it. Boys were at the top of the list, but hairdos, makeup and clothing also were regular topics. Barbara asked for tips about improving her appearance, and Laura trimmed Barbara's pageboy cut to a shorter, more flattering style, which Barbara would tint blond later in the year.

Early that fall, Laura met Steve Hamrick,* a sophomore, an education major from Lexington, and they soon began dating. Steve's roommate was a close friend named Larry Ford. Larry often ate in the campus cafeteria with Steve and Laura and two other friends, forming a comfortable group. Laura was impressed with Larry, whom she thought to be smart, levelheaded, sincere, a really nice person who knew where he was going. "He was like a big brother you could just sit down and talk to," she recalled.

Larry, she knew, wasn't dating anybody, and neither was Barbara. In the first weeks of school Barbara went home every weekend, and after returning from one of those trips, she had told Laura that she had broken up with her boyfriend. Laura thought that Larry and Barbara might hit it off, and she invited Barbara to join their group for lunch one day.

Barbara didn't say much about Larry afterward, but she did continue joining their group for activities. It wasn't until Laura saw Larry and Barbara talking quietly in the student union one day that she thought something might happen between them. By winter, Barbara and Larry, who never had dated anyone steadily, were being thought of as another campus couple.

Larry had grown up in rented houses in the rolling countryside near the community of Colfax in Guilford County west of Greensboro, about sixty-five miles from Durham. His parents,

Doris and Henry Ford, had known each other from childhood in the small textile-mill town of Randleman in Randolph County, where Larry was born. The first of their five children, he was quiet, thoughtful, always helpful to his parents and his sisters and brothers. "He was a gentle child from the beginning," his mother recalled years later. Teachers' remarks on his report cards throughout his first years at Colfax School were the kind to make parents proud: "very polite," "works well with others," "an outstanding student."

The Fords had attended a Friends church in Randleman in the early years of their marriage, but there were no Quaker churches in Colfax, so they joined Shady Grove Wesleyan Methodist, the center of community activity. Larry went to Sunday school there as well as regular services and took part in the youth activities. He joined Boy Scout Post 370 at the church and eventually achieved Eagle rank.

As a teenager, Larry caused his parents no worries, even after he got his driver's license. "He drove just like an old man from day one," his father said, "just as stable. He was just that kind of person."

Although he liked sports and was a member of the track team, Larry was more gifted in the classroom. Not only did he excel academically, he also became a school leader, president of the Beta Club, treasurer of the Inner Club Council, secretary of the Junior Civitans. During his senior year—the year his family moved into a hillside two-story farmhouse on eighty partially wooded acres along Cross Creek, nearer the center of Colfax— Larry and Linda Pope were chosen most dependable in their classes.

Larry decided that he wanted to teach, and the Fords began rearranging their lives so they could afford to send him and their other children to college. Henry quit driving a delivery truck for Holsum Bakery in Winston-Salem to take a higher-paying job at Guilford Dairy in Greensboro; Doris went to work at Belk's, a department store in downtown Greensboro, riding the bus back and forth every day. Larry also got a full-time summer job at Guilford Dairy to earn money for college.

He wanted to go to North Carolina State in Raleigh, but he also applied to Appalachian State Teachers College in Boone. Appalachian was quick to accept him, and after several weeks passed without hearing from State, Larry sent off a deposit to Appalachian. Later an acceptance arrived from State, but Larry already had committed, and he stuck by his fateful choice.

Larry liked Appalachian and especially the Blue Ridge Mountains in which it was situated. On visits, his family would accompany him on outings along the Blue Ridge Parkway and hiking trips on nearby trails. Larry did well in his first year of college, attaining high grades and the plaudits of his instructors. He spent long hours studying and had little time for dating or other outside activities. His parents never worried about Larry, confident that with his likeable and easygoing nature, his intelligence, dependability and willingness to work hard, his future was bright. They had no foreboding that his sophomore year would bring forces into his life that would end in tragedy.

Laura could not have imagined that Barbara and Larry would become involved in a sexual relationship. Baptist girls just didn't do that. But years later Barbara would tell a friend that she had wasted little time with Larry, having sex with him the first time they were alone together—in the instruments closet of the campus band room. Her eagerness, her almost desperate hunger for affection and approval, though, produced only a cautious wariness in Larry.

He made no mention of a girlfriend in letters and visits home that winter, and even Laura got the feeling that he wanted to back away from Barbara, that she was pushing him too hard and too fast. That was confirmed for her after an incident on a snowy Saturday night in February.

Barbara returned to the dorm room that night in a state that Laura could only describe later as "bizarre."

"Barbara, are you all right?" Laura asked.

Only guttural sounds came, "almost animal-type."

"What's wrong?" Laura asked, but she got no response other than the strange noises.

Barbara slumped on the edge of her bed, her hair in her face, her head shaking, moaning eerily—"almost like a cry inside that wasn't coming out," according to Laura, who hurried to the room next door for help when she couldn't get Barbara to tell her what had happened. Dormmates were of no assistance in snapping

Barbara out of her spell, and the dorm mother was summoned. When she, too, was unable to get a response, she called the campus police, who took Barbara to the hospital in a security car. Laura went along to be of help if she could.

"I have never seen anything like it," she said. "I felt like I needed to be there if she wanted to talk."

Barbara did not want to talk. Doctors sedated her and kept her at the hospital overnight.

Laura called Barbara's parents to tell them she was in the hospital. "They really didn't say a lot," she said. "I was surprised."

Barbara was okay the next day but subdued when Larry and Steve went to the hospital in a station wagon they borrowed from a friend to take her back to the dorm. Barbara never talked about the incident, and within a couple of days she seemed normal again. Only later did Steve tell Laura that Barbara's bizarre behavior had been precipitated by Larry telling her that he wanted to break off their relationship. But by then Barbara and Larry were back together. They had resumed the relationship the day Barbara got out of the hospital.

Barbara's parents did not come to check on her, and Laura could not help but wonder if that was because they had seen Barbara display this type of behavior before. Was Barbara's episode a genuine breakdown in the face of stress, a dark secret the family did not want to acknowledge? Or was it just a device Barbara used to get her own way when things did not please her, something the family knew would quickly pass as soon as it had achieved its purpose?

Doris Ford was surprised in early May when she looked out the window of her farmhouse and saw Larry driving up unannounced in a car he had borrowed from a friend. Something must be wrong, she thought, and she knew that she was right as soon as she saw his worried face.

Larry kept most problems to himself, but when he was so deeply troubled that he had to talk to somebody, he always turned to his mother.

Doris and her son went upstairs to his old room and sat on the bed. Larry was nervous and ashamed, and it was hard for him to tell his mother what he had to say. He'd met a girl. Her name was Barbara Terry. They had been going together for several months. There was a pause. The next words seemed not to want to come. She had . . . become pregnant. She was about two months along now. She had told him that he didn't have to marry her, but he wanted to do the right thing.

Doris reached out and touched her son's hand. For long moments there was silence.

"Do you love her?" Doris asked.

"Yes," he said without hesitation.

What about college? she asked him. She knew how much he wanted his degree. He would try to go on and finish, he said. Barbara had agreed to that. They both knew it wouldn't be easy. They would get by the best they could.

"Well," Doris said after another long pause, "if you love her, then you should marry her."

Barbara had become pregnant only a couple of weeks after Larry had tried to break off their relationship, but if he thought that she had allowed herself to get pregnant to entrap him, he never mentioned it. Larry's father had that feeling, though, and soon afterward Larry told him, "Dad, I wish you had told me about women like that." It was too late for him to say anything now, Henry knew, for Larry had accepted his responsibility and was facing up to it with stout resolve.

The wedding was not announced. Their parents would not learn about it until later. It was held on May 21, 1968, at First Presbyterian Church in Boone, near the campus. Laura and Steve were among the small group of friends quickly assembled for the informal ceremony.

Larry had confided in Steve about Barbara's pregnancy, but Laura didn't know. Barbara never mentioned it, and Steve didn't tell her until later. Laura suspected it, though, because of the suddenness of the whole affair and the lack of joy in it. Barbara was very determined about it. Larry seemed subdued, almost reluctant. Something had to be wrong, Laura knew, because Barbara's grades had been dropping that spring, and she had taken to skipping classes.

Only a week of classes remained when Larry and Barbara were married, and both remained in their dorm rooms afterward. But Barbara stopped going to classes altogether. She was going to drop out of college and get a job, she told Laura, stirring her concern. Laura had thought that Barbara really wanted to get an education and become a teacher. She hoped that she wasn't messing up her life.

Larry and Barbara drove to Colfax soon after the wedding, Larry again driving a borrowed car, to tell his family about the marriage. Although they had never met their new daughter-in-law, the Fords went out of their way to make her feel welcome and part of their family. Still, the situation was strained. Barbara was anxious and didn't talk much. And the Fords thought that she was too openly affectionate with Larry. When she started kissing him passionately in front of them, they were shocked.

"I never had seen anything in my life that came close to that," Doris later recalled. Did Barbara have no modesty or sense of proper behavior? Or was she showing her new in-laws that she would do whatever she wished?

Doris wanted to like her new daughter-in-law. She always gave everybody the benefit of the doubt, but there was something about Barbara that bothered her, although she couldn't put a finger on it. "You know, you get a feeling sometimes when you meet people," she said years later. "You're going to keep both eyes open."

That feeling soon would be confirmed for Doris. In becoming pregnant, marrying Larry and dropping out of college, acts that seemed calculated to bring grievous disappointment to her mother, Barbara had broken sharply with the strictures of her past. Now that she was out on her own, she would do exactly as she pleased.

# Chapter Five

In the same way Larry had backed into his relationship with Barbara, he would continue having reservations about their marriage. His unhappiness with it as time went on would lead him to withdraw ever more inward. Neither would Barbara find marriage what she hoped it would be, but she would react in a different way, her dissatisfaction and overpowering desires pushing her outward for gratification that could never be achieved.

The need to please and impress others that Barbara had absorbed from her mother would evolve into twin compulsions that would prove Larry right in his reservations. Barbara's strong sexual urges would drive the first wedge into their relationship, but it would be her second compulsion—her spending—that eventually would prove more damaging.

No signs of the coming strife were evident in their early days together, however. They were consumed by the immediate problems they faced. With a baby on the way, Larry had to find a job. He and Barbara had to have a car, a place to live, furniture and all the other accoutrements necessary to start a household, a family. There would be obstetrician bills to pay, baby things to buy. For a brief period after Larry finished his sophomore year, he and Barbara moved in with his parents. He got a job at Varco-Pruden, a manufacturing plant in nearby Kernersville. Barbara went to work at Wesley Long Hospital in Greensboro, filing insurance forms for emergency room patients.

Although less than pleased about their daughter's hasty marriage, Barbara's parents stood by her, making the best of the situation. Her father helped her and Larry to buy a used mobile home in Durham, and Larry had it moved to a rented lot not far from his parents' house. With a finance company loan, Larry also bought a used car, his first, a Rambler. With their combined incomes, Larry and Barbara made enough not only to get by but to save a little for the baby and to ensure that Larry would be able to return to college in the fall.

When summer ended, they decided that Barbara should keep her job and remain in Colfax so that she would be near her doctor. Larry would return to Boone alone to start his junior year at Appalachian, going back to life in the dorm. His parents would help to look after Barbara.

Larry's sister Jane, a senior in high school, sometimes spent nights with Barbara to keep her company and to help out if she could. Jane liked her new sister-in-law, found her to be perky and peppy and sometimes giggly. She could talk with Barbara about things that she would have been embarrassed to bring up with her mother or others, and Barbara made her feel good about herself. Jane looked up to her. "I guess I really put her on a pedestal," she said years later.

But Jane recognized that despite her upbeat facade, Barbara was unhappy with the way her own life was going. Only a year before, Barbara had been excitedly starting college with a bright future. Now she was out of school, married, seven months pregnant, feeling that she had let her mother down, living among strangers in a trailer in the country, driving miles to work at a job that was mostly drudgery. Larry, meanwhile, was off at college, seeing his friends, having a good time, as if nothing had changed.

Barbara never voiced her feelings to Larry's parents, but they knew that she was unhappy. She clearly resented her situation, hated living in a trailer, detested her isolation, disliked the hovering presence of her watchful in-laws. She was resentful that Larry was able to go on with his life while she was trapped by economics and the child in her belly. Larry's place, she thought, was at her side, and she said so to Jane. But he remained at college, coming home only on weekends.

In October, Barbara quit her job at the hospital, citing complications with her pregnancy, although the Fords would not be able to remember any complications other than that her feet sometimes swelled. After that, she spent most of her time alone in her trailer watching TV, growing more miserable by the day.

Barbara finally gave birth to a boy on December 2, 1968, at Moses Cone Hospital in Greensboro. She was twenty, the same age her mother had been when she was born. The child was named James Bryan in honor of her father, and he would be called Bryan. Larry barely made it to the hospital before his son was born. His mother had called to tell him that Barbara was going into labor, and he drove home so fast that he thought he might have set a new speed record for the stretch of U.S. 421 that separated Boone from Greensboro. On the way in, he stopped at his parents' house and picked up his sister Jane, who became terrified of his driving, especially after he ran a red light.

His family couldn't recall seeing Larry quite so exultant as when he first gazed upon his son.

"He was proud," Jane recalled, "really excited, just on cloud nine."

When Doris and Henry went with their son to see the baby on the day after his birth, they were startled that Barbara grabbed Larry and began kissing him passionately, even trying to put hickeys on his neck as he pulled away, protesting good-naturedly.

"It wasn't normal," Henry recalled. "It just wasn't normal."

After Christmas, Larry got a job managing Ivy Hall, an ivy-covered brick building on the edge of the Appalachian campus. It was owned by Barbara's Greensboro obstetrician, who operated it as a private men's dorm. The job offered a small salary and a free three-room apartment on the first floor. Larry sold the trailer and moved his family into the apartment. They had to share a bath with the students on the hall.

The new parents were having a tough time making ends meet, so Barbara found somebody to keep Bryan and took a job as a clerk at Sears. As for Larry, the pressure of living on a tight budget while being a husband, father, full-time student and boardinghouse manager was showing. His grades fell from their usual high marks. He wasn't able to carry as heavy a schedule of classes. To make up for this, he decided to remain in Boone after finishing spring classes in 1969 so that he could attend summer school. Larry's parents saw him only when they went to the mountains for occasional visits. Larry couldn't afford trips home.

Larry's sister Jane enrolled at Appalachian that fall and spent time when she could with Larry and Barbara, sometimes baby-sitting for them. One change that she noticed right away in Barbara was that now that she wasn't pregnant, she was brazen about sex.

One weekend, Jane recalled, she and her new boyfriend went for a ride on the Blue Ridge Parkway with Larry and Barbara. Barbara kept teasing Larry, grabbing at his crotch and giggling about it. Larry protested lamely, clearly embarrassed. It was obvious that he did not share Barbara's openness. Worse, although he had not yet admitted it to anyone, he now realized that Barbara's sexual needs were far greater than his, and the first indications that she would transgress all marital bounds to satisfy them soon began to appear.

That fall, Jane baby-sat one Saturday while Larry and Barbara went to a campus football game. Afterward, Barbara claimed to have spotted a young man in the crowd whom she recognized. The man had attempted to rape her while she was in high school, she said. Now she was certain that he had come to Boone looking for her.

What concerned Larry about her story, he later told his mother, was that Barbara had seemed not so much frightened by the incident as excited by it, as if it were a scene in some TV show in which she was the star—or some high school fantasy coming true.

This was not the first time that Barbara had told him about men who supposedly had sexual designs on her. Several times she had mentioned that "dirty old men" had said suggestive things while she was working at Sears. Was it actually happening, or was she saying it only to make Larry jealous and whet his interest? Was she projecting onto stray men what she wanted herself?

In October, Barbara took a better-paying job as a teller at a Boone branch of the First National Bank of Eastern North Carolina, later to become Northwestern Bank. Soon Larry would begin hearing about men who made suggestive remarks to her there as well. Before the year was out, Barbara would insist that he do something about the sexual harassment she was suffering from her boss at the bank. "How many times did you do it last night?" she claimed he would ask her with a leer. Finally, Larry went to the bank and confronted the man, he later told his parents, only to have him deny it.

In the spring of 1970, Larry finally finished his classwork. All that stood between him and his career was a semester of student teaching, and that could be done anywhere in North Carolina. He and Barbara left their cramped apartment and returned to Guilford County to live briefly again with his parents, intending to work and save money that summer. Larry went back to work at Varco-Pruden. Barbara got a job as a secretary at Pilot Freight Company in Kernersville.

Larry was concerned about one thing that summer: the draft. With the war continuing to escalate in Vietnam, he was certain that he was going to face military service soon. His college deferment would be gone as soon as he finished his student teaching. He was fascinated with airplanes, and long had dreamed of becoming a military pilot. When he mentioned this to Barbara, though, his parents later claimed, "she threw a fit."

"You'll be gone four years," she said.

Nevertheless, Larry took Air Force aptitude tests. When he was told that he was qualified for navigator training but not pilot training, he tried to hide his disappointment, but decided that he didn't want to commit four years to become a navigator.

One day early that summer, Barbara returned from a trip to Greensboro and said that she had checked by the draft board and had bad news. Larry was about to be called up.

Larry talked to his father, who urged him to see about a deferment. After all, his father noted, he had a wife and child and was still technically a full-time student, at least for another six months.

But Larry said that he would have to face his military obligation sooner or later, and he might as well go ahead and get it behind him. He didn't want to go into the army and risk becoming fodder for jungle patrols in Vietnam, so he joined the Marine Reserves. That way, he figured, he only would have to be away for six months of active duty, then he could return to do his student teaching and finish his degree.

Later, the Fords would learn that Larry had been in no danger of being drafted. Clearly, Barbara had made up the whole thing. But to what purpose? Was she trying to get Larry to make some bold move to break from his home and parents, much as she had done? Was she simply trying to get him away to free herself to see others? The Fords would come to suspect the latter.

Late that summer, Larry went to San Diego for basic training, leaving Barbara and his twenty-month-old son to live with his parents, who still had three children at home. Doris and Henry were glad to have Barbara, but she was resentful and frustrated about being there. Sometimes she would go out at night, leaving Bryan in their care, and would return late, "all bubbly." They suspected that she was seeing other men, but they had no proof and were reluctant to confront her about it. They were equally reluctant to mention their suspicions to Larry for fear that they might be wrong and he might think they were trying to turn him against Barbara.

In October, she announced that she had a dinner appointment for a job interview in High Point. She got a permanent and left for the appointment in her best clothes.

"She came in excited," Henry later recalled. "Boy, she was high." She had gotten the job, she said. It was at a bank. She showed off a set of sheets and pillowcases that she had gotten for taking it, along with $300 in cash that she said was a salary advance. This would be only the first of several times that Barbara would claim to have received expensive gifts from grateful employers.

She would have to live in High Point, and she started looking for an apartment immediately. The Fords were relieved that she no longer would be where they could observe so many of her activities. Some of them, they'd begun to believe, were things that they'd just as soon not know about.

Early in October 1970, Barbara moved all of her belongings out of the Fords' house and into a new two-bedroom apartment in High Point, a city famed for its furniture market, the largest in the world. On October 16, she started her new job at North Carolina National Bank, or NCNB, as a clerk in the consumer loan department of the bank's North Main Street branch.

Larry returned from his Marine training four months later, in February, and settled into the apartment with Barbara. It was too late for him to do his student teaching that year, so he took a job at Sears in downtown High Point, selling draperies, carpet and furniture.

The two fell into a low-key lifestyle dictated by their limited income and centered on their two-year-old son. They occasionally played cards or went out to eat with a friend of Larry's from work, James Whitley, and his wife, who lived in the same apartment complex. During this time Larry and James developed an interest in karate and began talking about signing up for classes. And on Sundays Larry and Barbara went regularly to visit his parents for the big dinners that Doris cooked.

This was not the kind of life that Barbara had envisioned for herself, and she soon felt stifled by it. She clearly wanted something grander, more exciting, more important. And she wanted to move toward it much faster than her means allowed.

To Larry's family, she was always "putting on airs." They thought that she considered herself to be from a higher social class, and that her mother thought Barbara had "married down" when she chose Larry. Barbara tried to prove that she was better than others by buying things.

She spent money so profligately that the Fords began to wonder how Larry, who was thrifty by nature, ever would be able to pay all the bills. Barbara was always buying something new— clothing, jewelry, things for the apartment. Larry's sister Jane came to believe that spending money excited Barbara. She was never happier than when she was buying something, Jane thought, preferably something expensive that she could show off to others. Yet once she had bought something, she never was satisfied with it, the Fords thought. Just as playing is more important to gamblers than winning, spending clearly was more important to Barbara than having spent. And just as gambling can become addictive, spending was growing into a craving that Barbara could not control.

Barbara didn't like her apartment—it wasn't good enough for her, the Fords believed—and less than a year after she had moved into it, she found a small yellow house for rent on North Main Street, a step up that offered more privacy as well, but the Fords couldn't help but wonder how long it would be before Barbara became unhappy with it, too.

The department in which Barbara worked at the bank was a large one, but she developed few friends. The department manager who hired her, Jack Kearns, thought of her as a good worker, a "clean-cut little girl," but Barbara's burgeoning sexuality was soon to assert itself and cause him to wonder if she was as clean-cut as she at first had appeared. He began getting complaints from other women in the department that her open talk about sex bothered them. She often wore miniskirts to work, and some of her female coworkers thought that she was flagrantly flirtatious with male employees and customers.

"Barbara could be with a group of women, acting perfectly normal," one acquaintance later would recall, "but if a man came around, she would suddenly become an entirely different person, all aglow. It was really something to see."

"Flirting was like a game with her," said another. "It was indiscriminate, a physical thing, just anybody who catches her scent."

Barbara would make friends with other women in the office, then do something that would alienate them, according to one woman. At times, for example, Barbara would seek help with her work from others, she said, then, with her work done, leave early, making her coworkers angry. But it was her open sexuality that bothered most of them, and as time went on, some women in the office would shun Barbara, calling her "loose." One, who knew nothing of Barbara's strict upbringing and religious training or of her teenage concerns about her looks, ironically would describe her as "a very cute girl who knew nothing about morals."

Men were certainly taking notice. Indeed, among her male coworkers and supervisors, Barbara was popular and highly regarded. All of them would speak well of her later.

Her title was wholesale clerk, and she handled loan applications and payments from car dealers. By the spring of 1973, almost five years after her marriage, it became obvious to her coworkers that she was getting very friendly with some of the bank's customers.

Larry would first get wind of this that spring, when Barbara told him that she was going off to spend a weekend with a group of girlfriends at the beach cottage her parents had bought when she was in high school. After she left, Larry got a late-night call.

"Do you know where your wife is?" asked a female voice. The caller hung up before Larry could question her.

Suspicious, he tried to track Barbara down. The beach house

had no phone, so he called the police on the island and asked them to check at the house for Barbara and have her call him. The police reported back that nobody was staying at the house that weekend.

"I ran the gauntlet of emotions," he later said to his mother when he told her about the call.

Doris knew how deeply troubled Larry had to be for him to talk to her about such a thing, and she didn't press him for details. She never knew if he confronted Barbara about that weekend, although she suspected that he did. Meanwhile, their marriage stumbled on, but Larry never seemed happy anymore and he was becoming more and more remote.

Doris assumed that things were going better when Larry told her later that spring that he and Barbara were going to buy a new house of their own. It was in a new subdivision in Randolph County, five miles south of High Point, a three-bedroom split-level, still under construction. They negotiated a loan with a savings and loan company and signed a contract for the house, agreeing to pay $27,000.

The house was clearly Barbara's idea. Larry's parents thought that he was going along with it just to appease her, and they worried that he wouldn't be able to keep up the payments. Barbara was eager to get into it, and she lost patience with the contractors as they worked to finish it. "Everything that she wanted, it had to be today," her father-in-law later recalled. "Like the house. She would say, 'They're going to have it ready in two weeks—or else.' "

Barbara began buying new furniture even before the house was ready and had it delivered when she and Larry finally moved in in early May. Then she didn't like the electric stove and refrigerator that came with the house, and she traded them for more expensive models in colors that pleased her. She bought a new washer and dryer and on and on.

The obsession for perfection that Barbara had brought from her childhood was expressed in her new house. She had longed for this symbol of status, and now that she had it, she was determined that it would reflect her taste and refinement, her superiority to the circumstances in which she found herself. Everything had to be perfect about the house, and she pushed herself to make it so. While she fussed about inside, arranging and clean-

ing, Larry cleared the back yard of weeds and vines, bought a tiller and put in a late garden. He erected a gym set for Bryan and
built a utility shed for his tiller and lawn mower.

Larry's family looked on with concern. Barbara never would
be happy with what she had, no matter how good it might be or
how much it cost, they told themselves. Larry was so deeply in
debt now that they couldn't imagine how he and Barbara would
pay for all of these extravagances. After all, Larry soon would be
giving up his job so that he could finish his degree and begin
teaching, as he had long dreamed of doing.

Larry left Sears that summer to do his student teaching in a
class for slow learners at Trindale Elementary School, only a few
miles from his new house. On the occasional weekends when he
went to his parents' house that fall, he didn't speak of any troubles, but Doris and Henry knew that something was wrong and
they suspected that the new house and all her new possessions
had not been enough for Barbara. Not only did Larry seem more
worried and withdrawn, he was even thinner than usual. He
complained of stomach troubles, and at twenty-five his hair was
already turning gray.

Not until later would Larry's parents learn that with her
spending carried as far as she felt it could go, Barbara's needs to
break boundaries would turn in a different direction. Months afterward, Larry confided to his mother that he had discovered that
Barbara was having an affair during this period and they had
stopped sleeping together. He did not say with whom she was
involved, and Doris didn't know if Larry knew the man's identity.
But others did. Barbara's affair was common knowledge at the
bank.

Several of Barbara's coworkers had met Larry at various times
when he stopped by the bank. They all thought him a quiet, gentle, thoughtful man, and that was one reason they could not understand why Barbara became involved with Ken Hazelwood,
who usually was called by his nickname, Butch. Hazelwood,
eleven years older than Barbara, was brash and aggressive, nothing like Larry.

Bob Gray, Barbara's supervisor since 1972, knew Hazelwood
well. Hazelwood had worked for him at a car dealership in High
Point a few years earlier. Hazelwood was a "rough character."
Barbara's first boss, Jack Kearns, also knew Hazelwood and de-

scribed him as "hot tempered," with a "poor reputation." Hazelwood was often in trouble of one sort or another, and years later he would be murdered, shot in the head.

Earlier in 1973, Hazelwood had started a used-car lot called Bargain Autos. He worked out a plan with NCNB to provide financing for his customers. Barbara made the credit checks on those customers, and she was in regular contact with Hazelwood. Coworkers saw that she was getting more and more friendly with him, but nobody knew just how friendly until he came to Bob Gray that fall to talk about a problem that he wanted to avoid. Barbara was going to leave Larry and move in with him, Hazelwood said. Would that affect his business dealings with the bank? NCNB didn't involve itself in the personal lives of its employees or customers, Gray told him. Later, when Gray stopped by Hazelwood's house one day, Hazelwood showed him personal items of Barbara's and said that she was spending time there with him whenever she could.

Gray wasn't the only person at the bank who knew about Barbara's affair with Hazelwood. The husband of one of her female coworkers was employed at a finance company where Hazelwood took customers who couldn't qualify for bank loans. Hazelwood frequently boasted to him about his sexual exploits with Barbara. She was unlike anything he'd ever seen, he claimed.

He would not be the last to comment about Barbara's sexual appetites. "She was tremendously aggressive," another lover recalled years later. "I thought she was a nymphomaniac to some extent. She wanted to go all night long. It was incredible, like a machine or something."

Knowing the strain that Larry's marriage was under, his parents were surprised when they learned before Christmas of 1973 that Barbara was pregnant again. Larry said little about it, and at the time Doris and Henry could only surmise that he and Barbara had worked out their problems.

Larry finished his student teaching just before Christmas and was awarded his degree and teaching certificate in February. He was promised a job teaching in the Randolph County schools starting in the fall. Meanwhile, he had to look for other work, and a far more lucrative opportunity presented itself. He got a job as office manager at Prehler Electrical Insulation Company in

High Point, a division of the 3M Corporation. The job turned out
to be better than he had hoped. It provided good benefits and
paid more than he ever had made, more than he could make
teaching. Once again teaching would be put on hold.

Barbara's second child, Jason Andrew Ford, was born July 27,
1974. He would be her last. After the delivery she underwent a
tubal ligation to prevent future pregnancies.

The baby offered no relief from the strain of a faltering marriage. Relations between Larry and Barbara continued to deterio-
rate. Larry fell into an even glummer mood and remained in it as
fall arrived. His parents didn't know how to help him. One weekend they took him to the mountains, as they had when he was
much younger, for a hike along the New River, hoping to revive
happy memories. Nothing seemed to help.

The estrangement he felt was redirected into a newfound passion. The year before, he had signed up for tae kwon do lessons
taught by Lou Wagner, a financial consultant and fellow Marine
reservist. The classes were held weekly at the High Point YWCA.
Tae kwon do is a Korean martial art that espouses self-awareness
and detachment, and Larry became absorbed in it that fall, drinking in the philosophy and working out hard.

Barbara was directing her passions in different directions.


Butch Hazelwood still came to the bank, still chatted with
Barbara, but her coworkers had detected a distance between
them since Barbara's pregnancy. She had not tried to hide the
troubles in her marriage, and since she had returned to work following Jason's birth, her coworkers had noticed that she had
become much closer with another of the bank's customers.

Joe Albright,* who was Barbara's age, worked for a car dealership and brought his customers to NCNB for loans. Barbara,
who had been handling his account for a year, always greeted
him with a big smile, was always especially nice to him. After her
baby was born, she became even friendlier. Late that summer, he
later would claim, Barbara told him that she was separated.

He asked if she would like to come to his house and go for
a swim in his pool one afternoon. She accepted, and their swim
led to sex on her first visit. After that, Barbara came regularly to

his house, sometimes even bringing Bryan with her. Albright was astonished at her sexual hunger.

Her desire, Albright soon realized, was not only for him. Word reached him that he might be treading in dangerous waters. Barbara, he was told, was also involved in an affair with Clement Wilson,* described by those who knew him as a "high roller," a "big-time operator." Like Butch Hazelwood, Wilson was eleven years older than Barbara, a man accustomed to getting what he wanted. He had a loan at NCNB, but he came to the bank far more often than was needed to attend to it, and he always ended up talking and laughing with Barbara. Years later, Wilson would deny having an affair with her, saying that he came to the bank frequently because he was selling his business and getting ready to move from High Point, but he wouldn't have been able to get anybody who worked with Barbara at the time to believe that.

Barbara never mentioned Wilson to Joe Albright, but when he heard that she was involved with him, he stopped inviting her to his house. He didn't want trouble, and she, after all, kept saying that she was thinking of going back with Larry. Albright did not know at the time that she had not even moved out of the house she shared with Larry.

Finally, Barbara did leave early in November, when Jason was three months old. Larry's family and friends would never know what precipitated the separation. His parents didn't find out about it until he showed up for dinner one Sunday alone. Even after he told them that Barbara had left and taken the children, he remained mute about the reasons for it. They didn't press him for details because he seemed so distressed about it. Instead, they tried to console him with normalcy. He must miss Bryan, his parents thought. They knew that Larry had been trying hard to make his marriage work for Bryan's sake, and he was clearly devastated by his failure.

The Fords figured that Barbara had turned to her mother for help, as she usually did in times of trouble, and had gone back home to Durham. They knew that Barbara had conflicting emotions about her mother. Her mother always tried to control her life, she had told Larry, never would let her make her own decisions. Yet, while resentful, Barbara still seemed almost completely dependent on her.

The Fords were surprised when Larry told them that instead of going back to her mother, Barbara had moved into a small apartment on Lexington Avenue in High Point, not far from the bank where she worked. There had to be a reason for that, the Fords knew, and they would soon discover what it was.

If they had talked to any of Barbara's coworkers, they could have learned the reason much earlier. His name was Gary Spangler,* and everybody at the bank knew that Barbara had had her eye on him since he had come to work in her department as a collector nearly a year earlier. He was twenty-four, two years younger than Barbara, good-looking, conservative, bright, serious-minded, a young man who clearly would go far. He also was, by his own later admission, naive about women and sex, making him vulnerable to Barbara's bold forwardness and growing sexual abandon. People at the bank were gossiping about Barbara and Gary even before she left Larry, but after they learned of the separation, they had no doubt of her intention. The only speculation was about how long it would be before Gary moved in with her.

Despite his misgivings, Larry filed for a legal separation, and it was granted on November 21. Later, he would tell his mother that until the separation he really hadn't known how much in debt they were. Bills he thought had long been paid actually never had been, he discovered. And there were bills he'd never even known about. Under the terms of the separation, Barbara got the 1970 Mustang that she always drove, Larry got the 1972 Datsun. She got the children's furniture and half the rest. He got the bills, the house and the mortgage.

Barbara received full custody of the children. Larry promised to pay $175 a month in child support. He could see the children one weekend each month, for a month each summer and for one week during Christmas vacation, but he had to give Barbara a week's notice before any visit.

Wanting to see their grandchildren and hoping to learn more about what was going on, the Fords dropped by Barbara's apartment unannounced one weekday afternoon. Bryan, who soon would be six, answered the door. Jason was in his crib. The TV was playing. Bryan sat on the sofa with his grandparents to talk. His mother was there, Bryan said, motioning toward the bedroom, where the door was closed.

A long time passed before Barbara emerged, wearing a housecoat. The Fords had the feeling that someone else remained in the bedroom. Barbara explained that she had gotten sick at work and fainted; a friend from work had brought her home. The Fords were fairly certain who the friend was.

"I'm going to have a new daddy," Bryan had told them a few minutes earlier.

At work, Barbara seemed giddy about her new romance, although her coworkers had no idea that she was thinking about marrying Gary. To her only female friend in the department, Barbara seemed to be pushing the relationship, while Gary was holding back, uncertain and reluctant. Nonetheless, he went with Barbara and the boys to Durham to meet her parents in December.

After Christmas, Barbara's mood changed. It became clear in the office that her romance with Gary had cooled. Later, he would not admit that there had been a romance at all. He acknowledged going out with Barbara, visiting her apartment, having sex with her and going to meet her parents, but he called it "a casual relationship" that had lasted only a couple of months. Barbara, he said, was more involved than he.

Gary's rejection was traumatic for Barbara, and on January 20, she wrote a letter to her boss at the bank. "Due to the personal problems concerning my separation, I feel it would be better for myself and my children to move and be near my parents for their help and support. My termination date will be Jan. 31, 1975. My work experience has been very enjoyable and rewarding. Thanks."

In his report on Barbara's resignation, her supervisor recorded that she had been a very good employee, capable, congenial, efficient, cooperative. "She is blessed with better than the average looks, personality and quick mind," he wrote, noting that he would not hesitate to rehire her. She would not be leaving if not for her separation, which had not affected her work, he wrote, adding that she had simply decided that moving back to Durham would be the best thing for her and her children, especially in view of the fact that she recently had discovered that she was pregnant again.

Barbara's supervisor had no way of knowing that she no longer could become pregnant. Why she told him that would be

cause for wonder years later. Had she hoped that word would fil-
ter down to Gary, frightening him or causing him to come back
to her? Was she losing her grip on reality, as she had when Larry
had rejected her years earlier?

Before she left, Barbara tried to find a position with an NCNB
branch in Durham, but none was available. However, she had no
trouble getting rehired as a secretary at the Duke University Medical Center, where she had worked all through high school, and
where her mother was still employed.

After she left, Larry's mood dipped even lower. He threw himself ever harder into tae kwon do, each kick and blow striking
out at his unhappiness. He didn't talk about himself with his fellow students, and few of them were aware of his marriage problems. He trusted Lou Wagner, though, and had told him about
the breakup. Wagner could tell that he was deeply troubled.
Larry mentioned to him how much he missed Bryan, whom he
had brought to class a few times, and Wagner knew that he
wanted to get his family back together if only for his son's sake.

Larry's parents could offer little comfort for his distress and
were reluctant to offer advice. But one cold Sunday, standing on
his front porch as Larry was preparing to leave, Henry suggested
that maybe it was better this way. Perhaps Larry should just let
her go, start anew.

"With what she's done," Henry said, "you can get the boys
and raise them yourself."

Larry was silent for long moments, as if deep in thought.

"I can't do it, Daddy," he finally said. "The kids need their
mother."

His father never pressed him after that.

Soon afterward, Larry told his parents and Jane that he had
gone to Durham to try to get Barbara to come back home. She
had declined. She was getting settled in her new job. She had
started going with her parents to their new church, Ebenezer
Baptist, and was helping with youth activities. She didn't want to
come back to Randolph County and more strife. Strangely,
though, she offered a compromise. They would remain apart.
But Larry could take Bryan. She would keep Jason.

Larry said no. He wanted his family whole. He came home
convinced that it was mainly Barbara's mother who stood in his
way. "These things happen, Larry," he said she had told him, as

if everything had been settled. There was a smugness about her, he thought, a sense of victory that Barbara was now back under her control and could be set again upon the right path.

Although he had entered his marriage reluctantly, Larry turned around to become its proponent. He was willing to forgive Barbara's infidelities and overlook their mistakes. If both were willing to change their attitudes and work at it, he was certain that they could make a go of the marriage and provide a stable and happy family life for Bryan and Jason, and he didn't intend to give up until his family was reunited. He kept trying, and in March Barbara gave in and agreed to try a reconciliation.

It was quickly clear to Larry's family that Larry had not been the only one to suffer from the troubles in his family.

"The biggest change was in Bryan," Jane later recalled. "He was so sad. The look in his eyes was just a haunted look. I'd never seen that in a child before."

If Larry thought that reuniting his family would bring them happiness, he was mistaken. Barbara's compulsions would continue to grow and would make their next break permanent.

# Chapter Six

The pattern that had emerged in Barbara's life would be evident later. She had to push the boundaries, one way or the other. When she was not having affairs, she was spending money. When she was not spending, she was having affairs. Soon after she moved back to Randolph County to try to salvage her marriage, she resumed spending.

Larry's family marveled at the things Barbara bought and wondered how she could keep doing it. She made only $175 a week at the job she took as a customer service representative at a newly formed company in High Point that supplied upholstery fabric to furniture manufacturers. And Larry wasn't making all that much more. How were they going to pay for everything when their budget was already stretched to the breaking point?

"If they'd been millionaires, it wouldn't have been enough," Larry's brother Ronnie said years later.

Barbara's new boss could have told them how she was able to get away with it to some extent. She had made it clear to him that she was the boss at home and controlled the finances.

If Larry was distressed by Barbara's spending at this time, he didn't show it. He seemed relieved just to have his family back together, and he was trying hard to keep the peace and make the marriage work. Although his parents no longer trusted Barbara because of the pain she had caused Larry, they suppressed their feelings for his sake. They still went for visits to their son's house. Larry, Barbara and the children still came for Doris's Sunday dinners. But Larry's siblings started to avoid them. They not only resented Barbara for the way she had treated their brother, they didn't like the way she looked down on them and their parents. And they didn't want to hear Barbara bragging about the new things she had bought.

Barbara became friends with Shirley Gilbert* at work, and Shirley visited at her house on several occasions, once going for a cookout. She got the impression that Barbara and Larry had a good relationship, and they both were clearly devoted to the children. Later, though, Barbara began telling her about a woman with whom Larry worked, implying that he had had an affair with her. Shirley was surprised. Larry just didn't seem the type to do that.

Although she couldn't have known, Barbara's implication of an affair by Larry was justification for further sexual adventures of her own. Barbara restrained herself for more than a year after going back to Larry, but in March 1976, she found new opportunity. She left her job at the fabric company and became a receptionist for a big manufacturing company, a job that paid only $25 more per month. But she had been promised, she said, that this was only a foot in the door, and greater things were to come.

Larry remained in his office manager's job and continued his martial arts classes. He was now a red belt, helping Lou Wagner teach beginners and volunteering his time at the Boys Club in High Point, where he took Bryan for activities.

Bryan was now a first-grader at Trindale Elementary School and had formed a close friendship with another boy from his neighborhood, Locke Monroe. Bryan had started going to Sunday school with his new friend, and Barbara had gotten to know Locke's mother, Brenda, because of their children. She invited Barbara and Larry to join Bryan at church one Sunday. They accepted and soon began attending services regularly at Cedarcrest Friends Meeting,* only a few miles south of their house. Larry's parents were pleased when they learned that Larry and Barbara had turned to the Quaker faith that had been their own heritage. Maybe this was indeed a new start for both of them. Maybe this was what they had needed to strengthen their marriage.

Barbara's promise of bigger things to come at work was fulfilled when she became secretary to the company president, Daniel Morefield.* He was a self-made millionaire. A man of great confidence and a personable nature, he harbored high political ambitions. Married, with children, he also had been involved in a long-term off-and-on affair with a younger woman, Susan Deaton.*

Although her promotion didn't bring much more money, Barbara celebrated by trading in her Mustang for a new Ford LTD. Her new job required her to attend business meetings with her boss, travel that sometimes took her away on weekends. She frequently returned with expensive items that she showed off to her in-laws—gifts from business associates, she said; it was the way business was done nowadays. But the Fords had seen such gifts before, and they doubted that they had anything to do with business. Barbara, they feared, was returning to the old habits that had hurt Larry so much.

Not long after Barbara went to work for Daniel Morefield, Susan Deaton sensed that he had turned cool toward her. He didn't call anymore. When she called him, he couldn't talk, couldn't find time for her. Finally he told her that so many things were going on that he wouldn't be able to see her again for a while. Susan was angry and hurt.

"I knew he was having an affair with Barbara," she said years later. "I just *knew* it, woman's intuition."

Susan had developed a close friend at Morefield's company, and she called her about it. The whole plant was swirling with gossip about Barbara and her boss, her friend reported, and everybody was certain that something was going on between them. Barbara seemed to go out of her way to make it obvious.

Susan confirmed the affair in her own mind later when she saw Barbara and Morefield leaving a convention together arm in arm.

In August 1977, however, Barbara left her job abruptly. As soon as Susan heard about it, she called her friend at the company. The word was that the gossip about Barbara and Morefield had finally reached his wife.

When Morefield showed no sign of renewing their relationship after Barbara left the company, Susan began to suspect that he was still seeing her, and she knew that was the case when she saw them together two months later.

Susan had never met Barbara, and she was certain that Barbara didn't know about her affair with Morefield. Wanting to size up her rival, she got a mutual friend of hers and Barbara's to invite the two of them to lunch.

"Money, money, money," that was all she talked about, Susan later recalled. "She was going to have a Mercedes, she was going to have a beach house, she was going to do this, she was going to do that. A golddigger, that's what I thought she was. She wanted what Daniel's wife had, the big house, the fine cars. She didn't care anything about him."

If Larry was ever aware of the reason Barbara left her job, he never told his parents. The explanation that Barbara later offered was that she wanted to make more money and had decided that the way to do that was in real estate.

She began studying to get a real estate broker's license, and she got it before Christmas. But not until January would she get a job, and then it would pay by commission only.

With Barbara out of work, the family budget had been stretched even tighter. But her spending had not abated. Their credit cards were at their limits and they were deeply in debt. Larry told his parents that the bank had tried to repossess his Datsun. Barbara was supposed to have made the payments, but she hadn't done it and hadn't told Larry about it, using the money for other purposes. He had to get an emergency loan from his company's credit union to save the car, and it had embarrassed him.

Matters didn't improve after Barbara went to work at Kay-Lou Realty in Archdale, a bedroom community south of High Point. Kay Pugh ran the agency, which she had founded with a partner. She later had bought her out, but recently she had sold half of the company to another real estate broker who had affiliated it with the Century 21 network. Six agents were already working out of the office, and Kay really had no need for another, but she had little say in the matter. Her new partner, Wayne Mabe, who owned another real estate agency in north High Point, not far from where Barbara once had lived, had hired her.

Kay liked Barbara and although they were not close, the two got along well, perhaps because in Kay Barbara had found someone to admire. Only in her twenties, Kay seemed to have everything. She was beautiful, ebullient and charming. She wore only the most expensive clothes. She lived in a big house with a swimming pool and a heart-shaped lake in the back yard. She alternately drove a flashy yellow Cadillac, a Datsun 280Z, a Ford Thunderbird. Men loved her and many pursued her. Years later, when Barbara would try her hand at writing a romance novel, she would turn herself into Kay as her heroine. But Barbara didn't know that it all was a facade, that Kay, who had come from a poor fundamentalist religious family, had made a lot of money but had spent much more, and that her personal life was in great turmoil—turmoil that eventually would boil over into Barbara's own life.

Kay was not nearly as impressed with Barbara. She told friends that Barbara was "strange," and that she didn't seem to have what it took to be successful in real estate. Barbara came to the office regularly but rarely stayed for longer than half a day, sometimes only a few hours. She didn't get many phone calls and developed few prospects. Her first month at work passed without her making a single sale—or getting a paycheck.

Other agents thought that Barbara was quiet and withdrawn, perhaps not outgoing or confident enough for sales. She spoke of being close to closing with some clients, but something always happened to subvert the sale. Sometimes she sat on a reception room sofa reading and not saying anything to anybody.

Another new agent, Carlton Stanford,* was best at bringing out Barbara, telling jokes, laughing, teasing in suggestive ways. "Carlton was just terrible about the way he cut up with Barbara," an older female agent later would say. A pudgy, gregarious man, four years older than Barbara, Stanford liked to smoke marijuana and snort cocaine, although nobody at the agency later would admit to being aware of it, and within two years he would go to prison for a year for selling a small amount of cocaine. Barbara, who neither smoked nor drank and was now regularly attending services at a Quaker church, began going out with Stanford to make appraisals on houses. Sometimes she spoke to the other agents of showing houses at night, which most agents didn't do. Her sales record, however, did not improve. A second month passed with no paycheck.

Early in March, Barbara joined others from Kay-Lou at a Saturday real estate convention at a hotel in Charlotte. It was only a one-day meeting and she would not be away overnight. Carlton Stanford also attended the seminar, which conflicted with a crucial Atlantic Coast Conference college basketball game that he wanted to see. He decided to skip some of the real estate sessions in favor of the game and rented a room so that he could watch it in comfort. He asked Barbara if she wanted to join him, and she accepted.

Settled on the bed in front of the TV, Stanford lighted a joint and offered it to Barbara. He was surprised when she accepted and took a drag. After they had finished, he was surprised again when Barbara began kissing him. Soon, Stanford later recalled, they were out of their clothes, but just as they were beginning intercourse, Barbara mentioned that she had just finished her period. "It just completely turned me off," Stanford said years later. He lost his erection and couldn't get it back even after lengthy oral stimulation. That, he claimed, was the end of his "one and only" sexual encounter with Barbara.

Later, he wouldn't be able to recall who won the game. Or even who was playing.

Barbara didn't talk much about her new job on Sunday visits with her in-laws, but on one visit, out of the blue, she hinted to Doris with an aura of mystery that strange things were going on in the upstairs rooms at the real estate agency, things she couldn't talk about. Why did she bring it up? Doris wondered. Was something actually going on? Or was it happening only in Barbara's mind? If Larry knew anything about it, he never mentioned it, and Doris was reluctant to bring it up with him. Was Barbara becoming unstable again?

It certainly seemed so. Barbara had never had much to say to Barbara Landrum, who was the receptionist at Kay-Lou and Kay's sister. But one day soon after the seminar in Charlotte, Barbara was sitting on the reception sofa and began chatting. She wound up telling about coming home from a Tupperware party recently and finding her husband in bed with another woman. Since then, she said, she had been sleeping on the couch.

Barbara Landrum couldn't understand why she was being told this. It was the kind of thing confided to a close friend, not to somebody with whom you'd never really had a conversation. She mentioned it to her sister. More of Barbara's strangeness, Kay thought.

Not long after this, Kay told a friend that she was concerned about Barbara. She had run up a lot of bills, she said, and was doing a lot of financial finagling to plug holes and keep her husband from finding out about it, borrowing to pay off loans, writing bad checks, shifting money from bank to bank to keep the checks from bouncing. She was afraid that Barbara was going to get into trouble, she said.

While Larry may not have been aware of all of Barbara's financial shenanigans, he at least knew that their debt was overwhelming, and he confidentially told his father that he was worried about it when his parents dropped by for a visit on a Sunday afternoon in early March. On this same visit, Doris noticed another peculiar thing. Larry had posed with the boys for a new portrait at a photo studio. Barbara had made it the center of a grouping of family photos on the living room wall. There were other individual photos of Larry, Bryan and Jason, but not even one of Barbara. Doris couldn't help but wonder why Barbara would leave herself out of the happy family circle.

As the Fords were leaving, Doris saw that Barbara had put her arm in Larry's. She seemed to be more affectionate toward him lately, often touching him or holding his hand. Maybe going back to church had brought about a change, Doris thought. Maybe, after all, Larry was going to have the happy family life that he longed for and deserved.

From the time Barbara had gone to work at the real estate agency, Larry's energies had been concentrated on getting ready for the strenuous tests he would have to pass to win his black belt in tae kwon do. He devoted many hours to it, and Toby Wagoner, a friend from the class who helped him get ready for the tests, knew how hard he worked. Larry had time for little else, Wagoner said later.

Larry won his black belt in mid-March after more than four years of effort, becoming the first black belt Lou Wagner had taught in High Point. His entire class was proud and happy for him. Larry was the most popular member of the class, always good-natured, even-tempered. He never used profanity and was always helpful and patient with those of lesser abilities and experience.

"Didn't matter how hard he was working on his own techniques, he would stop and help anybody," Toby Wagoner said.

"This was the nicest guy in the world," said Lou Wagner. "He never had a problem with anybody. That fellow didn't have a bad thought in his head or a mean bone in his body."

Two female members of the class were impressed by Larry's family orientation, his obvious love for his sons, whom he sometimes brought to class. One of them, Emily Cornelison, had a daughter whom she brought to class with her so that her daughter could take swimming lessons at the Y pool, and she and Larry frequently talked about their children. Larry almost never discussed his personal problems with class members, but after he got his black belt, he mentioned to Emily that things weren't going so well at home, although he didn't elaborate. Larry had indicated the same thing to another class member, Kathryn Pugh (no relation to Kay Pugh), when the two of them were helping to teach a beginner's class.

Larry was talking with Toby Wagoner and Kathryn after class on March 14 when he mentioned that somebody had been following Barbara home from work at night and that she wanted him to buy her a pistol because she was frightened.

"Why don't we corner the guy at the end of your road and have a little karate chat with him?" Toby suggested.

Larry laughed. "I'll just buy her a gun."


On Monday, March 20, 1978, Barnie Pierce, minister at Cedarcrest Friends Meeting, got a call from Barbara. He rarely heard from the Fords, who had been accepted for membership but had not yet taken the final step to join the congregation. He had visited briefly at their house a few times but didn't really know them well. Neither Larry nor Barbara had ever come to talk with him about any problems.

Now Barbara was telling him that twice in recent days somebody had followed her home from work at night, frightening her. She wanted to buy a pistol for protection, and she needed somebody to be a character reference so that she could get a permit. Would he sign? She would be happy to come and get him and drive him to Asheboro. It would only take an hour or so.

Pierce said that would be all right, and he would go with her.

The following morning, Barbara arrived at work and told Carlton Stanford that she needed a favor. She wanted him to go

with her to buy a pistol to carry in her purse. She had told him
more than a week earlier about people following her home.

"You have to get a permit," he told her.

"I've already got it," she said, showing it to him. He noticed
that a minister had signed as a character witness.

Barbara said that she didn't know anything about guns, and
she needed his guidance.

That afternoon they went to Hunter's Haven, a small gun
shop just down the street from the real estate office. Carlton suggested that Barbara get a .25. It would be small enough for her
to carry and handle yet powerful enough to offer an effective defense. Together they picked out a blue Sterling Arms .25 semiautomatic. It was a decent weapon, Stanford told her, not a piece of
junk like the cheap Saturday-night-special .22s that were so common. Barbara also bought a box of shells.

After they left the shop, she asked Carlton for another favor.
Would he show her how to use it?

He agreed, and they drove to the house of a friend of his in
an isolated area of Randolph County, where he showed her how
to load and handle the weapon. Both fired it several times.

As Stanford was demonstrating how to unload the pistol, he
later said, he showed Barbara what he considered to be the
number one cause of accidents with semiautomatics. People
would sometimes remove the magazine without realizing that a
shell would be left in the chamber. He showed her how to oper-
ate the slide and eject the cartridge that remained, then presented
her with her newest possession.

"Be careful with it," he said.


Larry showed up at the YWCA at seven-thirty as usual that
night. He seemed to be in good spirits, and as always, he took
time to help others with their workouts. During a break he told
Emily Cornelison that he and his family were planning to go to
the beach for the weekend, and he hoped that would help things
at home.

Afterward, Larry sparred with Lou Wagner. Everybody who
worked out with Larry was cautious about kicking him high because he wore braces on his teeth. As the two sparred, Larry took
a kick high in the ribs, slowing him for a moment.

"You caught me a good one," he told Wagner.

Both were winded when the class ended at nine-thirty.

Some of the class members always went out to eat after their workout. Larry rarely went with them, but they always invited him anyway. When they asked this night, he declined as usual. Two class members later would remember him saying that he had to go by his parents' house, but he didn't do that. He said good night, waved to his fellow class members and headed for his car wearing scruffy tennis shoes and his *gi,* the loose-fitting white uniform that he now tied at the waist with a black cloth belt.

None of them suspected that he was on his way to a violent encounter in which his extensive martial arts training would offer no defense.

# Chapter Seven

Another shooting. In three and a half years of riding ambulances in Randolph County, Bob Perry had seen his share of carnage from gunshots. Those calls often came late at night, as this one did, the result of drunken confrontations or desperate despondency. Usually, though, these calls weren't to middle-class subdivisions.

The call came from the dispatcher in Asheboro at 12:36 A.M. on Wednesday, March 22, 1978. Perry and his fellow emergency medical technician Jim Owen were working a twenty-four-hour shift at the Guil-Rand Fire Department in Archdale.

They jumped up immediately at the alarm and donned bright yellow helmets. Five minutes later, with red lights flashing and siren blaring, the Ford van ambulance turned into the Windemere Heights subdivision, occupied mainly by young families living in three-bedroom brick ranch houses and split-levels.

The house Perry and Owen were looking for was set on a small rise beside an identical house on a dead-end street. A steep concrete drive led to a carport where a yellow 1976 Ford LTD and a 1978 Datsun 510 were parked. The carport lights were on, and as Owen cut the siren and pulled up the drive, outside lights began popping on throughout the quiet rural neighborhood.

Perry was first to reach the carport door, medical kit in hand. The glass storm door was closed, but the inside door stood open to the dining room and kitchen at the back of the house. As he opened the door, a short blond young woman wearing blue jeans and a sweatshirt emerged from the kitchen to greet him.

"My husband's been shot," she said. "He's upstairs. I think he's dead."

Perry and Owen headed for the short staircase that led to the upstairs bedrooms. The woman followed to the foot of the stairs and stopped.

The victim was tall and thin with dark hair and a neatly trimmed beard. He lay on his back in bed wearing gray pajamas with red and black stripes. The covers were pulled over his chest. His eyes were closed, and at first glance he might have been sleeping. Perry knew differently. He recognized death when he saw it.

Perry jerked back the rose, aquamarine and white bedcover. The stylish top sheet, patterned in multicolored stripes, was blotched with dried blood. Blood also had dried on the man's pajama top. Perry reached for a pulse but found none. The man's face was white. Parts of his body were already purpled where blood had settled.

The man was sprawled across the bed, his head on the right edge of the pillow on the opposite side of the bed from which he lay. His right leg was hanging partly off the bed, his right arm at his side, his left arm flung back.

Perry raised the pajama top to reveal a small bullet hole in the man's chest, a couple of inches above and to the left of his right breast. There was relatively little blood. Most of the bleeding, Perry saw, had been internal.

Under the covers, near the man's left hip, was a loaded clip for a semiautomatic pistol. Perry saw the pistol on the beige carpet beside the bed, as if it had fallen from the man's right hand, the barrel facing the bed. He recognized it instantly as a .25 caliber. His wife had one that looked just like it.

Perry left his helmet and medical equipment on the bed and returned downstairs, where the woman waited. "There's· nothing we can do," he told her. "I'm sorry. We're too late."

Years later, he still remembered how she took the news. "She was fairly cool about it."

Perry didn't question her about what had happened, and she offered no explanation. The police, he knew, were on the way, and he went to the ambulance and radioed the dispatcher that the call was code forty-four: dead on arrival.

He thought that his supervisor, Eddie Hoover, should come

out. He knew that his wife's .25 caliber would not fire without the clip, and he suspected that somebody other than the man in the bed had fired the shot that killed him.


Larry Allen was on patrol in northern Randolph County when he received the call. He was thirty-one, the father of two young children, and he had been a sheriff's deputy for seven years. Later, though, he would acknowledge that his training, while no different from that of most other deputies in the department at the time, was woefully insufficient, consisting of just four weeks of rookie school before he went on patrol.

"Randolph County was probably fifty years behind then," Allen said. "We had no equipment. I'm not sure investigators were much more trained than the patrolmen were, and that was sad."

The bedroom at the back of the house seemed too small for the bulky, darkly stained wood furniture that dominated it. On one side of the bed was a nightstand, on the other a long dresser with a tall mirror and nine drawers in three rows. Against the wall at the foot of the bed was a four-drawer chest.

"He's dead," Bob Perry said as Larry Allen came into the room.

Allen went to his patrol car to call his supervisor, Sergeant A. C. Bowman, commander of this patrol zone, then returned to the bedroom to try to determine what had happened.

Perry and Owen pointed out the loaded clip in the bed, the pistol on the floor. They raised the body to look for an exit wound but found none.

On top of the chest of drawers, a small green box lay open. It had contained the pistol. In the bottom of the box was a pamphlet marked with bold black letters—WARNING; READ—offering safety instructions.

A receipt beside the box revealed that the pistol had been bought less than twelve hours earlier at Hunter's Haven in Archdale. The price: $79.95. A box of shells had cost $9.15. The open box of shells was on the chest, too, several rounds missing.

Two small red suitcases—both packed, one unzipped—and an upright shopping bag were set in the narrow space between the dresser and the back wall, under a window that looked out onto a children's gym set in the back yard. A pair of woman's stack-heeled shoes had been casually tossed beside the bag.

When Sergeant Bowman arrived, he and Allen made a diagram of the room. Allen went to his car for the Polaroid camera his wife had given him and took color snapshots of the scene.

Eddie Hoover, the county's emergency services director, came in as Allen was taking photographs. Hoover thought that he was coming on a suicide call, but Perry told him he didn't think the man had deliberately killed himself. Hoover called Dr. Marion Griffin, the Randolph County medical examiner, but Griffin told him that he'd just look at the body at the hospital the next day.

Griffin suggested trying to reconstruct what had happened, and the officers and EMTs searched for the spent casing, finding it at the base of the dresser beside a scruffy pair of tennis shoes. Allen picked up the pistol and tested it several times to see in which direction it ejected a shell. He wanted to try to determine the gun's position when it was fired.

Hoover recently had attended a seminar on preserving evidence conducted by Dr. Page Hudson, the state medical examiner, and he tied clean plastic bags around the man's hands before Bowman and Allen gave the okay to load the body onto a stretcher and take it to the hospital morgue in Asheboro, the county seat, fifteen miles away.

Allen went to the kitchen to question the woman while the body was being removed. The man, he learned, was Larry Ford, age twenty-nine. The woman was his wife, Barbara.

Larry had been to his regular tae kwon do class the night before, she said, and had been kicked in the groin. After he got home, they watched TV for a while, then went to bed about eleven. But Larry was so uncomfortable from his injury that he kept tossing and turning.

She offered to go downstairs and sleep on the sofa. He said that he would be more comfortable if she did. She turned the TV back on to watch a movie and had drifted off to sleep when she was awakened by a noise that sounded as if something had fallen upstairs.

She thought that a picture had slipped off the wall and went to investigate. When she found the picture in place, she thought that perhaps Larry had knocked the lamp off the bedside table. She went to the bedroom and found Larry on the bed with blood on his chest, gasping for breath, and she ran downstairs and called for help.

What she didn't mention was that before calling for an ambulance, she had called her mother in Durham.

"Larry's hurt, and I think he's dying," Marva Terry later recalled her saying in an agitated state. "I knew she did not have a good sense about her," Marva said of Barbara's condition at the time. She told her daughter to call the rescue squad.

Allen asked about the gun. Barbara said she had bought it just the day before for self-protection. Her minister, Barnie Pierce, had signed for the permit.

The story sounded plausible to Allen, and Bowman concurred. Allen figured that Larry, unable to sleep, had gotten up to look at the gun because it was new. Like many people, he probably figured that it wouldn't fire with the clip removed. But when he took the clip out, a round remained in the chamber. Thinking it unloaded, he might have idly pulled the trigger with the gun aimed toward himself.

Allen and Bowman spent less than an hour at the house. Before they left, Allen told Barbara that he would have to take the gun, the clip and the shells and hold them for thirty days.

"Take it," she said. "I don't ever want to see it again."

When Allen typed his report at the end of his shift, he closed it by writing, "As a result of my investigation, I determined the shooting was accidental." Sergeant Bowman signed his concurrence.

# Chapter Eight

Ina Mae Hamblin didn't make note of the time when her telephone rang, awakening her. She only knew that it was after midnight, and she couldn't imagine who would be calling.

It was Barbara Ford, who had lived across the street from her for nearly five years. Mae, as most people called Ina Mae, was older than Barbara and wasn't close to her. They usually spoke only in passing in their yards. All that Mae knew about Barbara came from her fourteen-year-old daughter, Diane, who often baby-sat for her and was fond of her and her two sons.

Barbara sounded frantic. Larry had shot himself, she said. Could Mae come and get the boys and keep them while she rode to the hospital with Larry in the ambulance?

Mae woke her husband, Edgar, to go with her, and they dressed quickly and hurried to help. An ambulance was pulling to a stop in the Fords' driveway as they left their house.

Barbara had directed the medical technicians to the bedroom by the time they got there. The children were in the living room. Bryan, who was nine, looked frightened and bewildered. The younger child, Jason, three, was crying. Mae took Jason from Barbara, trying to soothe him, and Edgar got Bryan in hand. The Hamblins left with the children before the medics came down to tell Barbara that there would be no need for a trip to the hospital. The Hamblins left the children with their daughter and went back across the street to see if they could be of further help.

Larry was dead, they learned, and sheriff's deputies were on the way. There was nothing to do but wait for them to arrive, and they sat with Barbara waiting anxiously, uncertain of what to say or do.

When a deputy finally arrived, the medical technicians told him what had happened and took him upstairs.

In the meantime, Brenda Monroe and her husband, Wayne, who lived several hundred yards beyond the Fords on the same dead-end street, had not been awakened by the clamor that had aroused many of their neighbors. Their phone rang around one o'clock and Brenda answered to find a neighbor, Arnold Farlow, on the line.

He told her that an ambulance and the police were at the Ford house. He had talked with Edgar Hamblin, who told him that Larry had killed himself.

Brenda told her husband to call their pastor to make sure that he was aware of what had happened. She knew that Barnie Pierce would come immediately. Brenda's immediate concern was Bryan and Jason. She hurried to Barbara's house to see if she could get them and bring them back with her.

The emergency technicians and the sheriff's deputy were upstairs with the body when Brenda arrived. The Hamblins were with Barbara, who curled on the living room couch with her feet tucked beneath her.

Brenda hugged Barbara and sat on the couch beside her. She could feel Barbara trembling through the cushions. "I don't know what we're going to do without him," Barbara said.

The unspoken feeling among the assembled neighbors was that Larry had deliberately shot himself, although they had no idea why he would do such a thing. He and Barbara had seemed a loving couple with everything going for them. Nobody gave voice to those feelings, but they realized that Barbara must have sensed their thoughts, because several times she said, "Larry wouldn't kill himself. He wouldn't commit suicide."

When Brenda asked what she could do, Barbara asked if she would mind calling her parents and Larry's. Brenda agreed to call Barbara's parents because she knew they had been called already. But she didn't think she could bring herself to call the Fords and tell them that their son was dead. She'd prefer to wait and let their pastor do that, she said.

Brenda and the Hamblins had listened as Barbara told the deputy what had happened. Her story sounded plausible to them. It struck a special chord of truth with Mae when Barbara said she thought the sound she heard was the picture falling in the hall. Her daughter had told her that the picture had fallen on two occasions while she was baby-sitting, frightening her.

As the deputies were preparing to leave, somebody mentioned that the bedroom should be cleaned. Brenda and Mae volunteered to do it and checked with the deputies to make sure that it was okay. The sergeant told them to go ahead.

They were surprised that there was so little blood and disarray. They stripped the bedding, turned over the mattress and remade the bed. Mae took the soiled sheets home to wash them.

As Brenda and Mae cleaned the bedroom, Brenda noticed the packed suitcases in the corner. Curious, she asked Barbara about them later. Barbara said that she and Larry had been planning a trip to her parents' cottage at Long Beach on the coming weekend. Brenda found nothing unusual about Barbara being packed so far in advance. She knew how meticulous and well organized Barbara was.

Henry Ford's week had gotten off to a bad start. Demand was up for dairy products, and he'd been working long hours. On Tuesday, he'd had to make an extra two thousand gallons of cottage cheese and sour cream. It was something you had to stay with once you started it, and he'd worked nineteen hours that day. He was worried about Larry. When he and Doris had last visited him and his family, Barbara had mentioned that she hadn't had a paycheck in months. Larry had spoken to him about their debts. Clearly, he was worried. Henry wanted to help but didn't want to embarrass his son. But as he worked that day, he decided that he would ask Larry if he wanted him to go to the credit union and get a loan to help relieve his financial bind.

Henry didn't get home until well after midnight. Exhausted, he had eaten a sandwich and fallen into bed. He had just gone to sleep when the phone woke him. He reached blindly for the receiver and muttered a groggy hello.

"This is Reverend Barnie Pierce," said a voice he didn't recognize. "It's about Larry."

"What is it?" Henry said, quickly coming awake.

"He's had an accident."

"Where is he?"

"He's at the funeral home."

Later, Henry wouldn't remember what was said after that. He only remembered being dumbstruck. He stood by the bed after hanging up the phone, silent, dreading telling Doris, who had stirred from sleep and was looking at him anxiously.

"What's the matter?" she asked.

He couldn't help himself. He broke into tears as he blurted the words. "Larry's dead."

The preacher had not told Henry what had happened, telling him only to come to Larry's house. Henry woke his youngest son, Scott, who was seventeen, and after dressing as quickly as possible, the three of them set out, riding in dazed silence.

"It's like you're numb," Doris explained later. "It's like it's not real."

At a little after three o'clock, Henry turned into the steep drive at Larry's house. As the Fords were getting out of the car, Barbara's parents pulled in behind them, arriving from Durham, seventy-five miles away. Barbara came out and rushed past the Fords to her parents, huddling with them, it seemed to the Fords, and ignoring them.

"Her parents took her over," Doris recalled later. "They surrounded Barbara. It's been a strange thing, evidently, all through Barbara's life, a need to protect her. Her mother did not look at us and say, 'I'm sorry your son's dead.' I don't think she ever spoke a word to us."

Barnie Pierce told the Fords that Larry apparently had shot himself accidentally, but Barbara offered no details and barely acknowledged their presence.

The deputies were gone. Larry's body had been taken to the hospital morgue in Asheboro. The room in which Larry had died had been cleaned, the bed stripped and remade. Only Brenda Monroe and the minister remained at the house.

The Fords got the impression that everything had been done without any consideration of them. In their anguish they didn't know what to do. Later, they would recall walking back and forth from kitchen to living room, seeking comfort and finding none, thinking only one thing during those agonizingly long hours until dawn: "He's gone. He's gone, and he'll never be back."

\* \* \*

Near dawn, the Fords began to call their children to tell them what had happened. Their son Ronnie lived not far away and he soon arrived at the house.

Brenda Monroe later would recall that he came in and went straight to the bedroom where Larry had been shot. She followed.

Ronnie was filled with questions. Where was the gun? The police had taken it, Brenda said. What about pajamas? Larry was still wearing them. Where were the sheets? The neighbors had taken them to wash. Were there holes in the sheets? None. Was there much blood? Some, not much. Was there blood on the mattress? A little, and the mattress had been turned over. Ronnie raised the mattress to look at it. Why had the bed been made?

Soon Ronnie went downstairs and sat at the kitchen table talking with his parents. Doris called Barbara to come into the kitchen, but Brenda couldn't hear what was said.

An air of suspicion and accusation suddenly had invaded the house, Brenda thought, but Barbara wasn't sensing it. "I thought that something was going on and Barbara was not catching on," she recalled later. But she didn't bring it up to Barbara; she didn't think it her business.

Before leaving the house that morning to attend to her own family's needs, Brenda recommended Cumby Mortuary in Archdale, and two representatives of the funeral home came to the house Wednesday morning to talk with family members.

Barbara wanted to have the funeral the following day. "Bryan and I have decided that we don't want Larry open," she said.

Larry's mother was quick to object. "Barbara, Larry's not deformed. We want to see him. People will want to see." She also thought that the funeral should be put off until Friday, at least, so that people with great distances to travel could arrange to come. Barbara insisted on having the funeral the following day, but finally relented on allowing the coffin to be open.

Both families had to go to the funeral home to help Barbara pick out a casket and to take the clothes Larry would be buried in—Barbara had allowed Bryan to choose the clothing and he had picked out a three-piece white leisure suit with a bright multicolored sport shirt. Doris and Henry Ford rode to the funeral home in the same car with Barbara's parents. The two families had had very little to do with each other during the ten years that their children had been married, having visited only once.

On the way to the funeral home, Barbara's mother said the only words that the Fords would recall her speaking to them in the days immediately following Larry's death.

"Our family is closer than yours," she observed.

The Fords did not respond.

"I thought, How cruel," Doris recalled later.

John Buheller, a dapper detective who favored expensive suits, had been getting ready to go to work at the Randolph County Sheriff's Department in Asheboro early that Wednesday morning when he got a call from Sheriff Carl Moore.

"John, we had a shooting last night," the sheriff told him. "The body's at the morgue. You'd better get over there."

"Good way to start an investigation," Buheller muttered after hanging up.

Standard procedure required that a detective be called to any shooting, but that hadn't happened, and Buheller was angry about it. The sheriff's department was rife with friction between patrol deputies and the three-man detective squad that Buheller headed, and he was especially ticked off when he discovered the name of the deputy who had investigated the shooting.

"There was no love lost between me and Larry Allen," Buheller said years later. "Larry Allen was a report-taker. He wasn't an investigator at all. An investigator should have been called to the crime scene before anything was moved, especially the body."

He suspected that Allen had deliberately failed to call him. That wasn't true, Allen said years later. He had asked the dispatcher for a detective, he said, but was told none was available, and he then asked for his supervisor.

Buheller, a Vietnam veteran who had worked for the Asheboro Police Department and the North Carolina Highway Patrol before joining the sheriff's department six and a half years earlier, went to the hospital and took a look at the body.

He found a tall, thin man with dark hair and a full beard, obviously young. All Buheller knew was that the man's name was Larry Ford and that he had a small bullet wound in the center of his chest. He couldn't tell much from looking at the body. The man supposedly had shot himself accidentally, Buheller knew, but just to be safe, he decided to run a basic investigative test.

He removed the plastic bags that had been tied around the man's hands the night before, opened a standard forensics kit and, using acid and swabs, he took wipings from several areas on both hands. Carefully labeling each one, he enclosed them in plastic bags, which he would send to the State Bureau of Investigation lab in Raleigh. The wipings would tell one simple fact: whether or not the dead man had fired a gun.

The two families had returned from the funeral home when an unmarked sheriff's department car arrived and a short detective in a suit got out and walked to the house. He apologized for intruding at such a time and asked to speak with Mrs. Ford. Barbara took him into the kitchen to talk. Afterward, the detective went to his car to get a Polaroid camera and returned. Barbara showed him to the bedroom, where he took several snapshots. He left after spending only twenty minutes at the house.

After the detective had left, Barbara asked her father-in-law if he would mind doing her a favor. She produced two plastic garbage sacks filled with what appeared to be paper trash, old bills, junk mail and personal papers, and asked if he would take them out back and burn the contents. It was too windy to burn anything, so Henry put the bags in his car and disposed of them later at a trash dump. Afterward, he would regret that he didn't check to see what was in them. Bills and financial records, he suspected.

Another suspicious note was sounded when the two families returned to the funeral home for the first viewing. Barbara and her mother were standing by the coffin when Larry's brother Ronnie and his sister Janice walked into the room. Barbara was crying.

"What have I done?" Ronnie and Janice heard her saying. "What have I done?"

But her mother quickly hushed her, they said, and led her away.

Larry's family was not alone in wondering whether Barbara was actually grieving for Larry after seeing her at the funeral home as the families received visitors Wednesday night.

"Barbara acted like it was a social gathering," recalled an acquaintance who was a close friend of Kay Pugh. "She was just flitting around greeting everybody. It was unreal."

Leaving the funeral home, Larry's tae kwon do instructor, Lou Wagner, remarked to his wife, "She's not taking it hard at all."

Barbara's behavior would raise questions the following day, too, after the funeral, which was held at Cedarcrest Friends Meeting at four o'clock with burial in the cemetery beside the church.

After the ceremony, both families returned to Larry's house, where some neighbors and friends also gathered. Larry's family got upset at the way Barbara was acting. She was laughing and talking, playing the role of hostess, showing no grief at all, they thought.

Before dark, everybody returned to the cemetery to see the flowers displayed on the grave. When the Fords came back to Larry's house afterward, they saw Barbara's brother Alton walking out with Larry's leather jacket. Barbara called in Larry's brother Ronnie and gave him some of Larry's shirts, pants and sweaters.

"She gave away everything of Larry's right there on the spot," Henry recalled.

As the Fords started to leave, James Terry, Barbara's father, hurried to their car.

"I hope there won't be any hard feelings," he told them.

# Chapter Nine

Barbara could not shake Larry from her life as neatly as she had shed his belongings. Although his death would solve her financial problems temporarily, opening new opportunities for grander spending and sexual exploration, it also would create new problems and worries that would weigh heavily before she could overcome them.

After Larry's funeral on Thursday, Brenda Monroe suggested that Barbara go on to her parents' cottage at the beach as she had planned to do with Larry that weekend. Brenda would go with her, and they could take the kids. Diane Hamblin, the fourteen-year-old neighbor who baby-sat for the children, could go along. All the children loved her. It might take their minds off the sorrowful events of the week. Barbara agreed, and they left on Friday afternoon in Barbara's LTD.

The idea turned out to be not so good. No one talked about what had happened, but nobody could forget it, either, and the somber aura of death engulfed everything they tried to do. Brenda and Barbara took the children to buy Easter baskets on Saturday, but there was no joy in it.

"Protect Larry, Lord," Barbara prayed, "and be with him wherever he is." Then she burst into tears and cried so hard that she couldn't continue.

Everybody was so glum and unhappy that Barbara and Brenda decided to leave for home Sunday afternoon. Barbara wanted to go back through Durham to be with her parents, and she suggested that Brenda drop her and the boys off there and drive her car back to Randolph County. She would get somebody to bring her home later.

Alton's wife, Mary, an accountant, drove her back two days later and stayed to help with insurance and business matters involving Larry's estate.

On Wednesday, March 29, one week after Larry's death, Barbara walked into the Randolph County Courthouse in Asheboro and filed his will with the clerk of superior court. It was handwritten on the back of a Marine Reserves form used to request permission to miss regular drill. "I hereby bequeath my house and all its furnishings to my wife Barbara Terry Ford," the will said. "Said house located at Rt. 2, Box 226T, Windemere Heights, Trinity, N.C. This statement is noted to be my last will and testament and the above is to be executed upon my death."

It was dated July 12, 1975, only a few months after Barbara and Larry got back together after their separation. It was not notarized and had been signed by only one witness: Barbara Ford. The will was unnecessary. Under North Carolina law, Larry's share of the house had automatically become Barbara's at his death.

That same day, Barbara went to Kay-Lou Realty to tell Kay that she wouldn't be returning to work. That was a relief to Kay. Barbara had never made a sale, and well before Larry's death Kay had been trying to come up with some way to let her go without hurting her feelings.

After Barbara had talked with Kay, Barbara Landrum asked what she planned to do.

"I'm going to sell my house and move back to Durham," Barbara told her.

As she was cleaning out her office, Stan Byrd, another sales agent, dropped by to offer condolences. Byrd barely knew Barbara and had thought of her as "quiet, a regular little homemaker" until he had learned of her fling with Carlton Stanford in Charlotte three weeks earlier.

"If I can do anything for you, just let me know," Stan told her.

"You know what you can do for me," she said with an alluring smile, and Byrd had no doubt about her meaning.

"Scared the hell out of me," he recalled later.

* * *

Larry's parents had been so stunned immediately after his death that they couldn't think clearly or rationally. The whole thing had seemed surreal. They kept telling themselves that their son could not be dead, gone forever from their lives. They had learned few details of his death, they said later, and hadn't really begun to question the circumstances of it until the empty days that followed.

Doris had turned her family's thoughts in that direction as they were leaving Larry's house on the day of the funeral. "Something is terribly wrong here," she said, expressing a feeling that had been growing in all of them.

They forced themselves to talk about it, and when they did they found that they were of like mind. There were but three possibilities. Either Larry had shot himself accidentally or intentionally—or somebody else had shot him.

They dismissed one possibility immediately. They could not believe that Larry had deliberately killed himself. His religion didn't condone suicide. Beyond that, they knew that he loved his children too much. He loved his parents and the rest of his family too much. He was too sensitive to the feelings of others to bring them such grief.

Accident seemed the most plausible explanation for his death, yet that, too, seemed unlikely to the Fords. Larry had never even liked guns. He wouldn't be playing around with one, especially at that time of night. He always came home tired from his workout, they knew, took a shower and was in bed before eleven o'clock because he had to be up early for work. Even if he was in pain and couldn't sleep, as Barbara had claimed, Larry surely wouldn't be fooling around with a gun in bed. Besides, he knew too much about guns to be careless with one. Henry had taught Larry how to handle guns when he was just a boy, and Henry had emphasized safety. Larry always had been careful with guns. He also had been trained in the use of several types of weapons in the Marines. He knew how to handle guns. And he was safety-conscious about everything.

If he had not shot himself accidentally, that left the only other possibility, and it was almost unspeakable for the Fords. Could somebody have shot Larry? If that were so, they realized, Barbara would have had to be involved. Either she had shot him or she had to know who did.

Larry's parents simply didn't want to believe that. They knew that Barbara had problems and that she had mistreated Larry, but to think her capable of murder? The mere possibility of it seemed like something from a movie or a TV show, not something that could touch their lives, and they felt bad for even allowing it to enter their thoughts.

They were not about to point any fingers of accusation. They simply would try to deal with it one day at a time.

The Fords knew that Barbara had gone to the beach, and they called her after she got back to find out how she was doing. She invited them to come for lunch the next day. Mary Terry was still there, and Doris and Henry talked more to her than to Barbara. Barbara barely mentioned Larry.

The Fords invited her to come to their house for Sunday dinner three days later, and she did, bringing the boys and Brenda Monroe's son, Locke, as well. Ronnie was there, and the tension between him and Barbara was palpable.

The most close-mouthed of all the Ford children, Ronnie usually kept his thoughts to himself. He was by far the most suspicious about Larry's death in the days immediately following.

After dinner, Ronnie told Barbara that he had found a key to Larry's locker at the Boys' Club in the clothing that she had given him after the funeral. He would just drop it by the club, he said.

Barbara said that whatever might be in the locker belonged to her and the boys and asked for the key. When Ronnie declined to give it to her, she became angry.

Later, as she was standing on the back porch about to leave, Ronnie began asking questions that indicated he had doubts that Larry had shot himself accidentally. Barbara told him that there were only two possibilities: accident or suicide.

"And Larry didn't have the guts to kill himself," she said coldly.


Earlier that week, Detective John Buheller had asked Barbara to come to his office in Asheboro to try to clear up her husband's death.

"I felt like it sounded suspicious," he later said of her story, "but I really didn't have anything to go on."

Barbara came alone.

"She was sort of cagey," Buheller recalled years later. "She didn't give up a lot of information. Just cool. She was concerned about when we were going to close the investigation so she could collect the insurance."

Buheller asked her to take a lie detector test. She said she'd have to think about it. Several days later, a lawyer called Buheller from High Point. He represented Barbara Ford, he said, and she definitely wouldn't be taking any lie detector test.

Fifteen days after Larry's death, Barbara's former boss, Kay Pugh, and Kay's close friend Brenda Wilmoth, who was about to leave her husband, Tommy, were accosted by him as they rode in Kay's yellow Cadillac. Both were shot. Kay died of a bullet through the heart. After his arrest, Tommy Wilmoth, who later would plead guilty to second-degree murder, told authorities that he had shot the two women because he thought his life was in danger. He believed that Kay, Brenda and Barbara Ford were involved in a lesbian triangle and had plotted to kill their husbands. Larry's shooting had convinced him of this, and he believed that he was the next to die. Although no evidence ever would turn up that this was anything more than the product of a fevered imagination, rumors about Wilmoth's claim soon swept through High Point and Randolph County, and they would complicate matters for years to come.

Not until these rumors reached the sheriff's department, Buheller later would say, did he have the first real indication that Larry Ford's death might have been something more than the accident his department's reports had proclaimed it to be. The rumors, which he heard from several sources, reminded him that he had not yet sent to the SBI lab in Raleigh the evidence packet containing the wipings he had taken from Larry's hands. He mailed it, along with the pistol, on April 10, nineteen days after he performed the tests.

There was no point in taking any action, Buheller knew, until he could be certain whether or not Larry had fired a weapon. If he had, that was evidence enough that his death had been an accident or suicide and no cause for further concern. If he hadn't, then he would have to investigate.

SBI forensic chemist Michael Creasy examined the pistol and

processed the hand-wiping samples on April 26. All the tests
were negative. In his opinion, he wrote in his report, Larry hadn't
fired the gun that killed him.

When Buheller learned the results, he knew for certain that
Larry's death had not been suicide and he thought it unlikely that
it had been an accident. Only by dropping the gun, causing it to
discharge, could it have killed him without him holding it in his
hands. The position of the gun and empty shell and his location
on the bed made that possibility doubtful, if not impossible. Indeed, Larry's position on the bed made it appear that he had
been trying to rise when he was shot. Had he been awakened by
a sound only to discover a pistol aimed at his chest?

Buheller drove to Windemere Heights to talk again with Barbara. He found her at Brenda Monroe's house. Barbara had put
her own house on the market soon after Larry's death, and it had
sold quickly. Brenda had invited Barbara and the boys to stay
with her family until Bryan's school year was up, and Barbara
had trucked her furniture to Durham and stored it in the basement of her parents' house, then moved in with the Monroes.
The boys had been bunking with Locke, and Barbara had been
sleeping on the couch in the den. On weekends Barbara and the
boys had been returning to Durham to stay with her parents.

Brenda was present as Buheller talked with Barbara, and she
later described the visit as friendly. Buheller indicated that he just
wanted to clear up some details about the shooting. He asked a
few questions and talked about the location of the empty cartridge before he broke the news about the gunshot residue tests.
He led Barbara and Brenda to think that he still thought the
shooting was an accident, however, that Larry no doubt had
dropped the gun, causing it to go off.

In fact, Buheller now strongly suspected that Barbara had
shot her husband, and he called Doris and Henry Ford and asked
them to come to his office in Asheboro. The Fords were not especially surprised when Buheller told them that Larry had not
fired the gun. But they were stunned when the detective went on
to tell them about the wild rumors that were spreading about the
case. Although their son Ronnie was aware of the rumors and
was conducting his own investigation of his brother's death, this
was the first that his parents had heard about them.

Buheller said that he was almost sure now that Larry had

been murdered and Barbara had done it. He intended to prove it, he said, and he wanted to begin by having Larry's body exhumed for autopsy. Would they sign their approval? They would, said the Fords, who were almost speechless after the things he had told them.

Randolph was in a judicial district with another county at the time, and Buheller went to Assistant District Attorney Ron Bowers in Salisbury, forty miles away, to ask him to request a judge's order for the exhumation and autopsy. The autopsy, Buheller said, would reveal the angle and projection path of the bullet, which still was in Larry's body, and might also tell how far away the gun was when it fired. This information might eliminate the possibility of accident.

Bowers took Buheller's request before Superior Court Judge Thomas Seay Jr. of Spencer on May 16, and Seay approved and issued the order.

Newspapers in Asheboro and High Point reported the order, and Barbara was upset when she heard about it. She told Brenda that she didn't want Larry's body to be mutilated, and she didn't see any need for it.

"I don't know what that will prove," she said.

A week after the judge's order was issued, a backhoe scraped away the red dirt from the steel vault containing Larry's bronze coffin. Workers hired by the funeral home that had buried Larry removed the coffin and opened it for Deputy Larry Allen to identify the body. Moisture had entered the coffin and green mold had begun to form on Larry's skin. The coffin was resealed, placed in the back of a hearse and delivered to the office of the state's chief medical examiner in Chapel Hill, sixty-five miles away.

Allen and Buheller drove to Chapel Hill that afternoon to serve as witnesses while Dr. Brad Randall, the assistant chief medical examiner, performed the autopsy.

Randall found the bullet that killed Larry in his spine. The bullet had pierced Larry's right lung and right pulmonary artery, and Dr. Randall deduced that Larry had bled to death within minutes.

The wound suggested that Larry was shot at close range, Randall thought. The muzzle of the gun might even have been touching his chest when the bullet was fired, but it was too late to tell for certain because Larry's body had been cleaned and embalmed, and a plastic plug had been placed in the wound. That ruined any chance for a close estimate about the distance of the gun from Larry. That two months had passed since Larry's death didn't help either, he noted.

"FORD DEATH RECLASSIFIED AS MURDER," a headline in the *Greensboro Daily News* reported on Thursday, May 25. The short article quoted Randolph County Sheriff Carl Moore. He had no choice but to reclassify Larry's death a homicide, he said, although he had no idea who had shot him.

Brenda Monroe didn't see that headline or hear anything about it. If Barbara saw it, she didn't make it known, and Brenda saw no signs of special concern in her. Barbara blamed the detective for the unnecessary autopsy and investigation. "She felt like it was all Buheller," Brenda recalled later. "That was the bad word, Buheller."

Brenda couldn't understand why Buheller had focused on Barbara either. She could not imagine that Barbara had killed Larry. Barbara was living with her. She could see her grief, see what a caring person and loving mother she was. Barbara took part in her family's daily devotionals. She read her Bible and prayed every day. Those were not the actions of a murderer.

School was out at the end of May, and Brenda kept the boys while Barbara went off to a church camp in Indiana as a chaperone for the young people's group at Cedarcrest. After her return, Barbara took the boys to Durham, saying they were planning to go to the beach with her parents. The Monroes later joined them for a few days at the Terrys' cottage at Long Beach. It was not until near the end of June that Barbara returned to Trinity to pick up the rest of her belongings at the Monroes'.

Larry's parents had not spoken with Barbara since Buheller had told them that she was the target of his investigation. After that Sunday dinner, they had seen her only once. They had picked her up at Brenda's and taken her and the boys to Hanes Mall in Winston-Salem for an afternoon. Barbara had not seemed to enjoy the outing, and afterward the Fords felt that she was avoiding them.

Now that Larry's death had been publicly proclaimed murder and Barbara was the prime but unspoken suspect, they didn't know what to do about their relationship with her. They knew that suspicion didn't equal guilt, and they still didn't want to think her capable of what they now were convinced she had done, but despite all of that, they didn't want to appear to be accusing her or to be abandoning her and their grandchildren either. When they heard nothing from her following the news reports reclassifying Larry's death, they put off trying to contact her. Finally, they decided to drive to Randolph County and drop in on her to try to get a feel for the situation.

Finding nobody at the house, they went on to the Monroes' house and were amazed to learn that Barbara and the boys already had moved back to Durham. Not only had she not bothered to say goodbye, she hadn't even told them that she was intending to leave.

After Barbara fled to Durham, the Fords expected to hear any day of her arrest. When days passed, then a week, then another, and they still had heard nothing, they drove to the sheriff's department in Asheboro to find out what was going on. Buheller met with them and assured them that the investigation was proceeding. But there were many other crimes in the county, he pointed out, including other murders, and only himself and two other detectives to look into them. He had to fit in the investigation of Larry's death as best he could. It might take a little time.

The Fords left dissatisfied but still hopeful that something would be done soon.

Years later, Buheller would acknowledge that his investigation had come to a halt soon after the autopsy had come back. "The only thing we really had to go on was the gunshot residue," he said. "Other than that I couldn't get anything." Moreover, the assistant DA with whom he had conferred did not seem interested in pressing the matter. "I just didn't get any cooperation from the DA and really didn't have a case," he recalled. "One piece of evidence is not enough to take somebody to death row on."

The Fords were not the only ones concerned about the progress of the investigation. Insurance companies also were interested.

On April 20, Barbara had received her first insurance payment as a result of Larry's death, a check for $26,326.17 from a group life policy that Larry had with his company. The policy, which had been issued by Equitable, had a double indemnity clause for accidental death and she had filed for that as well, sending newspaper clippings to verify that Larry had died accidentally.

Eighteen days after she had received the first insurance check, Barbara had received another, much bigger one, from Metropolitan Life for an individual policy Larry had taken out. The check for $44,902.55 included $10,000 for an accidental death clause. She also had filed to get $20,000 from an accidental death policy that Larry had with the Exxon Travel Club.

Equitable was hesitant to pay Barbara's claim for accidental death, and on June 6, Ernest Atkinson, the company's account benefits manager, interviewed Sheriff Carl Moore about Larry's death. Moore told him that he had originally thought that Larry had committed suicide but had changed his mind after learning the results of the hand-wipe test.

"The sheriff does feel that someone did kill the insured," Atkinson later wrote in a memo to his supervisor.

The following day, Atkinson interviewed Buheller.

"He said insured's wife is under investigation in connection with the possible homicide," Atkinson wrote in his report. "He feels that if the death was due to homicide she had something to do with it. He stated another insurance company whose name he would not release had a $100,000 policy on the deceased. Mr. Buheller said his investigation will determine if the death was due to homicide or accidental. He said the deceased definitely did not commit suicide."

The $100,000 insurance policy did not exist, except in the rumors that were flying about Larry's death. But Equitable had more than $26,000 at stake on the double indemnity clause of Larry's policy, and it could attempt to reclaim the money it already had paid Barbara if she could be proved responsible for his death. The company not only put a hold on that payment but tried to stop payment on the check it had issued. Barbara already had cashed that check, however.

Like the Fords, the company kept waiting for word of Barbara's arrest. June turned into July and still nothing was heard from the Randolph County Sheriff's Department. At the end of July, Ernest Atkinson called Buheller again.

"Buheller said the case is still open," he wrote to his supervisor. "They have several suspects. He would make no statement beyond this."

Buheller had no new suspects at all. He hadn't even conducted another interview. Years later, other investigators would speculate that he had become so wrapped up in the complexities that were presented when Kay Pugh's death became entangled with Larry's that he simply had thrown up his hands.

As fall approached, Atkinson was still trying to find out if Barbara was going to face charges. He called Buheller again on September 7.

"He said the case is still open," he wrote in his report. "He still is unable to discuss the case. Call back in 30 days."

Atkinson called back as directed, and again thirty days after that. Each time he dutifully noted the results in his file: "Same as above."

The final blow to Larry Ford's homicide investigation came that fall. In Randolph County, Sheriff Carl Moore was an aberration, a Democratic office holder in a county where Republicans far outnumbered Democrats. Four years earlier, Moore had beaten Robert Mason, a twenty-year veteran of the Asheboro Police Department, for the job. This time, Mason was running again, with stronger support from the Republican Party. And this time he prevailed. With the new sheriff would come new top officers in his department.

Doris and Henry Ford had not been able to get anything out of the sheriff's department in months, and after the election they wanted to make sure that the investigation of Larry's death continued. They drove to Asheboro one day and searched out John Buheller.

He had worked hard on the case, Buheller told them, but there was not yet enough evidence to make a case against anybody. The investigation would now be left up to the new sheriff.

"I've done all that I can do for you," he said, throwing open his arms in a gesture of helplessness.

The Fords left realizing that they might have to start all over again if they were to have any hope of seeing justice in Larry's death.

Ernest Atkinson also made one last try with Buheller to find out something about the Ford murder investigation early in December.

"Dec. 15 is Buheller's last work day," he noted in his report. "The case has been turned over to Charles Hatley, SBI. Buheller said call Hatley in 30 days."

The case had not been turned over to the State Bureau of Investigation, however. It had been shunted to the sheriff's department's inactive file.

The insurance company did not stop trying to get a resolution about Larry's death, and neither did the Fords. The company began pressing the new sheriff for action, and the Fords, who were unaware of the insurance company's activities, took the same tack. Nearly a year after Larry's death, they finally arranged a meeting with Sheriff Mason, but they left it disappointed and angry. "He practically told us to go home and forget it," Doris recalled.

The Fords would not do that. They called the new district attorney. They tried to get the State Bureau of Investigation to look into it.

The pressure from the Fords and the insurance company prompted Sheriff Mason to make a determination about the case at the end of March, just over a year after Larry's death.

His officers had interviewed witnesses and family members, the sheriff told reporter Bob Williams of the *Courier-Tribune* in Asheboro. "They are now more satisfied than they were, if not completely satisfied, that it was accidental," he said.

The Fords were disgusted. They appealed to the state attorney general. They tried again to interest the SBI. Later, they would even try to get the FBI to intervene, but they were rebuffed at every turn.

Finally, for their own peace of mind, they would decide that they had to leave justice for their son's death in the hands of God.

Barbara was free.

# PART THREE

# New Beginnings, Old Endings

# Chapter Ten

As summer began, Barbara and her sons were living once again with her parents in Durham, where nobody but her family knew the circumstances of Larry's shooting, but Barbara intended for the stay to be only temporary.

With more than $70,000 in insurance money, she planned to invest in a house. She wanted to be near her parents for the children's sake, and she began looking in their neighborhood. The first house she went to see was a neat brick bungalow at the corner of Bramble and Genesee. She had noticed the "FOR SALE" sign in the front yard soon after she returned home. The house, only a couple of blocks from her parents' home, belonged to Russ Stager and his estranged wife, Jo Lynn. Russ had been living there alone with his German shepherd, Sampson, for three months when Barbara first came to his door.

Although Russ didn't mention it when she showed up, he was having doubts about whether he really wanted to sell the house. He was showing it mainly to satisfy his obligations to the real estate agent. Barbara liked the house, but she wanted to take her time about choosing, and before she could make a decision Russ made a settlement with his wife and took it off the market.

While Barbara was house shopping, she and the boys began going to services regularly with her parents at their church, Ebenezer Baptist. The church members were aware that Barbara had only recently become a widow—her husband, some had heard, had died in an accidental shooting—and they went out of their way to make her and the boys feel welcome.

As part of this effort, the young adults group at the church asked Barbara to join and invited her to attend a weekend retreat at Topsail Beach. The members thought it would be a good chance for her to get away, to make some new acquaintances and perhaps to get over some of the trauma of her husband's death. The group stayed in a big rented house on the beach, the women upstairs, the men down. Barbara was a little standoffish and quiet, but the group had expected that, considering the ordeal she had been through. Everybody made a special effort to include her in conversations and activities.

Jim Browder* was one who went out of his way to talk with Barbara. Two years younger, he was a relatively new member of the group himself. A native of Greensboro, he had married and moved to Texas. When his marriage broke up, he returned home. He had moved in with his brother in Durham until he could recover emotionally and financially, and was starting a new business as a building contractor. He was lonely, and one of the reasons he had joined Ebenezer was his hope of meeting a decent young Christian woman with whom he might start a relationship.

Jim was introduced to Barbara by her brothers, with whom he had become acquainted at church. He knew that she had been in real estate. To make conversation, he had approached her at the beach and asked her advice about a building project he was working on in Durham.

Jim was tall and slim, like Larry, with the same understated, quiet personality. Barbara was friendly toward him, and they had no trouble talking to each other. Jim liked her immediately. She impressed him, he said later, as "just a good old country girl." He invited her to go for a walk on the beach after supper. He sensed that she might need to talk to somebody about her husband's death, and as they walked on the hard sand, keeping above the surf's foaming edge, he said, "Look, I don't mean to pry, but if you ever need to talk about what happened, I'd be glad to listen."

She seemed touched by the offer, and they stopped and sat in the sand, watching the waves break, while she told him how she had gone to sleep on the couch on the night of Larry's death and was awakened a short time later by a loud noise. It had sounded like a gunshot, she said, and she had rushed to the bedroom and found Larry shot while he was cleaning his pistol. She cried as she recalled the horror of the moment, and Jim reached to hug and console her. She clung to him crying, and before Jim realized what was happening, they were on their feet and moving toward the dunes. There Barbara kissed him deeply, and soon they had pulled aside their brief clothing and were in wild conjunction in the sand.

"It just came on, a natural thing," Jim recalled later. "I didn't intend to do that. I didn't want to do that. That wasn't my nature. One thing just led to another and there you are."

Jim did have the presence of mind to ask one important question before things had gone too far. "Are you on the pill?"

"Don't worry," she told him. "I had my tubes tied after my last baby."

Afterward, Jim was astonished at the level of Barbara's passion. He never had known a woman so sexually aggressive. Her husband had been dead just two and a half months, he knew, and she had been through great strain. He thought she had just been letting go of all her pent-up emotions.

He enjoyed it, he had to admit, was glad that he had helped Barbara through a moment of need, but it left him feeling guilty, too, and later he prayed for forgiveness for his moment of weakness.

Jim thought that what had occurred that evening had been a one-time thing. Not wanting others in the church group to suspect anything, he acted the next day as if it hadn't happened at all. But that night, at Barbara's suggestion, he joined her for another walk along the beach and it turned as passionate as the night before.

Not long after they returned home from the beach trip, Jim got a call from Barbara inviting him to go out to eat. He was financially strapped at the time and told her jokingly that he didn't know if he could afford to take her out.

"You pay for it," he said, laughing, "and I'll go."

No problem, she told him. She had plenty of money.

Jim picked her up at her parents' house, and Barbara paid for dinner. With Barbara staying with her parents and he living with his brother, they had no place to go to be alone later, and sex did not resume until July, after Barbara had bought a new three-bedroom brick house at 5516 Genesee Street. The house was plain, with a low-pitched roof and high windows with ornamental shutters. A tiny concrete porch, hardly wide enough for a chair, was set across half the front of the house. The yard was bare except for a few scraggly pines. The house was diagonally across the street from the one Barbara had first looked at—the house owned by Russ Stager.

After Barbara moved to the new house, she frequently invited members of the young adults group from the church over for get-togethers after services. Jim was always there, and by this time other members could tell that Barbara and Jim were getting close. Before long he was going by regularly at other times, usually after the boys had gone to bed.

Knowing that Barbara was a regular churchgoer, Jim assumed that she had never had sex outside her marriage, and as her drive continued unabated and he grew to know her better, he felt comfortable enough to joke with her about her sex life with Larry.

"Are you sure you didn't screw him to death?" he asked one night.

Jim enjoyed her company, wanted to keep seeing her, but by the beginning of August she was already talking about marriage. She had been hinting at it before that, and Jim had been taken aback. Her husband had been dead only four months, and she was wanting to get married again? He thought that a normal person would be grieving longer than that, not even thinking of having someone else take the place of a husband lost so suddenly and unexpectedly. It made him wary.

By mid-August, he felt pressured. "It was like she was on a mission to get married," he recalled later.

Jim tried to deal with the matter reasonably. He thought that he might very well be happy making a life with Barbara, but they had known each other for only a few weeks, he pointed out. He wasn't sure whether he loved her or not. He didn't see how she could be sure that she loved him, especially after all she'd been through. Perhaps they could grow to love each other with time, he said. They might indeed be able to develop a successful marriage, but he had to be sure this time, and there were other considerations that he didn't want to deal with then.

Barbara seemed unaffected by his reasoning. She wanted marriage.

By the end of August, Jim felt that he had no choice but to break it off. "Barbara," he said, "this is not going to work. You've got two kids. I don't have any. You can't have any more. I want to have kids of my own. Even if I did grow to love you, I don't know if I could marry you because of that."

Barbara cried, but Jim knew that his words had had the intended effect. It was as if a curtain had suddenly dropped between them.

"When I said that, that was the end of our relationship," he said.

They remained friends, still chatted with each other at church. Barbara, Jim knew, remained intent upon her mission. She was looking for another man to marry.

The next time she would not make the mistake she had made with Jim. Never again would she tell a man who wanted children of his own that she no longer could have any. Even if she had to lie, she would get what she wanted. And she already had her eye on the man she wanted, her across-the-street neighbor, Russ Stager.

# Chapter Eleven

Like Barbara, Russ Stager was a Durham County native, born in the same hospital as Barbara, five months earlier. Like Barbara, he was a first child. His mother, Doris, was twenty-one, a tiny, delicate woman, and the birth was difficult.

"I was scared to death," she recalled years later. "I screamed so loud that I disturbed everybody in the hospital."

She clenched her hands so tightly during the long hours of labor that she later said she had feared that she'd squeezed them off. The baby finally arrived at 1:22 A.M. on Thursday, May 22. He weighed six pounds, eight ounces, had dark, curly hair and a lusty cry. His parents had decided long before that if their child was a son, they would name him for his father, and he became Allison Russell Stager III. To avoid confusion, his father, known as Al, would call his son Rusty.

Al Stager Jr. had been born and reared in Paterson, New Jersey, but by the time his son was born he was a dedicated North Carolinian. He had come to the state in 1944, a soldier on his way to war, training at Camp Butner, just north of Durham. He had met Doris at a USO dance not long after he arrived in the state, and their attraction had been immediate and mutual.

"She was a good-looking woman," he recalled forty-five years later, as she glowed in his presence. "Pretty. I liked southern belles."

Doris had graduated from Durham High School just five months earlier and was working as a secretary at Durham Realty Company. She had been born on a hardscrabble tobacco farm. The youngest of seven children, she had been only sixteen months old when her parents separated and her mother, Belle, had brought her and her older brother Earl to Durham to live with Doris's elder sister Erma, who was twenty-three years older than Doris and had moved to Durham several years earlier to work in a tobacco factory.

Al and Doris's romance was a whirlwind, and with his unit about to ship out to the war in Europe, they married on December 9, 1944, just two months after they met. Doris went to New Jersey to see him off on New Year's Eve. After fighting in France, Belgium and Germany, Al returned with a chestful of medals on their first anniversary, and Doris was waiting for him. "I didn't stand there and wait for him to get to me, either," she later recalled.

Doris was very close to her mother, her brothers and her sisters, who had been bound together by love and hardship, and Al, who had only a half-brother and always had longed to be part of a big family, thought that they should settle in Durham to be near her family, who had accepted him into their fold wholeheartedly. They moved in with her mother, sleeping on a foldout couch, and Al took a job reading water meters for the city of Durham. They had moved to a two-room apartment in Doris's sister's house and Al was selling life insurance when their first child was born.

When Russ was two, his father landed a job as installer and repairman with Durham Telephone Co., which later was to become part of General Telephone and Electronics. It was a job with promise, and Al would be quick to get promotions, remaining with the company until his retirement because of bad health thirty-four years later.

With the new job, Al moved his family into a house of their own, and three years later, just before Russ turned five, his parents bought a three-bedroom brick house at 1605 Delaware Avenue. This house was in a nicer neighborhood, shaded by huge trees, closer to schools and parks. There they would remain for the next twenty-five years.

Russ was a reticent and well-behaved child. When he started school at E. K. Powe Elementary, though, he proved to be less than studious. He was too fun-loving, wanted to play and talk too much to have patience for the rigors of learning, and he repeated a grade in elementary school.

As Russ was about to finish third grade, only weeks before he turned eight, the Stager family increased by one. A daughter, Cindy, was born and Russ became a doting older brother.

Russ was a natural athlete and mastered almost any sport with ease. He loved water sports, and on summer weekends the family often went to nearby lakes for swimming, fishing and skiing. Team sports were his favorites, though, especially football and baseball. He played on Little League teams, and by junior high he was the football team's star halfback.

"If he ever got two steps, he broke out into a gallop and he was gone," his mother recalled years later.

He did that once in a game at the county stadium, and the woman seated in front of Doris jumped up, whooping with excitement. "Hey, that's my son chasing him!" she cried.

Doris interrupted her own cheering to let her know, "That's *my* son he's chasing."

Injuries plagued Russ, and his mother would never forget taking him to football practice and seeing him get out of the car stiff with pain but determined to play. After an injury to his back, however, a doctor warned that if he continued to play football, he might be permanently disabled.

That kept him off the football team at Durham High School, but he did make the baseball team, playing outfield and catcher. By then Russ had decided what he wanted to be: a high school coach.

He developed into a trim and strong young man—five feet nine, 150 pounds—with an engaging and magnetic personality, a memorable smile and an infectious laugh. A fellow student later recalled that Russ had friends in all of Durham's High's three distinct social classes and was the only person at the school who could pass easily from one group to the others. He happily and unashamedly drove an old Ford Falcon, hauling great loads of his friends around in it, and many of them made his family's house on Delaware Avenue their home base. His mother sometimes felt that she was operating a fast-food emporium, forever frying hamburgers and french fries for Russ and his friends.

"He had a Robert Redford type of appeal," one female admirer later recalled. "Women loved him." He had many female friends and could have had his choice of dates, but throughout high school he had only one steady girlfriend, Linda Whitaker, whom he had begun dating in junior high.

Russ's parents never worried about their son's activities. They knew that he was levelheaded and firmly grounded in the values he had absorbed from family and church. The Stagers had belonged to Westwood Baptist Church when Russ was growing up, but when he was twelve he started attending Grey Stone Baptist Church after hearing the minister, Malbert Smith, speak at school. Grey Stone had a much bigger congregation than Westwood and more activities for young people, including many sports teams. Russ became such an enthusiastic member of the church that his family moved their membership there as well.

"Every time those doors opened, Russ was there," his mother later recalled of his early years at the church.

After his graduation from Durham High in 1966, Russ wanted to attend Campbell College, a strict, conservative Baptist institution, but his grades were too low to gain admission. Instead, he enrolled at Mount Olive Junior College in the eastern part of the state, where he had to complete a remedial English course before he could begin classes.

Russ's strong interest in Durham High's sports teams continued unabated, and he often returned home for important games. One weekend early in 1969, he drove to Raleigh to watch Durham High play a crucial basketball game with Sanderson High. At the concession stand, he started talking to a dark-haired, dark-eyed Sanderson student who was selling popcorn. Her name was Jo Lynn Ellen. He left with her phone number. A few days later, he called and asked if she'd like to go out for a pizza on the coming weekend. She said yes. She thought that Russ was cute and funny, and after one date she knew that he was full of life and loved to have a good time. They began dating regularly and would continue off and on for the next six years.

Sports and good times interfered with Russ's accumulation of credit hours, and by the time he began dating Jo Lynn, he dropped out of Mount Olive and enrolled for a semester at another junior college on the coast, College of the Albemarle in Elizabeth City. He was tired of struggling for grades, but the Vietnam War was raging and the draft was waiting for dropouts. There was, however, an alternative. He joined the Army Reserves and was sent to Fort Jackson, South Carolina, for six months of training. Afterward, he was ready to try college again, and this time he was accepted at Campbell, where he majored in physical education and played on the baseball, soccer and tennis teams.

After his graduation in 1972, Russ spent a term student teaching in Cary, near Raleigh, where he would be close to Jo Lynn. The following year, he applied to the city school system in Durham and was rewarded with the fulfillment of his adolescent dream. He became a physical education teacher and assistant coach at Holton Junior High.

It quickly became evident that Russ was born to coach. His players not only respected him, they nearly idolized him. He praised them and made them feel good about their abilities, even buying certificates and plaques to hand out for extraordinary individual efforts. His even temperament and good humor served him well for calming tempers, settling disagreements and soothing hurts. His persistence and optimism inspired perpetual hope and effort.

His Christian attitude showed itself in other ways as well. Many of his players came from poor families, and he often used his own money to help them buy athletic shoes and other gear they could not afford. He had them to his house for meals, black and white alike, and sometimes took groceries to their homes in hard times. He organized raffles, bake sales and other activities to raise money for equipment.

Russ was meticulous about personal appearance, and he passed this on to his players. Looking good was important ("If we can't win, at least we're going to look good losing," he liked to say), and to make sure that his teams always looked their best, he sometimes brought home their uniforms to mend, wash and iron, so that they would be just right. He taught his players to have pride in themselves, to struggle and endure.

"My whole philosophy in sports, period, is it's a preparation for life," he later told sportswriter Al Carson of the *Durham Sun*. "I think you have to get in there and fight, scrap and dig. Then when you get out in the world and things go wrong, you can hang in there. I try to teach my kids never to give up. You always have a chance until the last out."

Russ and Jo Lynn were married on October 18, 1974, in a ceremony at her parents' home in Raleigh. She was a senior at Meredith College in Raleigh, majoring in business education. After their wedding they moved into a three-room apartment connected to his Aunt Erma's house on University Drive in Durham. Six months later, they bought a small brick ranch house with a basement on Willow Drive. After her graduation, Jo Lynn went to work for the Liggett Group in Durham, the corporation that controlled some of the city's major cigarette manufacturing plants. Soon afterward, Russ took a step upward in his career, becoming an assistant coach at Durham High.

In 1976, Russ and Jo Lynn bought a larger brick house with three bedrooms, two baths, a huge master bedroom, den, fireplace and deck at the corner of Bramble Drive and Genesee Street in the Willow Hill subdivision off Guess Road, about five miles north of Durham.

Within a year of moving into the house, though, trouble had erupted in their marriage. Rumors reached Jo Lynn that Russ might be getting involved with a student, and one night when Russ didn't come home, she went looking for him and spotted his car at the apartment of his friend and fellow coach, John Biddle. She parked nearby and at 2:00 A.M., she saw Russ emerge from the apartment holding the hand of a teenage girl. After they had left in his car, she went to the door.

"John," she demanded when Biddle answered, "I want to know what's going on."

"You'll have to talk to Russ," was all he would say.

Given to occasional fits of temper, Jo Lynn waited until the next morning, when she was calmer, to confront Russ. The girl was a troubled student he was trying to help, he claimed lamely. Jo Lynn accused him of lying, stormed out and went to her parents' house, certain that her marriage was at an end. But a contrite Russ soon called, asking forgiveness, and after two weeks of pleading, he talked Jo Lynn into giving him another chance.

Things never would be the same again, however. Jo Lynn saw Russ in a different light now than she had in the early days of their marriage. The boyishness that once had been so charming now was simple immaturity that he refused to relinquish. He never would grow up, she thought. He wanted to remain a big, playful boy forever. Too late, Jo Lynn had realized that she and Russ had almost nothing in common. Russ's main interest was sports, and she couldn't care less about them. In addition, she didn't like his friends, and he didn't particularly care for hers.

There were few things on which they agreed. Although they remained together and still loved one another, they were drifting further and further apart.

Matters finally came to a head on a night late in the winter of 1978, a year after Jo Lynn had walked out. An ice storm hit, downing power lines. With no TV to watch, no stereo to listen to, no lights to read by, Jo Lynn and Russ found themselves sitting in uneasy silence in candlelight, unable to find anything to talk about. They went to the same bed feeling the same isolation.

"Do you think we ought to try a separation?" Jo Lynn asked the next morning.

Russ was all too quick to agree. He packed his clothes and left. Jo Lynn cried as she watched him drive away. They had been married not yet three and a half years, and now she knew that it was over for good.

Two weeks later, they got together at a lawyer's office and drew up a separation agreement. It was all very amicable, without bitterness or acrimony. Jo Lynn would move back home with her parents. Russ would return to the house to stay until he could sell it and they could divide the equity. They would go through the house together to decide who would get what from the possessions they had accumulated together. Russ would keep Sampson, the boisterous German shepherd they both loved. Jo Lynn didn't want to inflict the dog on her parents, and Russ was better able to care for him.

After Jo Lynn moved out, she did not see Russ again until summer, when he called to invite her on a trip to the beach with his parents. She thought he was inviting her because of his parents, who had been upset about his separation and wanted to make certain that he was doing the right thing. She went, but the situation was strained. She didn't know what to say to his parents, and she and Russ still found little to talk about.

Jo Lynn knew that Russ had been dating. He had gone out a few times with a fellow teacher at Durham High, an old friend. What she didn't know was that he had been doing this for the sake of appearances, to distract attention from his real romantic interest. Secretly he was seeing a former student.

Sybil Jackson* was seventeen, and Russ, who was thirty, had known her since her junior year. After her graduation that spring, Sybil saw Russ every chance she could get. They went on walks together and played tennis. Once, with the help of her best friends, she rendezvoused at the beach with Russ. All the same, she was terrified that her parents would find out about her relationship with Russ and had told only her two best girlfriends about it.

Russ was in love with her and told her so. He wanted her to tell her parents about him so that their relationship could be open. They argued when he kept pressuring her about it.

She thought that she was in love with Russ as well, although later she would realize that it was only an infatuation. She never had dated anybody seriously and Russ had overwhelmed her. He was hopelessly romantic, she later recalled, warm, considerate, generous, always giving her little things. Once he presented her with a St. Christopher medal that he said his parents had given him when he was eight. He brought her flowers and even sent flowers to her house, although he signed other names to the cards.

Russ wanted to marry her. He loved to talk about the life they would build together, the children they would have. She knew that she couldn't marry Russ. Her parents expected her to go to college. They would be devastated if she married, indeed if they even knew that she was dating a man so much older than she. She couldn't let her parents down.

At summer's end, she left Durham to attend college in another state. Russ went to see her on weekends. A couple of times she came home to see Russ and to attend the Durham High football games that he was coaching. She visited at the games with friends on the cheerleading squad and with the coaches and team members.

At one of those games, one of the coaches' wives introduced her to a new friend of Russ's who had started coming to the games. Her name was Barbara. She was just a friend, Russ told her, a neighbor who had lost her husband. Sybil was sure that that was exactly how Russ saw her, but she could tell by the way Barbara looked at Russ that she was after him "hot and heavy," as she later described it.

This could have serious consequences, Sybil knew. Russ's friends were aware of their relationship and if they knew, might not Barbara also? Sybil sensed that Barbara realized that she was her rival, and it concerned her. Would Barbara call her parents, perhaps anonymously, and tell them about her relationship with Russ in hopes of eliminating the competition? It was a worry she took back to school.

Russ still was pressuring her to marry him, and by the end of September she had decided to put an end to it. She had a deep affection for Russ, wanted to continue to be his friend, but she could not marry him. Her parents never would accept it. Besides, she had met a young man at college, somebody nearer her age. She liked him a lot, and he had asked her out. She was too young to be married and settled. She wanted to be able to date, have fun, enjoy her college years.

She told Russ all of this when he came to meet her for the weekend. He had given her many wonderful memories, she said, and she would never forget them. She could tell that Russ was crushed, although he tried to pretend otherwise. Later, she heard from his friends in Durham that he was having a hard time because of it.

Sybil was not surprised when soon after she broke off with Russ, she heard from her friends that he had started seeing Barbara.

Indeed, with the way cleared, Barbara was wasting no time. In mid-October, she brought Russ to Sunday morning services at Ebenezer Baptist Church and made a special point of introducing him to Jim Browder. Not more than two weeks later, Jim later recalled, Barbara approached him at church with a smile as wide as her face and told him she and Russ were planning to get married.

Jim congratulated her, and although he felt secretly relieved, he also felt a sympathetic concern for Russ, who seemed like a nice guy. Jim hoped that he knew what he was getting into.

# Chapter Twelve

Barbara's imaginative view of her early relationship with Russ later would be set down in thinly veiled fiction in a romance novel that she would attempt to write. Although she would change the names and locations, she and Russ clearly are the main characters. She is a sexy and highly successful real estate agent who drives a Mercedes, lives in a fabulous contemporary house and reaches into her fantastic wardrobe several times each day to change her expensive clothing. Russ is a recently separated high school baseball coach who is Barbara's equal only in sex appeal. Economically and socially, he recognizes that he never can be her match, but she brushes off his protestations of inferiority and wins him away from a high school cheerleader who is pursuing him. She feels a "strong sense of belonging" when she is cheering for Russ's team, but her main interest in him is physical, and at the end of the last chapter that Barbara would finish, they "melt together in passion."

With Russ as her new outlet for passion, things should have been going well for Barbara that fall. She was settled in her new house. Bryan was doing well at his new school, already on the honor roll, she boasted. Jason was in pre-school classes. She had made new friends at church, where she was taking part in more and more activities, as if she were trying to prove her piety and goodness. She also had a new job, her first since leaving the real estate agency in Archdale.

But as Barbara later would write of her romance novel heroine, "everyone who was acquainted with [her] was unaware of the turmoil inside her." That turmoil obviously was Barbara's, too, and it would lead her to brazen and bizarre behavior in the fall of 1978, when she began dating Russ. Later, it would seem almost as if she were subconsciously driven to take actions that were designed to have her castigated.

Barbara's job was at Security Federal Savings and Loan, where she had gotten a loan to buy her house. She applied for the job on September 5 and was hired the following day as a teller trainee at a salary of $575 a month. The job of training Barbara fell to Joanne Brockman.* Joanne got along well with Barbara in the beginning, but within a few short weeks she began to have concerns.

On October 4, Joanne had a $100 shortage from the cash drawer that she had been working with Barbara. It was the first shortage for Joanne in fifteen months on the job, and no matter how many times she went back through the day's transactions, she couldn't account for it. She decided that she would have to watch Barbara closer in the future.

Two weeks later, just after she brought Russ to church to show him off for the first time, Barbara had a shortage of $357.12 while working from her own cash drawer. Two checks that she had taken that day added up to that amount, and Barbara remembered that she had cashed the checks for the customers and mistakenly posted them as loan payments. But when her supervisor called the customers, each said that he had brought in the check as a payment and had received no money back.

A day later, Barbara missed work, calling to say that she had personal business to which she had to attend. She called in sick the following day as well.

On November 17, a couple of weeks after Barbara had announced her engagement to Russ, Joanne Brockman had an unprecedented shortage from her cash drawer of $500. Twenty-five twenty-dollar bills were missing. Twice that day, Joanne told her supervisor, Barbara had inquired how much money she had in her cash box. After the earlier shortage Joanne had thought that Barbara simply had made a mistake. Now she was convinced that Barbara was stealing.

After that shortage Barbara began to be moved from branch to branch, filling in where a teller was needed. In late November and early December, she had several discrepancies in her cash drawer, but no major shortages. The only real blot against her was that a check that she had written for $50 and gotten another teller to cash had been returned for insufficient funds. That turned out to be only an indication of what was to come.

At the beginning of December, Barbara wrote a check for $935 for her house payment, which she had allowed to fall behind. It, too, was returned for insufficient funds. A mistake, Barbara said, and the check was redeposited.

On December 14, just before Barbara took Russ to Randolph County to meet Brenda Monroe and other acquaintances, she asked for a $400 salary advance for Christmas shopping. It was granted, to be repaid when she got her paycheck on December 21. When Barbara hadn't repaid the advance by December 22, her supervisor asked her about it. She would be able to repay it soon, Barbara said. With Christmas so close, her supervisor didn't want to appear like Scrooge and press her for it.

By the time Barbara returned to work after Christmas, not only had she still not repaid the salary advance, but her house payment check had been returned once again for insufficient funds.

Confronted once more, Barbara said that she would take care of it.

But the next day, December 28, she called to say that she would not be able to come in because she had to undergo a D & C (dilatation and curettage of the uterus) and minor breast surgery at Durham County Hospital. She called shortly after noon to say that the surgery had gone fine and she was at home resting. She would not be returning to work until after New Year's Day.

Suspicious, her supervisor called her doctor and the hospital. The doctor said he knew nothing about any surgery scheduled for Barbara, and the hospital reported that Barbara had not been admitted and was not scheduled to be. Concerned, the supervisor audited Barbara's cash drawer and found two $100 bills missing.

When Barbara reported to work, she was summoned to a meeting with her supervisor and branch manager. Confronted with her lies, she had no explanation. The unpaid salary advance, she said, had been slipping her mind. A problem with an insurance check that was supposed to be deposited in her bank account had caused her house payment check to be returned, but that had now been worked out, she assured them. She couldn't understand how her drawer could be short $200 and asked for a chance to find it.

Barbara had run out of excuses as far as her bosses were concerned. If she paid back the advance, made good on the bad check and shortage, she would be allowed to resign, and no further action would be taken. Barbara agreed to the terms, and while her supervisor checked with her bank to see if her balance was adequate to cover the bad check and the new check that she wanted to write for the salary advance, she was allowed to search her records and cash drawer for the missing $200. Unable to find it, she was given one more day to come up with it and turn in her equipment and uniforms.

The next day, Barbara called to say that her son Jason had found the $200 in an envelope with some other papers in the trunk of her car. She would return it after a job interview that she had scheduled in Raleigh. Later, she called to say that she had been delayed in Raleigh and would be there as soon as she could make it. She arrived shortly before four o'clock and turned over her uniforms, office key and a Security Savings envelope containing two $100 bills.

Her supervisor was not surprised when, a week later, a check that Barbara had written to cash for $170 and cashed from her own drawer on her last day at work was returned for insufficient funds.

Later that year, Barbara's sister-in-law would tell a member of Larry Ford's family that Barbara's whole family had been concerned about her during this period. Barbara nearly had a nervous breakdown right after Christmas, Mary Terry said, and she had been making a lot of unexplained trips back to High Point. They figured that Barbara was still grieving over Larry's death and probably was going back to visit his grave, which by then bore a tombstone Barbara had ordered saying, "WE WILL MEET AGAIN."

Barbara, meanwhile, was careful not to let Russ know about any of these troubles. She clearly was intent on marrying him, and the only thing keeping her from it was Russ's upcoming divorce.

Russ's mother, though, was concerned about the impending

marriage. She thought Barbara was pushing Russ into it too quickly, that he hadn't really had time enough with Barbara to make sure she was the right choice.

Doris had first heard of Barbara the previous fall when Russ stopped by Vickers Electronics, where Doris then worked for her brother-in-law, Wesley Vickers, who was married to her sister Erma, Russ's favorite aunt. Russ started talking about this neighbor he had been taking out. She had two children, and he wasn't sure whether he should keep seeing her.

"If you have to ask somebody, don't," said Aunt Erma, who never was hesitant to speak her mind.

Soon afterward, Russ brought Barbara to his parents' house for Sunday dinner. Barbara's younger son, Jason, came with them. Jason was four and Doris was struck by how cute he was in his little suit and bow tie. Barbara seemed shy and didn't say much.

It was only a few weeks later that Russ came by the house alone and asked his mother, "How do you feel about a ready-made family?" Doris was a little taken aback. She knew how much Russ loved children and how much he wanted his own, and she realized how much he must care for Barbara to be considering this step. She hadn't expected Russ to become so serious so soon, but he had dated Jo Lynn for six years before their marriage and that hadn't worked out. She and Al had known each other for only two months before their marriage, and it had been lasting and happy.

"Russ, if this is what you want, it's all right with me," she told him.

What he liked most about Barbara, Russ emphasized to his mother, was that she was a good Christian, and that was the primary quality he was looking for in a wife. Doris had strong views about religion, and she didn't mind letting anybody know about them. She wasn't hesitant to ask others about their religious convictions either, particularly if they were going to matter to a member of her family. One day only weeks before Barbara and Russ were scheduled to be married, Doris called Barbara and asked if she would stop by the house and help her empty a rug cleaner because Al wasn't at home and she couldn't handle it herself. Doris waited until Barbara was about to leave to get to the real point of asking her over.

"Barbara," she said, "are you a Christian?"

For a moment, Barbara looked at her, saying nothing, then glanced away.

"Usually," Doris recalled years later, "if you ask someone that who's not a Christian, they'll hem and haw about it. When I asked her, she hemmed and she hawed. She said, 'I have been to church all my life.' I looked her straight in the eye. I said, 'That is not what I mean, Barbara.' She looked down, sort of rubbing her foot back and forth. She said, 'I know what you mean. I just came back from a retreat at Ebenezer Baptist Church.' She never said yes and she never said no."

This only confirmed Doris's suspicions. It worried her because she knew that Barbara had convinced Russ of her devout Christianity, and if she was deceiving him about that, what else might she deceive him about? But Russ was firmly committed to marrying Barbara, she knew, and nothing she could do would change that. A prospective mother-in-law had to be careful about what she said for the sake of future tranquility, and she never brought it up to Russ.


Russ and Barbara were married in the large Parlour Room at Grey Stone Baptist Church on March 17, 1979, only a few days after his divorce was effective and just five days before the first anniversary of Larry's death. Barbara wore a pale blue floor-length dress. Joe Wolfe, one of Russ's buddies on the men's softball team at the church, was best man. Malbert Smith, Russ's longtime pastor, presided. The ceremony was held at a portable altar placed before the fireplace. Bryan and Jason stood with Barbara's parents at their mother's side. Marva provided a silver punch bowl for the reception that followed, and Aunt Erma remarked that if she were so accustomed to such elegance, she should at least have known to have it polished. After the reception, Russ and Barbara drove straight to a room at the Ramada Inn on I-85 where he had worked as a lifeguard while he was in high school. Later that afternoon, they flew to Florida for a weeklong honeymoon, leaving Barbara's sons with her parents. "Are you really going to see Mickey Mouse?" Jason asked as his mother departed.

After the honeymoon, Barbara and the boys moved into

Russ's house, and she put her house on the market. She also took another job, the first since her dismissal from the bank. She became a secretary at Harris Inc., a beer distributing company. She would keep the job for fewer than six months, however. Later, her boss wouldn't be able to recall why she left, but on future job applications she claimed that she resigned to spend more time with her children.

Barbara had not told Russ anything about the problems that Larry's death had brought her, except to say that her in-laws had kept her from getting some insurance payments promptly. He knew only that Larry had accidentally shot himself and was unaware that Barbara had been suspected of murder. He knew nothing of what had been happening in Randolph County.

Barbara, however, had been keeping in close touch with the situation. And when she learned upon returning from her honeymoon that Sheriff Mason, prodded to do something by the insurance company, had publicly announced that the investigation of Larry's death was at an end, she was quick to act. She collected copies of news reports about Mason's decision and sent them to Equitable Insurance on April 2, along with a letter requesting payment of the double indemnity clause in Larry's policy.

"I feel, due to the enclosures, that there should be no further delay in Equitable making payment," she wrote. "Since the case has been closed as accidental, there should be no further investigation. After all, it's been well over a year. I would appreciate it if the check could be sent immediately. Please advise."

The insurance company already had heard about the sheriff's announcement, and a company representative, Albert Finney, called Mason on April 3, before receiving Barbara's request.

"He advised no new evidence had been found," Finney wrote in a report of his conversation with the sheriff. "The death has been ruled accidental. In his judgment, the case was closed and [he] did not think anything would turn up in the future."

The company saw no option but to pay off the policy, and on April 27 it mailed a check to Barbara for $27,791.61, including interest. All told, Barbara received $119,020.63 in insurance payments from Larry's death. She also was receiving more than $800 monthly in Social Security payments from Larry's account for the support of Bryan and Jason, payments that would rise over the years to more than $1,400.

* * *

As soon as Russ and Barbara returned from their honeymoon, Bryan and Jason began calling Doris and Al Meemaw and Papaw. It was clear that they had been instructed to do so. Doris had never heard the boys mention their paternal grandparents, and that concerned her. She pulled Barbara aside to talk about it.

"We don't want to take the place of their other grandparents," she said.

"They don't care anything about those boys," Barbara said.

"Any time the Fords came up," Doris later recalled, "she would talk about them like a dog."

In truth the Fords were longing to see their grandchildren and had made numerous attempts to reach them by telephone. Each time they had been told by Marva that the boys and Barbara were not available. The Fords hadn't given up. Doris had written a series of letters to Barbara and the boys and had sent all of them gifts at Christmas. But she wondered if Barbara had even let the boys have their presents, and early in the new year, she had written again to ask if the gifts had been received. Barbara finally had sent a letter of thanks that offered a bit of welcome news about the boys, but she had failed to mention that she was getting married again and that Bryan and Jason were about to have a new set of grandparents.

Russ knew how much his mother and father wanted to be grandparents for real, and only a couple of weeks after the honeymoon, as he and Barbara were having Sunday dinner with his family after church, Barbara shyly mentioned that she was pregnant. Russ was beaming happily.

Aunt Erma was there, as she often was, and she didn't hesitate to speak up. "There is no way you would be able to tell that this soon," she said.

Aunt Erma held old-fashioned ideas about morals and couldn't imagine her nephew sleeping with somebody before marriage. She was looking Barbara straight in the eye.

Barbara glanced away, saying nothing.

"Oh, she got one of those tests at the drugstore," Russ jumped in to say.

Not long afterward, Russ told his mother that Barbara had

miscarried, but Doris couldn't help but wonder whether she actually had been pregnant.

In Russ, Barbara had found somebody who was almost her equal as a spender, and combined with the insurance money she had received, this only exacerbated her compulsion and sent her into an even more reckless spree.

Soon after their wedding, Russ and Barbara decided to buy a new house. His house held too many memories of Jo Lynn and his failed relationship with Sybil. A new house would be appropriate for the new life he and Barbara would build together, and they began spending much of their free time searching for the right one.

By May, they had found it. The two-story brick and frame house was set amid pines, oaks and maples at 5514 Falkirk Drive in a subdivision called Heather Glen. It had three bedrooms, three baths, a huge living room and a study. The master bedroom was enormous, with a spacious sitting area. The house wasn't exactly what they wanted, but that could be fixed with remodeling. They paid $84,500 for it and moved in after Russ sold his house in June.

In July, Barbara received $9,115.78 from the final settlement of Larry's estate, and she and Russ began remodeling their new home. They enclosed the garage, making it into a recreation room with a pool table and a fireplace. The carpet in the house was perfectly good, Doris noted, but not good enough for Barbara. She had it pulled out and more expensive carpet put down. Doris and Al took the old carpet for their cabin at the lake. Russ had beautiful living room furniture, but he and Jo Lynn had bought it, and that, especially, had to go. To please Russ—who, like his family, loved Williamsburg and often visited there— Barbara was planning a subdued, traditional decor, although her own tastes were more modern. Doris and Al took the cast-out furniture for their family room, paying them for it, although they knew that the money they gave them would be only a fraction of the cost of the new furniture Barbara was buying. Later, Doris and Al also would end up with Russ's and Barbara's twenty-one-inch TV, after a big-screen television with a videocassette recorder was installed in the new recreation room. VCRs were not widely available then and few people could afford them. Soon Russ and Barbara had added a room with weightlifting equipment at the back of the house.

The period of remodeling was not the first time that Doris had taken note of Barbara's expensive tastes. Just before Russ's and Barbara's wedding, the women at Barbara's church had given a bridal shower for her. Barbara had offered Doris some towels that one church member had brought as a gift. They were cheap, Barbara had told her, and she wouldn't think of using them.

The house was not all that Barbara and Russ had been spending on. She was now tooling about town in a new pale green Cadillac Seville, which was almost identical to the car Kay Pugh had been driving when she was murdered. Russ, who always had liked fine things and fancy cars (he had been driving a Corvette when he married Jo Lynn) and always managed to find a way to possess them, usually by taking extra jobs or bartering, was driving a 280Z.

Brenda Monroe and her children joined Barbara, Russ and the boys at Barbara's parents' cottage at the beach that summer and found Barbara acting the happiest she'd ever known her to be. Barbara, of course, had reason to be happy. The troubles brought by Larry's death and the year of uncertainty that they had caused were now behind her. All the insurance companies had paid up. She had the big house and the fine car she had dreamed of having. Soon she would have her own beach cottage, too. And her new marriage was giving her new social standing as well as security.

Sex and security had been her main motivations for marrying Russ, and nine months after her wedding, she would acknowledge in a letter to her former in-laws informing them of her marriage that it had been one of convenience. Russ, she wrote, "provides for us very well and is a good father to the boys. We are very close friends, hoping that love will follow."

Nobody who saw them together would have known that Barbara wasn't in love with Russ, however. The two were openly affectionate. He always called her "Honey." She called him "Baby." They seemed well matched, enjoying the same things. They did everything together. Barbara seemed almost afraid to let Russ out of her sight. She attended all of his games and always hovered near him, especially when female students were about. At times she seemed almost desperate to please him. She took up jogging and weight lifting so that she could be with him when he worked out.

The marriage and the new exercise regimen had a transforming effect on Barbara. The hippiness that had long plagued her began to melt away. As her muscles toned, she got a tan and took on a lithe, healthy look. She cut her hair short and tinted it an even lighter shade of blond. She wore contact lenses instead of glasses. She became expert at makeup. She began dressing in ever more expensive clothes. The effect was remarkable. Longtime friends noted that Barbara never had looked better. Why, at times she was actually glamorous.

By their first anniversary, Russ's and Barbara's marriage seemed on a sound footing, even if others still had reservations about it that they didn't make known.

On Mother's Day 1980, Barbara sent Doris Stager a card in which she had written a personal message:

> Every day, I thank God for you and Dad. Sometimes, I just can't believe you're for real because of the animosity I always had from my previous in-laws. You made me feel loved, wanted and important. Slowly, I'm getting to the point where I know I can come to you for anything because I know you care.

If Barbara's sentiments for her in-laws were genuine—and Doris wondered if they were—the Stagers were more cautious in their feelings for her. They noticed that Barbara only called when she wanted something. When Russ asked his parents to join them in activities, Barbara sometimes seemed resentful, yet she always wanted her family around. Doris and Al wanted to be close to Barbara for Russ's sake, but they sensed that she didn't really want to be close to them. Barbara and Russ came to their house often for Sunday dinners after church, but Barbara never wanted to stay long and would soon be making excuses to leave. When Doris and Al were invited to their son's house, Barbara's family, or others, were apt to be there as well. While the Stagers tried to be congenial with the Terrys, they would never develop a comfortable relationship with them. They found it difficult to talk with James and wondered if he ever got a word in at home. Marva, they thought, was one of those people who knew everything and always had to have the final word. And mother and daughter were exactly alike. "Barbara had something to say about everything, unless she knew she was going to be cornered," Doris later would say. But in her mother's presence Barbara usually yielded. "Barbara folded her wings when Marva spoke," Doris recalled. Both usually had something bad to say about almost everybody, Doris noted, and she couldn't help but wonder what they said about her and Al to others. They had the feeling that both Marva and Barbara looked down their noses at them—"Mrs. Bigshot," Doris sometimes referred to Marva later—but they kept their feelings to themselves.

"She was Russ's wife," Doris later recalled. "We would go along with what we had to, to keep peace in the family."

She would hold her tongue as well when she inadvertently stumbled across another of Barbara's lies.

In the spring of 1980 Barbara was working at PATCO, a wholesale distributor of shipping supplies. She had taken a job as a part-time secretary the previous fall, working four or five hours a day so that she could be finished by the time the boys got home from school.

One evening a neighbor who also worked at PATCO called Doris and asked, "How's Jason?"

"He's fine," Doris said, wondering why she would ask such a question. The neighbor seemed a little taken aback. She had asked, she explained, because Barbara had called saying she couldn't come to work that day because Jason was in the hospital. Doris had just talked with Jason and knew that this was not so, a pointless lie. It disturbed her so much that she called Barbara's mother to tell her about it. Marva seemed unconcerned that Barbara would do such a thing. "She just sloughed it off," Doris later recalled. Not wanting it to seem that she was trying to interfere in his marriage, Doris decided that she shouldn't bring this up with Russ.

\* \* \*

Russ and Barbara had begun attending Grey Stone Baptist Church regularly, and they were becoming one of the most popular couples in the church, which boasted a membership of more than two thousand. Much of their popularity was due to Russ's long-term membership and his outgoing, fun-loving, boyish nature, but the members embraced Barbara as well, despite her reserved demeanor.

That summer, Russ and Barbara grew especially close to another couple at the church, Harry Welch and his new wife, Terri. Harry and Russ had met when both were playing for the church softball team and they had been friends for a couple of years. Harry was general manager of WTIK, a 5,000-watt country music and sports radio station in Durham. He was as outgoing and friendly as Russ and just as athletic.

Harry also had an odd ambition: He wanted to break the world's record for one-arm pushups. In July 1980, with Russ serving as verifier, he did it—3,821 pushups. Harry and Russ appeared in a news photo that was sent to newspapers around the country, and Harry made it into the *Guinness Book of World Records*.

That month, too, Russ officially became a father. At the end of October, he had filed legal papers to adopt the boys. On July 16, the adoption was granted, and Bryan and Jason Ford became Bryan and Jason Stager. Later, Barbara would apply for a new birth certificate for Jason, removing Larry's name as father and replacing it with Russ's.

No one could doubt Russ's feelings for his new sons. He was devoted to them and loved spending time with them. He was always teasing or tussling with them, or instructing them in sports. Discipline was left to Barbara, allowing Russ to be a pal to his stepsons, and all who saw them together could tell that the boys adored him. All onlookers also were impressed by how well behaved and well mannered the boys were. There was a good reason for this. "Barbara controlled Bryan mentally," Doris recalled. "He did exactly what she wanted. You can't imagine the control she had over Bryan." Friends noticed that a simple inflection in Barbara's voice would cause Bryan to alter his behavior. Jason, on the other hand, was her pet, and if Bryan corrected his younger brother in his mother's presence, Doris later recalled, "she would rake him over the coals." Yet Doris knew that Barbara often left the boys alone, with Bryan expected to look after Jason.

She learned that when Bryan called one day and said, "Meemaw, Jason won't mind." Doris thought that the boys were too young to be left alone, but she wasn't certain what to do about it.

Russ and Barbara joined a couples Bible class to which Harry and Terri Welch belonged, and they often went out after church for ice cream or pizza. They soon were joined by Bill Gordon, a dentist, and his wife, Carol, who was the daughter of Malbert Smith and had known Russ and his family for much of her life. The three couples grew close and visited frequently at one another's houses. They went to Duke University sporting events together, spent weekends at the beach, made other trips together. The three men became golfing companions.

As the friendship between the three couples grew, the Welches and Gordons became well aware of Barbara's need to impress, to gain approval and acceptance through her possessions. Now she had more people than ever to impress, and she bought accordingly.

The Welches and Gordons were amazed at the money that Russ and Barbara spent. Barbara traded her Cadillac, which had a leaky sunroof, for a new steel blue Mercedes. Russ bought a new four-wheel-drive Jeep, then a new Honda motorcycle and a Galaxy speedboat to use for waterskiing when he and Barbara and the boys went to Lake Kerr or Lake Gaston with his parents, as Russ and his family had done for years.

"Seemed like they were always doing something new," Terri Welch recalled years later.

Barbara bought new clothes constantly, shopping only at the most expensive stores. On trips with the Welches and Gordons, she always sought out trendy boutiques.

"She would pick something out and say, 'Gee, this is two hundred dollars. What do y'all think?' " Terri said. "We'd say, 'Well, looks good. If you can afford it, get it.' She always got it." Sometimes Barbara would pull a fat roll of bills from her purse to pay for her purchases, but more often she used credit cards.

The Welches and Gordons knew that as an assistant high school coach, Russ didn't make a big salary. And Barbara probably wasn't making more than minimum wage as a part-time secretary. Yet they kept spending as if they had been born to wealth. Russ surely had no family money, and neither, they thought, did Barbara. The only way that the Welches and Gordons could explain all the extravagant spending was that Barbara must have gotten a lot of insurance money from her first husband's death.

That was what Joe and Alissa Sommers also figured. Joe, too, was a coach at Durham High, and he and Russ had become close friends. When Russ had started dating Barbara, the two couples began doing things together. They went to ball games, took occasional trips and frequently got together at one another's houses for dinner or to watch Braves games on TV. Barbara told them that her first husband had died from an accidental gunshot wound, although she offered no details, and Joe and Alissa decided that had to be the source of all the money that Russ and Barbara were spending. Barbara was generous, frequently bringing clothes or toys as gifts for the Sommers' young daughter. But as Russ's and Barbara's spending increased, Joe and Alissa began referring to them as "our rich friends." By 1981, the Sommers decided that the Stagers' lifestyle had grown so extravagant that they no longer could afford to keep up with it, and they began spending more time with other friends.

Barbara left her part-time job at PATCO at the end of January 1981. Her coworkers had wondered what a woman who drove a Cadillac, then a Mercedes, was doing in a low-paying part-time job, and she had told them that she only worked to have something to do. Her first husband, who traveled in his work, had died in an accident, she explained, and she had received a lot of insurance money. Her coworkers assumed that her husband had died in a traffic wreck.

Barbara's supervisors at PATCO considered her a good employee, genial and quick to learn, but prone to skip work without adequate excuses and "to stretch the truth." She usually called in to say that she had a problem of one sort or another, often involving her children, that kept her from coming in, they would later recall. Not long before she quit, she said that she had to miss work because her husband was having surgery on his back that day. One of her supervisors saw her and Russ at the mall later that day, however, and noted that Russ was walking with a quick step for one who supposedly had been under a surgeon's knife only hours earlier.

In February, Barbara applied for another part-time secretarial job at Moore Business Forms. She began in March, working from eight to one. The company employed only one other secretary, and Barbara let her know that she didn't have to work. This woman would recall later that Barbara talked a lot about money. She said that she had gotten a lot of money from her first husband's death and that she got a very low interest rate on her home loan because she had so much money in her savings account at the savings and loan.

Barbara also talked frequently about religion and sometimes brought a Bible to work. She complained to her deskmate that some of the company's salesmen spoke suggestively to her.

The salesmen had a different version. As the weather grew warm, they said, Barbara began wearing low-cut sundresses to work, and it was quickly apparent that she never wore a bra with them. She would act teasingly with the salesmen, often saying suggestive things herself, then go back and complain to the other secretary when one of them responded.

Barbara's friends were unaware of any sexual comments at work, but they were well aware of her strong interest in sex. They had been surprised and bemused by her candor about it. She boasted about how much she liked it and laughingly said that she couldn't get enough.

Russ's close friends also knew that Russ and Barbara had a lusty relationship. When locker-room and golf-course talk turned to sex, Russ sometimes acknowledged that Barbara was quite a number. Almost more than he could handle, he laughingly admitted.

He even joked to his parents about it. One day when Barbara was complaining in their presence that she was tired, Russ grinned and said, "Yeah, she was tired all day yesterday, too—until she got into bed."

While Russ seemed satisfied with his sex life, strain was beginning to show in other areas. He needed to make more money than he was paid as a coach and driver's education teacher, and in June of 1981, he left the school system to take a job at Durham Sporting Goods. He didn't last a week before deciding that he was no salesman. He acknowledged to himself that he was born to coach, poorly though it might pay in the public schools, and he went asking for his job back. Somebody else already had been given his position, but he was rehired and assigned back to Holton Junior High School, where he had begun his coaching career. This time he not only would coach football and baseball, but also would serve as the school's director of athletics. This would hardly pay the mounting bills, though.

One reason for this was that Barbara decided to enter sales herself, even though she had done so miserably selling houses. That summer, Russ mentioned to Harry Welch her experience in real estate. Harry was always looking for good salespeople at the radio station. Russ said that he would send Barbara around to talk with him. She was only working part-time now as a secretary and not making very much money at it. Barbara came to talk to Harry soon afterward, and he hired her to sell commercials. She would draw $150 a week as an advance against commissions until she could get a clientele established. A good salesperson, Harry told her, could make a lot of money.

Barbara quit her job at Moore Business Forms the following day without giving proper notice, saying she'd found a full-time job. She didn't even bother to say goodbye to the other secretary, who didn't realize she'd quit until she asked what had happened to Barbara.

Barbara began her new job in late August bubbling with enthusiasm. She came to the station every morning and left with her sales materials, always expressing great confidence. She attended staff meetings religiously, often reporting that she was just about to land some big new account. But something always seemed to happen not only to keep the big accounts from signing, but the little ones as well.

A week passed. Then another. Then a month. And Barbara still hadn't sold a single commercial. As the weeks wore on with the same results, Harry realized he had made a serious mistake. He couldn't afford to keep paying Barbara $150 a week to produce nothing, but how was he going to handle this awkward situation without losing Russ's and Barbara's friendship?


Another aspect of Barbara's pattern of deceit emerged that summer as well, when Doris, Al and Aunt Erma went to Russ's and Barbara's new beach cottage with them. They had bought a three-bedroom house on stilts just two streets back from the ocean at Long Beach—where Barbara's parents also had a cottage—well away from the beach near the inland waterway.

Barbara went to the beach in a bikini that Aunt Erma considered to be scandalous, so brief that it even embarrassed Al. The skimpy swimsuit also allowed Aunt Erma to notice a tiny scar on Barbara's lower belly, and she asked her about it.

It was just from some minor surgery she'd had to have after Jason was born, Barbara explained.

"Doris, she's had her tubes tied," Erma said when the two of them were alone.

If that were so, had the pregnancy and miscarriage Barbara had announced soon after her marriage been real? Imaginary? Just a lie? Of course, Doris and Erma knew that tubes that had been tied sometimes could be untied, and perhaps that had been the case. Still, it was more reason to be wary of Barbara and anything she said.

That was why, when Barbara announced she was pregnant again, they were skeptical. They were also worried because Barbara seemed to be duping Russ, who was so easygoing and trusting.

Although he loved Bryan and Jason as if they were his own blood, he continued to want children of his own, and not long after Barbara went to work at the radio station, Russ excitedly announced that she was expecting again. Barbara talked about her pregnancy for several weeks and even discussed borrowing maternity clothes from Alissa Sommers. One day she came to her in-laws' house wearing a maternity top, although, Doris noted, she showed no signs of needing one. When she said that she had begun craving squash cooked with onions, Doris obligingly fixed them for her.

If the baby was a boy, she told one friend, he would be Allison Russell Stager IV; if a girl, still Allison. This friend knew that Barbara had had her tubes tied after Jason's birth, but Barbara had told her within a year after her marriage to Russ that she was planning to have surgery to allow her and Russ to have children, so she was not surprised when Barbara told her that she was pregnant again.

One Sunday morning in the Sunday School class that Bill Gordon taught, Barbara rose when the time came for special prayer requests. With tears welling, she emotionally spoke of how much this pregnancy meant to her and Russ, and asked the class members to pray that she would carry the baby to term.

Only a week later, Russ and Barbara came to church in a somber mood and informed their friends that Barbara had suffered another miscarriage. Words of consolation seemed to be of little help to Barbara, and although Russ was upset as well, he appeared to be more concerned about her emotional state than his own. After all, he confided to his friends, she could get pregnant again.

Although Barbara would indeed claim to be pregnant once more, again to suffer a miscarriage, causing Russ to give up the dream of having children of his own, he never would learn that she had been lying all along.

Russ was too trusting, which perhaps spurred Barbara on. Was there no limit to the deception she could carry off? Could that be what emboldened her to turn to an even more dramatic and implausible hoax?

# Chapter Thirteen

The audacity of it would intrigue people later. How did Barbara think she could possibly get away with it? What was the point of it? How could she do such a thing to close friends, and especially to Russ? Was it a symptom of a deep character flaw? A cry for help? A deep need to be found out, castigated and cast out of her marriage and circle of friends, which secretly she thought she didn't deserve? All of these were questions that people would be asking when the truth finally was revealed about Barbara's book.

Friends first began to hear in the fall of 1980 that Barbara was writing a book about her first husband's death. But it would not be until early in 1982 that the news would become an event.

That was at a regular Wednesday family supper at Grey Stone Baptist Church late in February. Russ couldn't contain his pride as he and Barbara joined Harry and Terri Welch in the buffet line.

"We've got some great news," he said.

"What?" Harry asked.

"It's really heavy-duty," Russ said, grinning, teasing the moment.

"Well, don't just stand there, tell us," Terri put in.

"Barb has sold her novel."

The title of the book was *Untimely Death,* and she had written it under the name B. T. Stager, Russ explained. It had been accepted by a major publisher, Doubleday, and Barbara was expecting an advance of more than $400,000.

The Welches could hardly believe their friends' good fortune, and they began spreading the word. Soon all of their friends and many members of their church were aware of it. Everybody was happy for them.

All of their close friends were eager to read the book, but Barbara was coy about letting anybody see it in manuscript. There was still work to be done on it, she indicated, telling some that the editor couldn't decide whether it should be told in the third person, as she had written it, or in the first person. She would rather everybody wait to read it until the book came out. She couldn't say yet exactly when that was going to be. Soon, she was sure.

When Harry asked Russ what the book was like, he said he hadn't read it yet either. Barbara didn't want him to, he said. But he was going to design the book jacket from her description, and he was excited about that. Later, he brought his design for Harry to see. It was the face of a clock with only one hand sprouting from a tombstone in the center. The hand pointed straight up at the hour thirteen. Sad faces around the clock's periphery looked onto the mounded grave spreading out from the tombstone. Harry was impressed.

In March, only a couple of weeks after telling Harry and Terri about the book, Barbara told Harry that she would have to quit her job at the radio station. She really didn't have to work, she said, now that she had all the money coming from her book. Besides, she needed time to plan for the book's release. She would have to be traveling a lot to promote it.

Harry was relieved. Not only had Barbara been drawing a weekly advance for months without selling even a single commercial, but he had begun getting calls from companies that she had been soliciting saying that Barbara had bought merchandise from them on credit and hadn't paid for it. Harry had known that he was going to have to get rid of Barbara, but he had been putting it off, trying to figure some way to do it without angering Russ and losing his friendship. The book was granting him a graceful way out.

Early in April, as if in celebration of their new prosperity, Russ and Barbara joined Croasdaile Country Club, the most exclusive in Durham. They were sponsored by the Welches and Bill and

Carol Gordon, who lived at Croasdaile. They paid an initiation fee of $1,250. Monthly dues would be $80.

Another person who wrote a letter of recommendation for Russ and Barbara's membership was Irwin Breedlove Jr., a lawyer who had been a high school friend of Russ's. He, too, was well aware of Barbara's book.

In February, Barbara had gone to Central Carolina Bank seeking a substantial loan on a ninety-day note. As proof of income, she had carried along a letter that bore the letterhead of Doubleday & Co.

The letter was signed by an editor named Frances Dubose, and it confirmed the acceptance of Barbara's book for a price of $100,000, of which $25,000 would be paid on first printing in March 1982, the remainder ninety days later.

"Sales of additional printings, paperback rights and royalties will be forthcoming in a separate certified letter," the letter went on to say.

Uncertain that the letter could serve as a legal contract, the bank passed it on to Breedlove for an opinion. He met with Barbara and reviewed the letter before informing the bank that "letter contracts are valid in form and are customarily used as the initial document in the publishing business." Barbara could rely on it for payments once her book was published, he said. The bank let Barbara have the money.

Soon after joining the country club, Barbara attended a ladies luncheon for new members. Carol was sitting beside her.

"Let's go shopping this afternoon," Barbara proposed. "I just completed a sale this morning that was so big that I probably won't have to work again for a year."

"That's great," Carol said, going on to congratulate her. Such success! And on top of her big book deal, too. Carol knew that Barbara worked at the radio station for Harry, but she wasn't sure exactly what she did, and now she asked.

"Oh, I sell ads," Barbara said.

Later, when the Gordons were alone with the Welches, Carol told Harry, "I want to work for you." When Harry looked at her as if he didn't understand, she said, "I want the same job you gave Barbara, where you sell one ad and don't have to work for a year." Harry, she noted, looked at her strangely, but he said nothing.

* * *

Both the Gordons and Welches liked Barbara's children and found them to be among the best mannered they'd ever known. But they thought it strange that they had never heard the boys mention their real father. Barbara never talked about Larry either, although she had told both Terri and Carol privately about the circumstances of Larry's death. Neither had any idea what Larry looked like, though, because they had never seen a picture of him.

After Carol had begun visiting regularly in Barbara's house, she realized that there was not a single photograph of Larry there anywhere, not even in the boys' rooms. She knew that Russ was not the jealous type and never would begrudge the boys a connection to their dead father.

"Have you got a picture of Larry?" Carol asked one day out of curiosity. "I'd like to see what he looked like."

Almost reluctantly, Barbara fetched a snapshot of Larry from a dresser drawer. He was standing by a sign on a mountain trail, alone, smiling. A nice-looking man, Carol observed, handing the photo back.

"I kept thinking she's going to say something about this man," Carol recalled later. "She never said, I loved him, he was a good father, nothing. Absolutely nothing."

Instead, Barbara quietly returned the snapshot to the drawer.

Carol couldn't understand Barbara's detachment about this man who supposedly was the subject of her book. But that wasn't all that she had been wondering about.

On drop-by visits, she never had caught Barbara writing, although Barbara had claimed that she was now working on a new book, a romance novel. Nor had Carol ever seen a typewriter or any signs of writing materials in Barbara's neat and meticulously clean house.

"Where do you do your writing?" Carol asked.

"Oh, anywhere and everywhere," Barbara said.

On a subsequent visit, after calling in advance, Carol arrived to find Barbara sitting in an easy chair writing on a legal pad. Several paperback romance novels lay close by. Writing romance novels was something she planned to do under an assumed name for quick money between her serious writing, she said. It was really easy. The publisher supplied a format. "All you have to do," she said, "is fill in the blanks."

Barbara still couldn't give her friends a publication date for *Untimely Death,* but she did confide in them that there was movie interest in her book. She was certain that it was going to be bought by a major studio.

As the weeks went on, Carol and Terri kept asking when the book would be coming out, but Barbara kept coming up with excuses for the delay.

Unbeknownst to Carol and Terri, she was also offering excuses at the bank. When her note came due, she couldn't pay it and asked to extend it for another ninety days. That had raised suspicion from her loan officer. The collateral letter had been clear about a March publication date and $25,000 of income it would bring. Irwin Breedlove, who had confirmed the letter, was asked to look into it. He called an acquaintance who worked at Doubleday, a woman from Durham, and she promised to investigate. What she found out was a shocker. She wrote to tell him that Barbara's letter was a mystery at the publishing house. Nobody there had ever heard of a Frances Dubose.

Pressed by the bank, Barbara managed to pay back the loan, but how she did it would become a mystery to Russ's family, who would not learn about the loan for many years. Russ never mentioned the loan to them, and they were sure that he never knew about it. They would come to suspect that Barbara had turned to her parents to pay back the money.


By August, with no book and no money forthcoming from Barbara, Harry Welch decided that he had better try to collect the money that she still owed his radio station for her salary advances. It was a ticklish matter because of the friendship, and Harry didn't want to have to ask for it. He got the radio station's bookkeeper to call Barbara instead. An agreement was drawn up in which she would pay back $2,903.59 at $100 a month. She came by the station and signed it on August 17.

Summer dissolved into fall, and still Barbara couldn't tell her friends when her book would be coming out. By now the Gordons and Welches had begun to suspect that there really was no book. Carol and Terri had discovered that in separate conversations Barbara had told them conflicting details about Larry's death. How could you get the details wrong about something so important as that, especially if you had written a book about it?

They decided to put Barbara on the spot. They told her that they wanted to have a big publication party for her book at Croasdaile Country Club, and they had to have a date so they could begin planning. Could she press her publisher for it?

When Barbara still couldn't give them a date, they were almost certain that the book was a fantastic hoax.

Harry decided to find out for sure. He knew a woman who worked in the publicity department at Doubleday, he said, and he would call her.

When she told him that she was certain that Doubleday was not publishing any book by Barbara, he asked her to doublecheck, he later recalled.

"I've checked," she said, when she called back again. "We do not have it."

Furthermore, she doubted that anybody was publishing it, at least not for the money Barbara was claiming to get. Nobody would pay that much to an unknown author for a first book, she said, unless it was such a hot property that the whole book industry had become aware of it.


If there was no book, did Russ know? No doubt he didn't, the Welches and Gordons decided when they gathered to discuss what they had learned. Should they tell him? How do you tell somebody so trusting as Russ that his wife was such a liar? What would he do? What would Barbara do? What would happen to the marriage, to the children?

The four never would forget that night, the seriousness of the matter, the anxiety, the uncertainty, the long agonizing. Underlying it all was a fear that they didn't really want to face. Carol, who had been the first to become suspicious of Barbara, was the one who brought it up.

"What if she does something to him?" she asked.

She wouldn't do anything, the others agreed, because they knew too much.

"You don't know what somebody might do when they're backed in a corner," Carol said.

Clearly, this was too much for them to face alone, and they sought help from a greater power. Both men prayed aloud, asking for guidance, for healing, for restoration. Afterward, there was a long silence, then Bill and Harry walked outside to the pen where the Welches kept a pet lion, talking quietly. When they returned, they had agreed that Russ had to be told, and that Harry, who was the closest to him and had known him longest, was the one to do it.

First, though, Harry wanted to consult with Malbert Smith, and when Malbert also agreed that Russ had to be told, they prayed about it again.

The call was one of the hardest things Harry had ever done, he said later, and he put it off several times.

"Russ, I need to see you," he said when he finally built up his nerve. "Why don't we get some coffee?"

They met at Shoney's on Hillandale Road and sat in a booth near the salad bar. It was late afternoon the week before Thanksgiving, and few people were in the restaurant.

"Russ, I hate to tell you this," Harry said as they stirred their coffee, "but I have reason to believe there's no book."

Russ listened in stunned silence as Harry told him what he had learned.

"Well, I guess we're lucky that she's still got her job at the radio station," Russ finally said.

"I wouldn't have been more surprised if he'd hit me," Harry recalled later.

"Russ, she hasn't worked there since March," Harry said.

Now Russ looked as if he had been hit. Tears came to his eyes and his voice choked. "What's she doing? She tells me she comes to the radio station."

Harry couldn't answer that question. He could only listen and offer comfort as Russ talked about his marriage for the next hour.

Other strange events had occurred in recent months, Russ told him. Several times police officers had come to his house and talked to Barbara and he didn't know why.

"She said there'd been mistakes and she'd take care of it," he said.

Barbara had indeed made mistakes. Twice warrants had been issued charging her with writing bad checks, once in February for a $16.63 check to Sears, again in June for a $146.78 check to

Winn-Dixie. In each case she made restitution and paid court costs, but Russ never knew about either warrant.

That wasn't all that she had failed to tell him, as it turned out. She also had taken another job. In August, she had gone to work as a secretary at Brame Specialty Company, which sold maintenance supplies for offices. An aunt of Barbara's had worked at the company for many years and had recommended her.

The long conversation between the two old friends was their last. Russ avoided the Welches and Gordons afterward. They were sorry about that. Although they wanted nothing more to do with Barbara and her lies, they still loved Russ and would have liked to maintain a relationship with him. But they were relieved that nothing drastic happened, that there was no big blowup, at least none that they heard about. They didn't blame Russ for avoiding them. They knew that he was hurt and embarrassed, and they felt sorry for him, but they weren't surprised that he would stand by Barbara. They knew his character.

To avoid any further embarrassment to Russ, the Welches and Gordons agreed that they would tell nobody else what they had learned about Barbara's book (others who knew about it were simply left to wonder why it never came out). But Russ had trouble facing his old friends at church, and he and Barbara soon joined Rose of Sharon, the church in which Barbara had spent her early years. She told Russ's parents, who were unaware of the book hoax, that they had quit Grey Stone because the boys in Bryan's Sunday school class were rough and used bad words. Russ never told his parents, either, but he went to Malbert Smith and explained why. Early in December, Russ also wrote a letter of resignation to Croasdaile Country Club, citing a recent increase in dues as his reason for leaving.

Although the Welches and Gordons believed there never had been a book, Barbara actually had begun one. She had written an outline and a first chapter that told her version of Larry's death in an amateurish and melodramatic fashion. The gist of the planned book was the ordeal she had undergone, not only because she'd lost her beloved husband and the father of her children, but because of the suspicions of Larry's family and the investigations they had spawned. The reason for those suspicions, she wrote, was the Fords' resentment of her because of all the fine things she and Larry had accumulated during their marriage and because she "had come from an upper-middle-class family and the [Fords] were lower middle class." Several times Barbara had sent her proposal to publishers in New York, but each time it had come back rejected.

Although her book was far from finished, Barbara already had written a dedication: "To my best friend, Russell, who believed in me and gave me the support and strength I needed to bring this story out in the open."

Despite their attempts to avoid Barbara, the Welches and Gordons had not heard the last of her or her book. Soon after Christmas, at Barbara's request, Terri met Barbara for lunch at the same Shoney's in which Harry had talked with Russ weeks earlier. Barbara told her that she was sorry about everything that had happened and she hoped that Terri and Harry could forgive her. She intended to go to see Carol and tell her the same thing, she said. While they were talking, Carol walked in and saw them. She took a table but was so upset at seeing Barbara and Terri together again that she couldn't eat and left the restaurant. An hour later, Terri called to tell her that Barbara was coming to see her to set things right.

Barbara showed up soon afterward. Carol was anxious but tried not to show it. Barbara was genial. She apologized for the problems she had caused and expressed hope that Carol could forgive her. Russ had, she said, and they were trying to make things work, which didn't surprise Carol, knowing Russ. Barbara went on to say that she was seeing a psychiatrist about her "problem." Carol assumed that the problem Barbara was referring to was lying, and couldn't help but wonder if this was the truth. Despite Barbara's seeming sincerity, Carol didn't believe anything she said anymore.

The meeting was awkward for Carol, who was trying not to appear overly sympathetic or friendly. She wanted it to end quickly, and she was grateful when Barbara made moves to leave.

They were sitting on a sofa and as Barbara pulled herself to the edge of her seat, she suddenly turned back to Carol.

"I know it was you," she said.

Startled, Carol stood.

Barbara didn't often get angry in front of people outside her family, but when she did, she turned the anger inward. Her body would become almost rigid. She would become silent and take on a deep, dark, teeth-clenching look—"that stare," her friends called it. Carol had seen that look several times, but the look in Barbara's eyes now was beyond that, darker, deeper, meaner, more determined, a look—there was no other word for it—of sheer evil.

"I want to know how you did it," Barbara said. "How did you know about the book?"

Frightened, Carol began walking toward the front door, urging Barbara along, thinking fast. She wanted this woman out of her house.

"Your story didn't make sense," she said, reaching the door and opening it for Barbara.

Carol then remembered an aunt who taught at Duke University and wrote psychology textbooks. She now told Barbara that her aunt, who was a writer, had told her that nobody would be likely to get such a big advance on a first book. It was clear that Barbara wasn't buying that story, but Carol thanked her for coming and bade her a quick goodbye.

As Barbara departed, Carol closed the door and locked it. She couldn't remember when she had been so scared.

# Chapter Fourteen

If his friends had known that they were about to deal a double blow to Russ when they informed him about Barbara's book hoax, they would have agonized even longer over their decision. But they had no way of knowing that just three weeks earlier Russ had stumbled onto other secrets of Barbara's on his own and that he was already suffering great anguish when Harry brought him more.

Russ never had paid close attention to all the spending he and Barbara had been doing. He just had turned over his paychecks to Barbara and left the bookkeeping to her. "I couldn't balance a checkbook with a pair of scales," he once laughingly told Harry. "Barb does all of that."

From the beginning of their marriage, they had been living on ever-expanding credit. Their credit cards had been pushed to their limits and beyond. As Barbara had done in the past, they had gotten loans to pay off loans. They had taken a second mortgage on their house. Their penchant for new cars saddled them with huge monthly payments that grew larger with every car they bought. Since her Mercedes, Barbara had had an Oldsmobile Cutlass Cruiser, a Mazda RX7, and now was driving a new Pontiac Grand Prix; Russ had had two Jeeps, a motorcycle and was also now driving a Grand Prix one year older than Barbara's. They also had two mortgage payments because of their cottage at Long Beach. They had been living far beyond their means for three years, yet they had done nothing to curtail their flashy spending.

Russ was unaware of just how deeply in debt they were until a Sunday night late in October 1982. He never said how he happened to find it, but after Barbara had gone to bed, he came upon a cardboard box hidden under an upholstered chair in the family room. The box, he discovered, was crammed with unpaid bills. There were bills he never had known about, others he thought had been paid long before. As he sat on the floor going through them, he began to grasp how dire their financial situation was. He realized for the first time that Barbara not only had been keeping secrets from him but had been outright lying to him, and he began to cry.

He heard a noise, he later told his mother, and looked to see that Barbara had come down from the bedroom and was standing in the doorway to the den.

"You're spying on me," she said coldly, and turned and went back upstairs.

Russ called his mother at work the following morning and asked if she could come home. He had to talk with her. He was distraught, thoroughly beaten, when she met him at her house and he told her about finding the bills.

Doris wasn't surprised at his disclosures. She and Al had worried about all the spending Barbara and Russ had been doing, had wondered how they could keep it up. But she also knew that Barbara had been letting bills slip. Three times she had involved Doris in her financial problems, each time begging her not to let Russ know about it.

The first time, a neighbor of Russ and Barbara's called Doris to say that a worker had come to cut off their gas while they were at the beach. They had no phone at their beach cottage, but when Barbara called from a pay phone, Doris told her what had happened. "Please pay it and don't tell Russ," Barbara said. Doris took $200 to the gas company and had the gas turned back on, and Barbara repaid her later.

The second time, Barbara called from work and said the telephone company was about to cut off their service, and she was worried that the boys would be at home alone and she wouldn't be able to reach them. Could Doris pay it—and please not tell Russ? To have Russ's phone cut off would be a greater embarrassment than Al, who worked at the phone company, could abide, and Doris hurried to pay it.

On the third occasion, Barbara called from the beach and asked Doris to go by her house, get a check from the mailbox and deposit it without telling Russ. She did it, although later she would not remember the amount of the check or from whom it came.

She did remember that soon afterward, Russ fell in beside her as they were leaving church and said, "Mother, where did that check come from that you put in the bank?" Doris didn't answer—she had told Barbara that she wouldn't tell Russ. "Well, if you don't want to tell me, okay," he said, disappointment showing in his face. That had shamed Doris and made her vow that never again would she let Barbara involve her in any of her financial shenanigans.

Russ did not want to tell his father about the mess he and Barbara had gotten into, not only because he was ashamed, but because he knew that stress was bad for his dad's heart condition. Everybody in the family had tried to keep bad news from Al since his triple coronary bypass five years earlier.

But Doris insisted that Al needed to know; this was too important to keep from him. Although the problems might seem insoluble to Russ, she assured him that together they could deal with them. The thing to do, she said, was to call a family meeting and tackle the situation rationally. She instructed Russ to call the Terrys and have them come to her house. He also was to fetch Barbara. Together they would analyze the situation and determine what would have to be done.

Marva arrived alone for the meeting. When Doris asked where James was, Marva said that he didn't know he was supposed to come. Doris said that she thought it would be better if everybody were present, and Marva called her husband. Russ had gone for Barbara and the bills, and he was a long time returning, leaving the others waiting uncomfortably. Later, he told his mother that Barbara had not wanted to come and he practically had to force her to accompany him. She was sullen when she arrived. Not wanting her to think that she was being blamed for the mess, Doris greeted her at the door by saying, "Barbara, I love you."

"Well, I don't know why," she later recalled Barbara replying.

"Well, we love you all, too," her mother quickly put in.

When all the bills had been sorted and all the set payments had been added up, it became clear that Russ and Barbara owed much more each month than they were making. Some emergency measures could be taken to relieve the situation temporarily, but if the problem were to be solved, the two simply would have to change their lifestyle and get rid of some of their obligations. Al and Doris picked out a few bills that they could pay immediately, those that would prove most embarrassing if they were unpaid, and Marva and James did the same. James suggested that he would take Russ and Barbara to his bank to get another bill-consolidation loan. The loan would not be a solution, just patchwork until the bigger problems could be worked out.

The bill-consolidation loan did not work out, however. After he and Barbara had filled out the applications, Russ later told his mother, the loan officer returned to ask Barbara if she had been Barbara Ford. After she acknowledged that she had been, the bank had turned down the loan, Russ said, and the loan officer wouldn't tell him why. No doubt the bank had checked with Security Federal Savings and Loan, where Barbara once had a house loan and where she also had been dismissed for suspected embezzlement four years earlier. Again, Russ didn't know anything about this.

Doris and Al offered to help reduce their son's debts by buying one of his cars. They would pay off the loan balance on it, they said, and give him one of their older cars. Russ agreed, but when he went to the bank to see about the transfer, he discovered that more was owed on the car than he had thought. Barbara had renegotiated the original loan and signed his name on the lien, he told his mother. It was such a good forgery, he said, that at first he thought it was his own signature. But he knew he hadn't signed it.

His parents couldn't buy the car because there was too much debt on it.

As part of her solution to the crisis, Doris insisted that Russ take over the handling of his family's finances. And to make sure that all of the bills came to him and that Barbara couldn't get hold of them, she suggested a post office box. She paid the first year's rent on the box and gave Russ the key, instructing him to keep control of it.

* * *

Not only did Russ and Barbara have to put their beach house on the market, they also had to give up their big house on Falkirk into which they had invested so many dreams and so much energy. The beach cottage went quickly, but the house was slower in selling. Not until the following summer did they finally find a buyer for the house.

In August, friends helped them move into a new house they bought not far away at 1918 Bivens Road.

The move was another humiliation for Russ, a step downward for all to see. The new house was small and plain, a tract house on a small lot facing a busy road. But Barbara, ever industrious and perfectionist, soon turned it into a showplace of tidiness, something she had come by naturally. "She's a lot like my mom in that she maintains an immaculate house," her brother Alton later would say. "You're almost afraid to walk in there with your shoes on." Russ, too, had grown up in such a house, and in her housekeeping Barbara was doing only what was expected from her.

Pam Spence, her husband and baby daughter moved to Durham from Maryland in the summer of 1983 and bought the house directly across the street on Bivens Road. Pam and Barbara soon met in passing. Pam thought that Barbara was very attractive, always "groomed to the nines," as she later put it, a woman who would turn a man's head. But Barbara seemed cool and reserved to her. "I thought Junior League, upper class, a little on the snobby side," Pam recalled.

She did not get invited into Barbara's house until a few months later. She had locked herself out of her house and needed to call her husband to bring a key and let her in. She knocked on Barbara's door and asked to use the telephone.

Pam's parents had visited model homes as a hobby, and Pam often had gone with them. When she stepped into Barbara's house, she got the same feeling that she always got when she entered a model home: It was a house to be shown and seen, not to be lived in. The house was not just immaculate, it looked as if an interior designer had been given a free hand with no concern for expense.

"Her house was as beautiful inside as any model home I'd ever seen," Pam said.

While she was using the phone, Jason arrived home from

school, and Barbara started yelling at him as soon as he stepped inside the back door.

"She spazzed out," Pam recalled. "She was yelling at him for wearing his shoes into the house. I was so embarrassed. There I was standing with my shoes on. If she would do that with me there, I hated to think about what the little guy got when nobody was around."

Later, though, Pam got to know both of Barbara's sons, and she had never known sweeter or better-behaved boys.


By the fall of 1983, Russ and Barbara appeared to have weathered the worst of their financial crisis. It was a particularly hectic time for Russ. School was back in session and he was busy coaching the football team at Holton Junior High. He had to look after the school's other athletic programs as well, in addition to teaching phys ed classes. At the beginning of the year, he had joined the National Guard, mainly to get the extra income that it offered, and one weekend out of each month was devoted to military drill. Russ also had realized that if he hoped to progress in education and coaching, he needed more education, and late that summer, he had enrolled in night classes at North Carolina Central University to work toward a master's degree.

All this activity also provided an excuse for the sexual coolness that now had grown between Russ and Barbara, and she retaliated for it as she had done with Larry: by having another affair.

Preston Adams* was twenty-seven, eight years younger than Barbara, married, a graduate of the same high school she had attended. He had come to work at Brame Specialty Company as a salesman two months after Barbara had started working there as a secretary in August 1982. That Christmas, Barbara invited him to the Christmas party at her house, and he met Russ. Early in 1983, Barbara and Preston had started going to lunch together. By spring they were still going to lunch regularly, but food was not on their minds.

Later, Preston would say that he never had known another woman like Barbara. He liked sex and wanted a lot of it, he said, but she loved it and wanted even more than he did. They sometimes slipped away to have sex every day, and she wouldn't allow him to leave until he had performed at least three or four times, he claimed. If he wasn't ready, he said, she would perform oral sex until he was.

Sometimes they would get together two or three times a day, Preston claimed, and afterward, he would hide from Barbara because he knew that she would want more and he simply couldn't stand it.

Barbara seemed to be without guilt about this, Preston said. She never spoke disparagingly of Russ, but she justified the affair by saying that Russ was always talking about other girls and she was sure that he had a girlfriend. This excuse was familiar as well.

Russ soon learned about this latest betrayal in a disturbing way. Barbara's maternal grandmother, Pearl Turner Rogers, died on January 26, 1984, and her funeral was set for Saturday afternoon. Early Saturday morning, Barbara said that she had to run some errands before the funeral. She left the boys with Russ, saying that she would be back in time to help them get ready for the service.

Later in the morning, Russ went to wash his car so that it would be sparkling for the funeral procession. On the way back home, he spotted Barbara's Oldsmobile sitting in isolation in the huge parking lot at Durham County Stadium. He pulled into the parking lot to make sure that it was Barbara's car. It was and it was empty.

Where was Barbara? And why had she left her car here?

Suspicious, Russ drove across the street to the National Guard Armory and backed his car into a spot from which he could watch his wife's car. Not long afterward, a car turned into the stadium parking lot and pulled alongside the Oldsmobile. Russ could tell that a man was driving the car and a woman was beside him in the front seat. He watched as they began embracing and kissing.

The amorous couple was startled when Russ's car came to a sudden halt alongside them. Looks of near panic came to Barbara's and Preston Adams's faces when they recognized him. Barbara straightened herself and hurriedly exited by the passenger door as Preston frantically cranked his car. No sooner had she closed the door, Russ later told his mother, than the red-faced man sped away.

Later that day, Barbara called Preston and told him that things were bad at home. She would tell him about it at work Monday. On Monday, however, she said that everything was okay. She had smoothed things over with Russ, and there was no need for this incident to interfere with their relationship.

Barbara did not break off the affair with Preston until several weeks later, telling him then that she was going to try to work things out with Russ and did not want to run the risk of getting caught again and further threatening her marriage. Preston left Brame Specialty shortly thereafter to take another job.

Barbara left the company in June. Her mother had helped her land yet another job at Duke University Medical Center, where Barbara had first worked when she was in high school. She would be a secretary in the Department of Utilization and Review. The job not only paid more than she had been making, it offered better benefits and a chance for advancement.

Barbara started work on June 16 and made a quick impression on her bosses. They thought her to be efficient, thorough, creative, self-directed and ambitious. Her coworkers found her to be friendly and helpful. She talked a lot about her sons and her husband, they would say later. She told them about gifts that Russ bought her and all the things they did together. All of Barbara's coworkers got the impression that she had an ideal marriage.

Russ was not viewing his marriage in exactly those terms that summer. He was more torn than his mother ever had seen him. He came to her in confidence one day and told her about catching Barbara with her lover at the stadium.

"Mother," he said, "she's sleeping all over town."

He had no proof of that, though, and indeed Barbara was successfully beginning to suppress this aspect of her personality. But aided by Russ's own weakness for spending, her other compulsion was as strong as ever. They had fallen deeply in debt again, Russ now told his mother. Once again they were members of a country club, this time at Willowhaven, just down the street from their house (the boys could ride their bikes there to swim, Barbara noted). Barbara had traded her Oldsmobile for a new one. She had had new hardwood floors put in the house, a Jenn-

Air range installed in the kitchen. Al had been noting these new extravagances and had been bringing them up to Russ, warning that he was heading toward trouble again. Now Russ was telling his mother that he couldn't control Barbara. She kept taking the key to the post office box and getting the mail before he could get to it, he said. He couldn't be sure what she was doing.

"Russell," his mother said, "leave her."

He was silent for a few moments.

"I can't," he said. "I can't hurt those boys. They're mine now."


Not long after spilling his troubles to his mother, Russ turned to the other woman who had played a major role in his life: his first wife, Jo Lynn.

After their divorce in 1979, she also had remarried later that year. She and her new husband had moved to Winston-Salem, then to Chicago. Russ and Jo Lynn had lost touch with each other for a few years, but late in 1982, soon after the financial crisis and the book deception, Russ had called Jo Lynn's parents to get her telephone number. He called her in Chicago. Although he likely called intending to talk about the troubles he was having, he apparently changed his mind, for he only chatted amiably and mentioned no problems.

When Jo Lynn told him that she was planning to come home for Christmas, Russ said that he would like to see her, and they made plans to get together.

They met for pizza at Crabtree Valley Mall in Raleigh. Jo Lynn saw immediately that Russ had changed.

"Russ always had a light around him that said, 'I'm so glad to be alive,' " she recalled years later. "That seemed dimmed."

Still, he spoke of no problems. They laughed and reminisced about happy times. Both realized that they still cared for each other and promised to keep in touch.

Russ called Jo Lynn again in the fall of 1983, after she had separated from her second husband. With a breaking voice he told her that Sampson, the German shepherd they had raised from a puppy, had died.

Jo Lynn returned to North Carolina soon after that. She got a job and moved into a small apartment in Raleigh with her young son by her second husband.

One Sunday evening in July 1984, Jo Lynn's doorbell rang. She answered to find Russ standing before her in camouflage military fatigues. He was just on his way home from his National Guard drill in Raleigh, he said, and thought he'd drop by.

Jo Lynn was happy to see him, but she could tell that something was wrong. Russ seemed worried. She invited him in.

Although she wouldn't realize it until later, she came to believe that Russ reached out to her instinctively when he was troubled, as if he needed to reconnect to the more innocent and happy time when they had been together.

When Jo Lynn inquired how things had been going, Russ indicated that they hadn't been going well at all. She knew how closemouthed Russ was, how he held so many things inside, and his admission surprised her. Soon it all was pouring out of him: the book episode, the unpaid bills under the chair, the rendezvous at County Stadium.

"Russ was a very trusting person," Jo Lynn recalled later. "To find out he had been deceived in so many ways, he was overwhelmed. It was almost a disbelief that anybody could do so many things."

He had thought about leaving Barbara, he told Jo Lynn, and if it weren't for the boys, he would. Jo Lynn knew from the way Russ had talked about Bryan and Jason that he loved them deeply. He was clearly devoted to them and he thought they felt the same way about him. They had already lost one father, he said, and he didn't want them to lose another.

Russ also talked about the father they had lost. Barbara had told him that Larry shot himself while cleaning a gun, he said, but he was beginning to wonder about that.

"I know it sounds crazy," he said, "but if anything ever happens to me, I want you to look into it."

Jo Lynn didn't know what to say. All she could do was offer a sympathetic ear and consolation, but his last comment unnerved her. Could he truly be in danger? Was Barbara just disturbed or truly crazy? It bothered her so much that after Russ left, she called a close friend to talk about it. Later she also told her parents about her concerns.

Several weeks after his first visit, Russ again showed up at Jo Lynn's door after a Sunday drill. Again she listened as he went on and on about Barbara. He couldn't believe that there were people like her, he said. He was sure that the ordeal he was going through was a payback for what he had done to Jo Lynn when they were married. He was to blame for the failure of their marriage, he admitted. If only he had been more mature, if only he had been a stronger person, they might still be together and happy.

"What goes around, comes around," he said, using one of his favorite expressions to explain his situation.

As he was getting ready to leave, Russ turned to Jo Lynn and paused, as if uncertain about what he was going to say.

"If you would give me another chance," he suddenly blurted, "I could be gone in a weekend."

Jo Lynn was taken aback. She was seeing somebody else, but she still loved Russ, wanted to be his caring friend and confidant. They could be closer as friends, she thought, than as husband and wife.

"We both made mistakes," she said, and his eyes told her that he understood. There would be no quick and easy escapes to happiness. He would have to find some other way out of the mire in which he had trapped himself.

# Chapter Fifteen

Russ always preached to his players never to give up when the going got tough, and he was not too big to heed his own lessons. After he realized that he never could return to his innocent and happy past, he resolved to work things out with Barbara. His determination would pay off, just as he had told his players that it would, and things would grow dramatically better for both of them in the next few years. But gradually, insidiously, old patterns would creep back that eventually would lead him to wonder if sometimes it was not better to be a quitter.

As he always had done in time of need, he turned to God for help, and by the fall of 1984, he and Barbara vowed to rededicate themselves to God, the church and each other. They began teaching Sunday school together at Rose of Sharon Church and took part in almost all of the other activities there.

As their relationship improved, they began to dream new dreams together.

Neither ever had been happy in the small house on Bivens Road, and fantasy house shopping became a favorite pastime for them. They often went riding through Durham's better neighborhoods, looking for houses that they liked. When they saw one for sale that caught their eye, they would call the realtor and make an appointment to look at it, just to see how their furnishings would go with the interior.

Early in the summer of 1985, they found a house that Barbara couldn't resist. It had the contemporary design that she favored above all others. Both liked the layout, the openness that the huge windows gave to the living areas, the stone fireplace and cathedral ceiling in the living room, and deck off the master bedroom.

The house was in a new subdivision, quiet and wooded, within walking distance of Willowhaven Country Club, only a mile or so from Russ's parents' house. And although the lot wasn't huge, the house's hillside location and the surrounding trees gave it a sense of privacy.

Best of all, the price was right. Russ and Barbara were sure that they could get it for not much more than $100,000. Their house on Bivens Road ought to bring at least $85,000. They would make money on their present house, and although they would have to take a bigger mortgage, their payments wouldn't be that much more than they were making now.

They made a bid on the house at 2833 Fox Drive, and a price of $101,500 was finally agreed upon. When Russ's parents heard about the new house, they were dubious. Al particularly made known to his son his doubts about the wisdom of this move, and as the time neared for signing papers and making a deposit, Russ began to have second thoughts. At Sunday dinner at his parents' house, he suggested to Barbara that maybe they should back out of the deal.

"We can't," Barbara said, pointing out that the real estate agent was a friend of hers and it would embarrass her.

"I thought I was your friend, too," Russ said.

He soon acquiesced, though, as his parents knew he would. What Barbara wanted, she usually got—and quickly. "She had no patience," Doris later recalled. "She wanted everything right now."

Russ and Barbara paid a deposit on the new house and put their house on the market. Their house sold so quickly and at such a good price—$89,500—that they found themselves moving much sooner than they expected, early in July.

They barely had time to get settled in the new house before their lives were overtaken by hectic new schedules.

Barbara's bosses had seen for some time that they needed to provide her with greater opportunities if they wanted to keep her. That summer she was offered a new job as an administrative secretary in the division of surgical nursing, a step up, with an increase in pay. One major benefit of the job was that Barbara could arrange her schedule to allow her to return to college.

That fall, sixteen years after she had dropped out of Appalachian State University to get married and have a baby, Barbara
enrolled as a full-time student at North Carolina Central University, where Russ was attending night classes, working on his master's degree. That decision had been made upon the advice of the
Christian counselor that Barbara's parents had arranged for her to
begin seeing to help her deal with her spending problems after
the financial crisis she and Russ had suffered through, she wrote
in answer to a letter from her former in-laws. They still were trying to keep in touch with her, still hoping to arrange a visit with
their grandchildren, although Barbara had been making excuses
to keep that from happening for more than seven years now. The
counselor thought that she was resentful because she had not
been able to finish college.

Barbara was convinced that her life was now set on a new
and far better course. "I think I am really getting myself into per-
spective, and am finally the person the Lord wants me to be," she
wrote to the Fords. "I have learned to be honest, totally honest
with myself."

In keeping with her new honesty, she acknowledged that she
had rushed into her marriage with Russ for the sake of her sons,
but she was not sorry for it. "We have a really good life now,"
she wrote, "although it was shaky for a few years."

Russ was much happier, too, not only because things had
turned around with Barbara, but because he was back at Durham
High, this time as coach of the baseball team, assistant coach of
the football team and instructor in driver's education—and at a
higher salary.

His hectic schedule had caused him to leave the National
Guard in the fall of 1984 and transfer back to the Army Reserves,
which he had left in 1976. He had been assigned first to a reserve
group in Durham, then to another unit in Garner, just east of Raleigh. In the summer of 1985, at his request, he had gone into a
control group in St. Louis, Missouri, which would allow him to
continue his service toward retirement but didn't require him to
attend drills. His life had become far too busy to spend weekends training.

By the beginning of 1986, however, Russ had only one semester remaining to complete his classwork, and at the end of January he rejoined the National Guard. Bryan, now a high school

senior more than six feet tall, joined with him, hoping to better his chance to win an ROTC scholarship. A serious and wry young man, Bryan once had entertained ideas of attending West Point, but now he was dreaming, like his real father before him, of attending flight school after college.

As a result of all their activities, Barbara and Russ were seeing relatively little of each other. Their schedules were keeping them apart until they fell in bed exhausted at night. But they were always together at church on Sunday morning, and during the week Barbara called Russ at his office in the basement of the gym to chat every day at lunch.

Keeping busy was good for Barbara. She was not only making top grades in her classes at North Carolina Central, she also was continuing to make good impressions at her new job at Duke. Her boss, Judith Rohlf, considered her to be especially bright and hard working, the fastest clerical assistant she had ever had.

She just didn't see how Barbara was able to do all that she was doing. She thought that Barbara felt obligated not only to be impressive at work and excel in her classes but to be a perfect mother, wife and housewife as well. Barbara tried to do everything for her sons and for Russ, whom she babied, Rohlf thought. "How do you do it all and still keep your house so spotless?" Rohlf asked after a visit to Barbara's home. To Barbara, the question had been a compliment.

Rohlf knew that Barbara was overqualified for the job she held at Duke, and she felt certain that it was only a temporary stop. Barbara had told her that she would like to become an administrator at the medical center after she got her degree, and Rohlf had no doubt that she could do it.

Indeed, Barbara's ambition was the source of the only problem that Rohlf had with her. Barbara seemed to want a lot of authority and often would do things without prior approval. Rohlf had had to tell her on several occasions to check with her first.

"Sometimes," Rohlf later recalled, "I just wanted to tell Barbara to relax and not try so hard."

As 1986 drew to a close, Barbara responded to birthday greetings from her former in-laws with a letter. "Therapy is still going very well for me," she wrote. "I've discovered many things about myself, past and present, that I hope I can fully overcome and be the kind of person the Lord wants me to be. . . . The worst problem was admitting that there was a problem. Pray for me. I feel I still have a long road to cover before I reach a point of satisfaction."

Russ finished his thesis in the spring of 1987 and defended it successfully. His family joined in celebration when he was awarded his master's degree in physical education in May, taking him and Barbara and the boys to a steak house for dinner after the ceremony. Barbara seemed pleased by Russ's accomplishment, but she was even more excited by the possibilities that were opening for her. She had been interviewed for a new position at Duke that month.

A new director was being appointed for the surgical nursing department. His name was Timothy Bevelacqua and he was thirty-one years old. He needed somebody to set up his office, a self-directed person who knew the Duke system well, a hard worker who understood the necessity of loyalty to a boss, and Barbara had been recommended to him. He offered her the job that summer.

Barbara's boss didn't want to lose her, but she didn't want to hold her back either. This was a good promotion, with another increase in pay. Barbara went to work for Bevelacqua in September. After she moved into her new job, Judith Rohlf had to hire two people to do all the work that Barbara had been doing.

Bevelacqua found her to be just what he was looking for, an excellent assistant, hard working and so efficient and loyal that it was sometimes annoying. Barbara tried too hard to please, Bevelacqua thought. He got the feeling that she wanted to mother him. She even tried to make his haircut appointments.

In anticipation of her new job, Barbara planned to take only a three-hour independent study course in English that fall. She was taking the class at Duke, but it would be applied toward her degree at North Carolina Central. After her first year of full-time study, she had been gradually cutting back. The previous fall, she had switched to evening classes and taken only three-fourths of a full class load. In January, she had changed her major from nursing to psychology and taken only two classes on alternating days, one in the morning, the other in the afternoon. Overall, she

was maintaining a 3.7 grade point average, although she told
people that she was making a 4.0, which at times she was. But
despite her new job and her success with her classes, new troubles were mounting for Barbara and Russ.

At the beginning of 1987, their spending again had begun
catching up with them. In the past two years, each had bought
two new cars. Barbara had gone from an Oldsmobile Cutlass
Calais to an Oldsmobile 88 and now was driving a new Ford
Mustang convertible. Russ had gone from a Sunbird to a Mazda
pickup truck to a Ford Bronco II, which he later would wreck
and replace with a Chevy Blazer. They had bought a Datsun
pickup truck for Bryan when he got his license, then a
Volkswagen Bug, followed by another VW. Both Russ and Barbara were wearing Rolex watches, and Russ's parents later would
be shocked to learn that his was worth nearly four thousand dollars. Barbara had a new refrigerator for the new house, new furniture. She had a new hardwood floor put in the kitchen and
hallway, her kitchen counters covered with ceramic tiles. Russ
also had bought a sparkling new boat, a nineteen-foot Bayliner
Bowrider with a 120-horsepower Volvo engine, which he now
kept at his parents' cottage at Hyco Lake.

"Honey, you won't believe what the Stagers have bought
now," Pam Spence's husband had said to her when he had seen
Russ pull his new boat into the driveway across the street, shortly
before Russ and Barbara moved to Fox Drive.

"Where do they get all the money?" Pam had asked.

Coworkers at Duke marveled at Barbara's spending, too.
Rarely did a Monday pass that she didn't come in talking about
the purchases made over the weekend: a new outfit, a new piece
of jewelry, something new she had bought for the house or the
boys, some new electronic gizmo Russ had picked up. They
couldn't help but notice how frequently Barbara came in wearing
new outfits, and it was clear that none of them had come from
discount houses. They just couldn't figure out where all the
money was coming from.

Barbara's former boss at Duke, Judith Rohlf, had run into Barbara and Russ at the mall several times on weekends, and she

teased Barbara that she had made a good catch in Russ. Few husbands liked to shop.

"Russ is a clotheshorse," Barbara had replied. He loved to shop for clothes, she said, and he bought most of her clothing as well. When Rohlf kidded Barbara about all the money she spent, Barbara just laughed it off.

All of this had not escaped the attention of Russ's parents. They knew that Russ could be almost as thoughtless with spending as Barbara was, and Al kept bringing it up to him, stressing that he had to get it under control. He went on about it so much at times that Doris would glare her that's-enough displeasure across the dining-room table at him.

Nonetheless, step by step, Barbara and Russ continued their slide back into old spending habits, lured to some degree, no doubt, by their increasing income. Both were making more money than ever. Barbara was getting nearly $18,000 a year at Duke; Russ was making about $30,000 from the school system, plus a couple of thousand dollars from the National Guard. But once again their income fell behind their spending, and as the gap grew, they reverted to old habits to deal with it.

In February 1987, shortly after both Russ and Barbara had taken out $50,000 life insurance policies, they refinanced their house, getting a better interest rate, but increasing their mortgage to $92,000. They got more than $20,000 in cash, though, to rescue them temporarily from their mounting debts.

Only a week later, however, they went back to another bank, negotiating a loan for $4,500 to buy another vehicle to replace Bryan's worn-out Volkswagen, a 1986 Mazda truck.

As 1987 wore on, Barbara particularly became more and more free with her spending. Several more times she went to banks to arrange loans to cover her debts. And still she could not stop buying.

That fall, she wrote checks almost every day to fashionable department stores such as Thalhimer's, Ivey's, and Belk's, as well as to expensive clothing shops, sometimes several a day. And more and more of those checks were being returned for insufficient funds, forty-two during one four-month period. The bank charges for overdrafts and returned checks on her account would amount to $275 for November alone. The $342 monthly payments on her Mustang convertible began going unpaid.

Friends began to notice that Russ seemed downcast much of the time, as if he had some great worry on his mind.

That fall Russ's first wife, Jo Lynn, saw a Dennis the Menace cartoon that amused her. In it, Dennis's friend Margaret was telling Dennis that she wanted him to be her first husband. Jo Lynn clipped it and mailed it to Russ at school. She hadn't heard from him in more than a year, since he had written a letter to the court in her behalf to help in her child-custody dispute with her second husband. She hadn't seen him in more than three years. She had assumed that he and Barbara had worked things out and that all was fine.

Russ called after he got the cartoon. They laughed about it and chatted briefly.

"Next time you're in Raleigh for Guard," Jo Lynn told him, "I'd love for you to come by and see me."

He came on the second Sunday in November. He looked tired and a little haggard. He had recently discovered that he had high blood pressure, he said, and he didn't understand it. He had even given up desserts because of it, and she knew how much he loved sweets, especially banana pudding and strawberry pie.

He talked about coaching and how he was becoming disillusioned with it, at least at Durham High. The school's student body was now almost entirely black, but most of the alumni were white and didn't support the school's athletic programs. Russ's teams were always just barely scratching by, and coaching seemed to be a constant struggle now.

"You know how it used to be everything to me," he said. "It's changing. Takes a lot out of you."

Jo Lynn asked about the boys, and his face brightened when he told about helping Bryan get ready to go to Fort Bragg to compete for an ROTC scholarship. Russ had pressed his uniform for him and helped him spit-shine his shoes. Bryan had looked really sharp, he said. He had gotten the scholarship and now he was a student at the University of North Carolina at Wilmington. Russ missed having him around the house.

Jason, he said, was beginning to really get into athletics—he was quite a golfer. He was proud of both of them.

Russ stayed only a short time and never mentioned Barbara and the troubles he had talked about before. But as he was getting ready to leave, leaning with his back against the door, he told Jo Lynn the same unsettling thing that he had mentioned three and a half years earlier.

"I know I told you once before, and I know I'm probably being paranoid, but if anything ever happens to me, I want you to look into it."

Surely he was just being paranoid, Jo Lynn agreed. After all, years had passed since he'd first said that and nothing had happened. What could happen to him?

Maybe the same thing that happened to Barbara's first husband, he suggested.

Surely she couldn't have murdered him, Jo Lynn told him, hoping to offer reassurance.

"There would've been an investigation," she said. "You can't just kill somebody and get away with it."

"But she would be clever about it," he said. "She would make it look like an accident. Just promise me that if something does happen, you'll look into it."

Surely Russ was just letting his imagination get carried away, she thought, but she promised. She was more concerned about his mood. He seemed to be sagging under a heavy sadness, his energy and enthusiasm for life completely dissipated. The light that once had surrounded him wasn't just dimmed now, it had gone out.

Before he turned to go, Russ looked at her in a way that he had not for a long time.

"I don't know how or where," he said, "but I think that someday we'll be together again."

Jo Lynn smiled, uncertain again what to say.

"The men I've been with since you make you look like a walk in the park," she said.

Twilight was fading as Russ left, and an overwhelming sadness overtook Jo Lynn as she watched him go, heading off into the darkness.

# Chapter Sixteen

I f Russ's National Guard unit had ever held a competition to pick its top soldier, few in the unit had any doubt that it would have been Russ Stager. His uniforms were always creased and starched. His boots and brass always gleamed. His equipment stayed in top condition and ready to go.

Russ was dedicated to the Guard and took great pride in serving in it. He was a by-the-book soldier: always showed up on time, always did his job without complaint, no matter how dirty or difficult it might be. He often volunteered for extra duty and even worked at recruiting on his own time. "He eagerly seeks responsibility and performs every task in a thorough and professional manner," one of his commanders wrote in an evaluation.

Younger soldiers looked to Russ for direction, and officers admired him. In December 1987 he was promoted to staff sergeant, raising his monthly pay from $160 to $184. Russ also had taken advantage of a new benefit offered by the Guard. Previously, members could get only $3,500 in life insurance through the Guard, but that had recently been expanded to $50,000, and Russ had signed up for it, paying $4 monthly for the new coverage. This raised his life insurance to $165,000 through five policies, enough to make sure that Barbara was taken care of if something should happen to him.

Russ had a long-time fascination with guns, and the Guard allowed him to indulge that hobby. In 1986, he had joined his unit's pistol team, which demanded that its members be as skilled in firearms safety as in marksmanship. He took pride in his abilities and often went practice-shooting with one or another of the team's members. In the spring of 1987 he had attended Combat Pistol Coaches School so that he could qualify to teach others in the use of military handguns. He had taught his boys to shoot and was trying to teach Barbara to safely handle the .25 semiautomatic he had bought a couple of years earlier for protection.

On Thursday, January 28, 1988, he took a sick day at school so that he could make a run to Fort Bragg to pick up equipment for his Guard unit. He made the run in an army truck with Kenneth Hanes, a member of the unit's honor guard who owned a frame shop and once had framed some Williamsburg prints for Barbara. Russ seemed his normal self that day, Hanes later recalled. They talked mostly about Guard matters.

When they returned that afternoon, Russ stopped by the supply room at four and checked out two Colt .45 pistols. One of them was for another member of the pistol team, Sergeant Gilly Boaz, also a member of the honor guard. He and Russ were planning to get together and practice for the upcoming meet.

Russ had become close friends with his assistant baseball coach, Mike Wood, whom he called "Coachy." They played golf together, and three times a week they worked out together in the weight room at school, each "spotting" for the other, standing by in the event one or the other got in trouble with a lift too heavy. Russ had been working out hard in the past year, his muscles expanding so much that he had outgrown many of his clothes. He was bench-pressing 375 pounds.

All through the fall, Wood had seen that Russ was not himself. He was quieter, seemed to be withdrawing. Once Wood had walked into the weight room and found Russ sitting on the bench with his head in his hands, as if in despair. Russ had been startled when Wood walked in.

"Something wrong?" Wood had asked.

"Nah," Russ had said, "my sinuses are just bothering me."

Wood thought that something was wrong, though, and he tried obliquely to get Russ to talk about it, but he never got anywhere.

When Wood went to work out with Russ on Friday afternoon,

January 29, he found Russ acting more like his old self, joking and kidding, as if a burden had been lifted.

"See you Monday," Wood had said, as he and Russ parted after their workout.

Only later would Wood learn the reason for his friend's relieved mood.


Russ did not get to go shooting that weekend as he had hoped. On Saturday, he went to the Virginia mountains with Barbara and her family to look at a farm the Terrys were thinking of buying there. Later, Barbara's brothers would recall him making jokes about the cow pies in the pasture.

On Sunday, Barbara and Russ taught their Sunday school class as usual. Russ wrote a $30 check for the collection plate at the regular morning service. That afternoon, he played golf with his friends and fellow teachers, John Biddle and Bill Page. Russ had a good round and was particularly pleased about shooting a birdie on the last hole. He was in a good mood when Biddle dropped him off at his house about five-thirty. Biddle saw Barbara in the driveway as he was pulling away.

This was Super Bowl Sunday: Washington Redskins vs. the Denver Broncos in San Diego, starting on TV at six. Russ had promised his parents that he would come and watch the game with them. He and Barbara and Jason arrived at their house just as the pregame coverage was beginning. On the way, they had stopped at Red Lobster to pick up a party tray of boiled shrimp. Barbara had paid for it with a check for $19.85 that later would bounce.

They watched the game in the family room and ate shrimp and key lime pie at halftime. After supper, Russ sat in his father's favorite chair by the lamp, and Barbara, who was seated on the sofa, suggested that he take the other chair so his father could sit there. After Russ took the other chair, which had been pulled to the center of the floor to give a better view of the TV, Barbara got up and went to sit on the floor by Russ's chair. She took his hand and held it, looking up at Doris as if she wanted her to see her affection for Russ. Doris had never seen her do anything like that before, and she noticed that Russ didn't respond at all.

Barbara had talked almost unceasingly that night about her

concerns for her boss. She was worried that Tim, as she kept calling him, was going to be forced out of his position, and she didn't know what she was going to do. She talked about it so much that Doris began to wish that she'd just shut up.

Russ seemed his normal self, joking and laughing, happy with his golf game but most unhappy at the way the football game was turning out. A staunch fan of the Dallas Cowboys, he was pulling for the Broncos. He gloated when the Broncos took an early lead, teasing his father, a fervent Redskins fan. But the tables soon were turned, and as it became more and more apparent that his team was going to be humiliated, his sister Cindy even called from Chattanooga to rag him about it. Later, she would take solace from the last thing she said to him: "I love you." Disgusted by the Redskins' blowout, Russ decided to leave before the game ended.

He needed to get home and to bed. Monday would be a busy day, the first day of baseball practice. He had a lot to think about, a lot to do. He needed to be sharp. He had great hopes for his team this year.

The parting was no different from any other, and later his parents would not remember what he said to them, or they to him. They returned to the TV to watch the Redskins finish off the Broncos forty-two to ten.

Not until days later would Doris recall anything unusual about that evening. Then she would remember how Barbara had sat on the floor by Russ, holding his hand and making certain that Doris saw it. She had seen nothing ominous about that at the time. After all, how could anybody have guessed that such an apparent show of affection really portended murder?

# PART FOUR

# Seeking Motive

# Chapter Seventeen

At forty, the father of a year-old son, Rick Buchanan was a short and dapper man with a touch of gray at the temples. Always neatly dressed, he favored blazers and tasseled loafers, which seemed to fit with the cocky attitude that some accused him of having. He had spent nine years with the Durham County Sheriff's Department at two different times under two different sheriffs. He had been with the department for five years on this stint, four as a detective. Buchanan had received extensive training in homicide investigation, his chosen specialty, leading to his promotion to sergeant and recognition as the department's top murder investigator.

He had investigated numerous killings in the past four years, some of which had turned into headline-making murder cases. As he sat in his office with Jo Lynn Snow on February 2, 1988, reading the letter she just had handed him, he realized that what had at first appeared to be an unfortunate accident might be a murder more sensational and bizarre than any he had ever investigated.

At the same time, though, he was a proud man who did not enjoy acknowledging mistakes, and despite his nagging uneasiness about Russ's shooting, he already had been quoted in the newspaper calling it an accident, saying that no charges were expected, and he had planned no further inquiries into it. Now here was this intense and frazzled woman with her letter suggesting that Russ might have been murdered.

He knew that he had riled her as soon as he said that Barbara's story was consistent with the evidence, for she fired off a flurry of antagonistic questions as rough as any he ever had faced on the witness stand from defense attorneys.

"What does the autopsy show?" she demanded.

He was forced to admit that no autopsy had been performed. Indeed, the body already had been cleaned, dressed, and embalmed and was now at Clements Funeral Home, where family and friends would be coming to view it later that day.

What about fingerprints or palm prints on the gun? Jo Lynn wanted to know. Did they show that the shooting could have happened as Barbara claimed?

The gun had not been examined for fingerprints, Buchanan acknowledged.

Jo Lynn was incredulous. "I was just shaking my head," she said later. "I was floored."

Buchanan always enjoyed a scrap, and he had some questions of his own. What did Jo Lynn know about this first husband?

Very little, it turned out. His last name, she remembered, was Ford. He had died ten or eleven years ago. He and Barbara might have lived in Burlington or Graham, she wasn't sure. The children were by the first husband, she knew. Russ had adopted them soon after he and Barbara were married, and he had married her soon after her first husband was killed.

There were other questions, and Buchanan wrote Jo Lynn's answers into his report later that day. "She readily admitted that during the five years that she was married to Russ, he ran around on her, but she was not the easiest person to live with either. She stated she had a terrible temper. . . ."

After describing Jo Lynn's memories of what Russ had told her about his problems with Barbara, Buchanan wrote: "Told her he thought he was being paid back for what he did in his first marriage and that what goes around comes around."

Jo Lynn was upset after her meeting with Buchanan. She had expected that a thorough investigation of Russ's death already would be under way and that Buchanan would be eager to hear what she had to tell him. But the realization that the police obviously had taken Barbara at her word rattled her. And Buchanan's questions, his detached and skeptical manner, had angered her, leaving her uncertain.

"I thought, maybe I've seen too much TV and it doesn't happen that way in real life," she recalled later.

Jo Lynn drove straight to the Stager home after leaving the sheriff's department. She hadn't seen her former in-laws for nearly ten years, but she was welcomed warmly with tears and hugs, as if she had never been away. She didn't know what the Stagers thought, so she didn't say anything about her suspicions or her visit to the sheriff's department. She soon discovered that Doris was accepting Barbara's version of the shooting. "I know that Russ would want me to forgive Barbara," Doris said, and that was her Christian intention. She seemed not to have even considered that Russ's shooting might have been deliberate, and Jo Lynn couldn't bring herself to suggest otherwise under the strain of the circumstances.

Not until she was leaving did she see an opening. Russ's sister, Cindy, accompanied her to her car, and as she was about to open the door, Cindy said, "Did you ever know Russ to sleep with a loaded pistol under his pillow?"

Jo Lynn knew immediately that in Cindy she had found an ally in her suspicions, and she poured out everything to her. Cindy hurried inside to get her husband, David, who at first said that they should leave the matter to the police. But they had accepted Barbara's story, Jo Lynn pointed out, and she knew that Russ had doubts about the death of Barbara's first husband and had expressed concerns that she might try to harm him. Hearing that convinced David that Russ's death had been no accident, and he agreed that the family had to go to the police. Worried about Al's heart condition, Cindy and David didn't want to involve him, but they knew that they needed to convince Doris that something was wrong so that she would accompany them, and Doris was in such a daze of grief that they didn't know how she would react. That job fell to Cindy, who returned to the house, crowded with relatives and friends.

"Mother, would you mind coming out here with me for a few minutes?" Cindy said.

They drove with David and Jo Lynn to a nearby Burger King so that they could talk without arousing the curiosity of their visitors. Doris had to hear only a little of what the others had to say before agreeing that something had to be done. Deep down, she said later, she had known from the moment she had walked into that hospital room and seen Barbara's face that the shooting of her son had been no accident. The four talked for more than an hour, putting pieces together, deciding what they needed to tell the police. Before they went to the sheriff's department, though, Doris wanted to go see her minister.

The women dropped off David at the house to stay with Al, and drove to Grey Stone Baptist Church, where they told Malbert Smith of their intentions. Before they left for the sheriff's office, Smith led them in prayer, seeking God's guidance for the course on which they were about to embark.

"We don't want vengeance, Lord," he prayed. "We want justice."

When the three women entered Buchanan's office at 3:50 that afternoon, Jo Lynn found a different person. Buchanan was courteous and sympathetic, eager to listen and quick with questions. Her earlier visit had prompted him to action, and he already had set several things in motion. He had arranged to have Russ's body picked up at eight the following morning and taken to the university hospital in Chapel Hill for an autopsy. He had learned that Barbara's first husband had died, strangely enough, from a .25-caliber bullet wound, and he had made an appointment to read the records of the case at the office of the state medical examiner in Chapel Hill the following day. He also had picked up a copy of Russ and Barbara's marriage license and had checked for gun registrations in their names. The .25 with which Russ had been shot was not registered, he had discovered, and he couldn't help but wonder if it was the same gun that had killed Larry Ford.

Doris now told Buchanan about Russ and Barbara's money problems, the book hoax, which Malbert Smith had just filled her in about, and Barbara's rendezvous at the county stadium. She'd heard, she said, that Barbara once had worked for a bank in Durham and had been asked to resign because of embezzlement. That might be the reason that she and Russ had been denied a loan without explanation during the time of their financial crisis, she thought. She also told about a theft at Russ's house the previous spring in which some jewelry supposedly had been stolen. Barbara had told her that was the reason Russ had become concerned about prowlers, but she knew that there had been no prowlers and that Russ was not concerned about that at all.

Buchanan quizzed Doris about the death of Larry Ford, but she could tell him little. Larry's parents, she thought, might live in High Point.

Buchanan thanked the women for coming and assured them that he would be looking further into Russ's death. This time Jo Lynn left the sheriff's department more hopeful.

Clements Funeral Home rarely had seen such a crush of people or such a mingling of black and white as it did that night. Family, friends from past and present, teachers, school officials, students and former students, players and former players, church members, neighbors, hundreds of people filed by the coffin where Russ lay in the dress-blue army uniform his parents had given him for Christmas just six weeks earlier.

Several people took note that Barbara did not stay in the room with Russ's body, where his bereaved parents and sister stood vigil, greeting the throng who had come to pay their respects. She remained in a separate room, with her family seemingly forming a protective circle around her. At one point when she became dizzy and went outside for fresh air, her family followed her even there.

While Barbara was in the separate room, Oma Smith and her husband, Everette, a Baptist minister, went to speak with her. Oma had worked with both Barbara and her mother at Duke. Barbara chatted lightly, telling her that she and Jason were planning to go to Wilmington Friday so that Jason could see Bryan's dorm room. And she couldn't wait to get back to work on Monday, she said. The sooner she got back, the better off she would be. And she was awfully worried about her boss, Tim.

After the Smiths had gone to Barbara's parents' house to see her on the evening of Russ's death, Oma had asked her husband a question. "Did you notice anything unusual?"

Barbara didn't appear to be all that grieved, he had said. The gathering had seemed like a social occasion instead of a wake.

"I was just wondering if I was the only one who had that feeling," Oma had said.

Now that feeling was even stronger.

# Chapter Eighteen

Rick Buchanan was on the phone before he left for work Wednesday morning, closely questioning the two deputies who had investigated the shooting on Fox Drive two days earlier. He wanted to know the condition of the bed, where the pistol and shell casing had been found. Had there been powder burns on the sheets or covers? He was pleased that the memories of the two officers were at least consistent.

As soon as he got to his office, Buchanan picked up a copy of Raleigh's morning newspaper, *The News and Observer*. A reporter from the paper had interviewed him the previous afternoon, and he wanted to see the story. It quoted him accurately. Barbara's version of the shooting was "consistent with everything we've seen at the scene," he had said.

Buchanan did not want Barbara to know that anybody suspected her. He had told the reporter that the pistol with which Russ had been shot had a "light trigger." Not much pressure was required to drop the hammer, he said. "I've seen accidental discharges of guns, but I've never seen one similar to this," the story quoted him. In fact, the trigger was not light.

Buchanan put the paper aside and took the elevator to the district attorney's office on the fifth floor. He called snappy greetings to secretaries and assistant DAs as he passed.

Ron Stephens was forty-three, tall and blue-eyed, with graying temples and a distinguished bearing. Thoughtful and soft-spoken, the father of two, he had been a decorated combat helicopter pilot in Vietnam. For the past seven years he had been Durham County's District Attorney.

Buchanan had come to alert Stephens that Russ Stager's shooting might be more than it appeared. He filled him in on what he had learned so far and told him the immediate steps he intended to take. It all sounded highly suspicious, Stephens agreed, and he told Buchanan to keep him informed of developments.

Eric Evenson had been talking to an assistant in his office when he saw Buchanan stroll past his open door on the way to talk with Stephens. Buchanan usually didn't come calling unless something big was up, and Evenson couldn't help wondering what.

Evenson was thirty-three, short and freckled with thinning red hair. He wore glasses and a narrow mustache. The son of a hardware store owner in Charlotte, he had been attracted to drama and journalism before gravitating to law school. He had worked as an assistant district attorney in Greensboro before coming to work for Ron Stephens seven years earlier. Since that time he had tried more than a hundred cases every year, and he had become one of Stephens's top assistants. Noted for his thoroughness and tenacity, he went at the big cases that came his way with a singlemindedness that bordered on ferocity.

Soon after Evenson saw Buchanan leaving, Stephens wandered into his office. "You know that Durham High coach who was shot a couple of days ago?" Stephens asked.

Evenson did. He had been in juvenile court when he first heard about it Monday morning. A teenager had been charged with carrying a gun, and Judge Orlando Hudson admonished him about how dangerous handguns could be. "Just this morning," the judge had said, "a woman accidentally shot her husband in bed."

That had stuck in Evenson's mind, and afterward he bought an afternoon newspaper for more details. Something just bothered him about it, he said later. A gun going off accidentally in a bed could hit a person anywhere, an arm, a leg, the torso. How had it hit such a relatively small target as the head? Evenson even had made a mental note to check with the sheriff's department about it when he got a chance.

"Well, it may not have been an accident," Stephens was now telling him.

Stephens went on to fill him in on all that Buchanan knew

about it. Buchanan was pursuing it, he said, and if the case developed, it would be a big one. He wanted Evenson to take it.


Buchanan called Russ's sister that morning to find out if anybody in the family knew Russ's normal morning routine. Barbara was always up first, Cindy told him, an early riser. She left Russ asleep while she showered and began getting ready for work. Russ, on the contrary, was awfully hard to get up. It was a joke in the family about how he would sleep away half the day if nobody nudged him out of bed. Once when a dogfight on his family's front porch had awakened everybody else in the house, he had slept right on. On another occasion, not only had he slept through the insistent bleatings of a smoke alarm, he had slept through a fire at a house he shared with a roommate. He hadn't even been awakened by the screams of his roommate, whose feet had been burned as he tried to escape over the malfunctioning floor furnace.

While Buchanan was talking with Cindy, Barbara was at the funeral home. She'd arrived carrying a rose, which she wanted to place in Russ's coffin, she said. She was surprised to find his body missing, taken earlier that morning, she soon learned, to North Carolina Memorial Hospital in Chapel Hill for an autopsy. One of Doris's sisters was there at the time, and she overheard the funeral home director asking Barbara if she would tell Russ's parents about the body being taken for autopsy.

Barbara arrived at Doris and Al's house shortly before noon with Bryan and Jason. The boys were hungry, and Doris went into the refrigerator to fix something for them from the vast amounts of food that people had brought to the house. Doris hadn't been able to eat a bite since Russ had died, but she noticed that Barbara joined the boys in eating heartily. Barbara left to get ready for the funeral without ever mentioning that Russ's body had been taken from the funeral home. The Stagers figured that she had been waiting to see if they would mention it, hoping to learn whether they'd had something to do with it.

Simultaneous services for Russ began at two. A memorial service was being held in the auditorium at Durham High under the direction of Principal Charles Warren. He had gone to Barbara's parents' house on the day Russ was shot to seek her permission for the service. Barbara had set two conditions: no music and keep it short. She didn't want to evoke emotion, she said.

Russ's players, all the coaching staff and his closest friends among the teachers were among the overflow crowd at the funeral in the chapel at Clements Funeral Home. The service was conducted by Larry Harper, his pastor at Homestead Heights Baptist Church, the church to which Russ and Barbara had moved less than a year earlier. He was assisted by Malbert Smith.

Following the service, a long procession of cars followed the hearse to a grassy hillside in sprawling Maplewood Cemetery, only a short distance from downtown Durham. Russ's fellow coaches carried his coffin to the tent that covered the open grave. A white-gloved National Guard honor squad wearing dress blues fired a final salute, and taps wafted forlornly over the somber gathering.

Sergeant 1st Class Joe Powell and Master Sergeant Robert Parker removed the flag from the coffin, folded it into a neat triangle and presented it to Barbara, causing her to break into sobs.


All the while, Rick Buchanan had been busy. After talking with Cindy that morning, he drove to Barbara's parents' house and talked with her father. He would need the bedding to help clear up the case, Buchanan said, and James Terry fetched the bloodied pillow from a trash can. The sheets had been washed, James explained, and were at Barbara's house. He would get them. When Buchanan learned that the bedcovers had been taken to a laundry for dry cleaning, he asked for the laundry slip. He picked up the bedcovers on his way back to the office and dropped them off before driving to the state medical examiner's office to read the autopsy report on Larry Ford and find out what Russ's autopsy had shown.

The autopsy had been completed by the time he got there. Dr. Thomas Clark had retrieved the bullet from the front of Russ's skull and had it waiting for him. He also had some interesting information. The trajectory of the bullet had been downward. That removed any doubt Buchanan still harbored that Russ's death had been an accident. The trajectory simply didn't jibe with Barbara's account.

Returning to his office, Buchanan next tried to find out how much life insurance Russ had. He had no luck, and after the funeral he called the Stager home and talked with Cindy. The Stagers didn't know anything about it. She gave Buchanan a list of names and addresses of family members and friends to question. Ten minutes later, she called back to say that Al had asked Barbara about life insurance. Barbara had told him that she didn't know anything about it. Russ took care of that kind of thing.

Cindy also remembered something she hadn't told Buchanan earlier. Her father had approached Barbara at the funeral home to talk about Russ having a loaded and cocked gun under his pillow. It just didn't sound like Russ, Al had said.

"I don't know where the information came from about the gun being cocked," Barbara told him.

"If he had a gun under his pillow, whether it was cocked or not, it was a stupid thing to do," Al said.


Doris and Henry Ford had just sat down to supper at the mobile home where they now lived near Colfax. Their son Ronnie had stopped by and agreed to stay for supper. They had just begun passing the dishes when Doris heard something that attracted her attention.

"Hush," she said. "Listen."

The six o'clock news was on the TV that was playing in the next room. The newscast was almost over, and the announcer was talking about the funeral that day for a popular high school coach in Durham who had been accidentally shot by his wife.

"My goodness," Doris Ford said, breaking the family's stunned silence. "She's killed Russ."

Before she knew what had happened, Ronnie left the table and grabbed the telephone. He got the number for the Durham County Sheriff's Department and began to dial.

# Chapter Nineteen

Rick Buchanan's phone was ringing when he arrived at work Thursday morning, the day after Russ's funeral. Ronnie Ford was calling. He had left messages the night before, but he didn't intend to wait for somebody to call him back. He and his family had been trying for years to get justice for his brother. Now, they thought, somebody would have to listen.

And Buchanan did, interrupting only now and then with a clarifying question as Ronnie poured out everything he had found out in his own investigation of Larry's death, all of his and his family's suspicions about Barbara. Buchanan had been a law enforcement officer too long to be surprised at anything he heard about human nature, but his twenty-minute conversation with Ronnie made him realize that in Barbara he might be dealing with a person unlike any other he ever had encountered.

After hearing the general outline of the circumstances surrounding Larry's death, Buchanan arranged to meet with the Ford family the next week to get more specific details. Then he called Larry Allen, the deputy who had investigated the shooting nearly ten years earlier. Allen, as Buchanan knew from his conversation with Ronnie, was now the police chief in Archdale, where Barbara once had worked for Kay-Lou Realty.

Allen said that he had only bare remembrances of the shooting. It was an accident, he recalled. He could check his files to see if he had kept anything about the case that might jog his memory or be helpful to Buchanan.

Did he know what had happened to the gun that killed Larry? Buchanan asked, wondering if the same gun had killed Russ.

He had turned it in to the sheriff's department, Allen said, and as far as he knew, it was still there.

After talking with Allen, Buchanan dispatched another detective to Barbara's parents' house to pick up the laundered sheets from Russ's and Barbara's bed. He took the pistol that had been the instrument of Russ's death to the sheriff's department's firearms expert and range officer and asked him to test it to see if jostling it could cause it to fire and to determine in which direction it ejected empty shells and at what distance. The empty shell lying so close to the weapon had seemed unnatural and inconsistent with Barbara's version of the shooting.


Buchanan had a long meeting later that morning with Cindy and Russ's cousin from Florida, Jane Wood. He was still trying to learn as much as he could about Russ's and Barbara's pasts, and Cindy had become his willing assistant in searching family memories for information that might prove helpful. If this was murder, as he now thought, Buchanan knew that he would have to establish motive to be able to convince a jury that a woman who to all outward appearances was a loving wife and mother, an active churchwoman, had coldly put a pistol to her husband's head and pulled the trigger. To find that motive, he would have to dig into every dark corner of her past, know everything that he could about her. From what he had learned so far, the motive could be any number of things.

That afternoon, Buchanan learned about the embezzlement. A woman who had worked with Barbara at Security Federal Savings and Loan nearly ten years earlier called to tell him that it had been common knowledge among the tellers that she had been stealing while she worked there, although she had never been charged. The woman also told Buchanan about another employee at Security Federal. This woman had worked with Barbara at another company, Brame Specialty. Buchanan should talk with her, she said. She could tell him something interesting.

Buchanan assigned another detective, Valerie McCabe, to work with him on the Stager case. At twenty-nine, she had been with the sheriff's department for four years but had been a detective for less than a year. Assigned to rapes, robberies and assaults, she never had been involved in a murder case. She went with Buchanan later that afternoon to a Security Federal branch to find the woman who had worked with Barbara at Brame. Everybody at Brame knew that Barbara was having an affair with one of the salesmen while she worked there, the woman said. The affair had gone on for a long time, and the salesman had sent Barbara roses when she finally broke it off. Since Russ Stager's death, she said, everybody who had worked at Brame at the time was talking about the affair and wondering if it had anything to do with the shooting. The woman couldn't remember the name of the salesman, but anybody at Brame could tell him, she said.

Soon after Buchanan returned to his office, he got a call from the woman he had just interviewed. She had found out the name of the salesman, but Preston Adams wasn't at Brame any longer. She gave him the name of another former Brame employee who might know Adams's whereabouts.

Buchanan called a company official at Brame who told him that while he had no personal knowledge of Barbara's affair, he certainly had heard about it. Everybody at his company was talking about it. He didn't think that the affair had been recently revived, though, because he had heard that Barbara was now having another affair, this one with a doctor at Duke University Medical Center.

Did he know a name?

He didn't, but he might be able to get one, he said.

Had Barbara killed Russ to get him out of the way and make room for somebody else?

It was not an uncommon motive for murder, Buchanan knew.


As the detective was pressing forward with his investigation, Barbara was busy at home. That morning she had called Chris Wagner, one of Russ's favorite players on the baseball team. Wagner had been very close to Russ, had visited at his house many times, and he had been devastated by Russ's death. When an assistant principal had pulled him aside to tell him about it on the afternoon of February 1, he had run from the room, down the hall and out of the school, running as hard as he could, not knowing why he was running or where he was going. The assistant principal, also a close friend of Russ's, had chased him down, grabbed him and held him close while Wagner cried and screamed out in distress. That night, he and two other players had gone to see Barbara at her parents' house and offered to help in any way that they could. When Barbara called Thursday morning, she asked if he and his friends could come that day and help her get Russ's clothes out of the house. As with Larry Ford, Russell Stager was being tidily removed from her life.

Wagner, Steve Bumgardner and Derrick Dickerson went to the house with a pickup truck. Barbara already had all of Russ's clothing packed into boxes. Some were in the garage, some still in the bedroom. Older clothing that Russ had outgrown because of his bodybuilding was packed away in the attic.

Barbara told them that Russ's baseball jackets should go to the baseball team. She kept a few of his warmup suits. The rest was carted away to the Goodwill store on Avondale Drive. It was a lot of clothing, Wagner later would tell the police. He and his friends filled the truck and two cars. Barbara had not asked for a receipt to deduct the donation from her taxes, he said.


Buchanan had much to report when he went to the district attorney's office that day to meet with Ron Stephens and Eric Evenson.

One thing seemed obvious after Buchanan had told all that he'd learned in the past two days. This shooting clearly appeared to have been murder, not an accident. If it had happened as Barbara had said, the bullet's trajectory would have been upward, not downward, as the autopsy had shown it to be.

The problem was that the officers had talked to Barbara in general terms about this, and nobody had taken a definite statement from her. They needed to get such a statement to have solid evidence, nail her down on details. If they could just get her to reenact exactly what had happened, maybe even get it on videotape, they would have something they could use in court.


Barbara's friend from Randolph County, Brenda Monroe, had not seen Barbara in some time. They had kept in touch over the years, had spent summer weekends together at the beach, visited each other now and then, exchanged cards on special occasions, and written infrequent letters, but the contact had lessened in recent years as their children, their primary bond, had grown apart.

When Brenda read about Russ's death in a small item in the newspaper, she was shocked. She worked now for her former minister, Barnie Pierce, who had been the Fords' minister. When she told him about this second husband lost to a gunshot, he remarked that it sounded strange. Brenda did not think it her place to question, but she thought that she should reach out to her friend.

Uncertain what exactly to do, she decided to call Barbara's mother, Marva, who told her that Barbara had been having a rough time and it might do her good to hear from her. Brenda called, and Barbara seemed pleased that she had.

When Brenda told her how sorry she was about Russ, Barbara responded, "It's just not fair. I can't take any more of accidentally losing husbands."

"Do you want me to come?" Brenda asked.

She would love to see her, Barbara said.

Brenda went the next day, Friday morning, two days after the funeral. Everybody was happy to see her, and Bryan and Jason introduced her to friends as their second mom.

Barbara and Brenda didn't get a chance to talk until after lunch. They sat at the table in the dining room, with its big windows that looked out onto the driveway and the wooded yard, and Barbara began talking about Russ's death and the sheriff's department's investigation.

Because of the similarities to Larry's death, Brenda mentioned, the officers probably would want to know whether she and Russ had had marital troubles.

"That won't be any problem," Barbara said.

Not long after she said that, two official-looking cars turned into the driveway and came to a stop near the windows where Brenda and Barbara sat. Brenda looked out and saw four men in suits walking single-file toward the back door. Cops. And clearly Barbara had not been expecting them.

"Well," Brenda said, "here comes the posse now."

\* \* \*

Buchanan never dreamed that Barbara would agree to reenact the shooting for him. He figured that she would beg off, saying that it would be too much of an emotional strain.

"I can't imagine somebody crawling back up in this same bed where her spouse was just shot and killed by her own hand and going through it all again," he said later. "I can't imagine it."

Still, he figured, there was no harm in trying.

He didn't want to warn her, to allow her time to think about it or to rehearse. He would just show up and spring it on her. If she agreed, he would ask her to allow it to be videotaped. If she shied from that, he would suggest still photography. If all else failed, he would settle for a close verbal description.

That morning he had lined up two crime-scene identification officers, Dave Frye and Lieutenant Bobby Ray, to handle technical matters. They assembled the cameras, tape, film and lights. Detective Tim Carroll agreed to go along to portray Russ, if they were lucky enough to get Barbara's consent.

Buchanan was friendly when Barbara answered the door, apologetic about having to bother her again.

"If you feel up to it," he said, "we'd like to reenact what happened so we can get it clear in our minds. So we can dispose of the case."

He was as surprised as he was pleased when she readily agreed, although he never would let himself show any emotion. He was even more surprised and pleased when she said that videotaping would be fine.

Brenda Monroe remained in the dining room as the officers and Barbara crowded into the bedroom. Barbara's brother Alton arrived and Brenda told him what was going on.

"You'd better go back there," she told him.

Alton went back to watch as Tim Carroll took Russ's position on the bed, lying on his left side, his holstered pistol protruding from his right hip. Barbara, who was wearing a dressy blouse with a long patterned skirt and boots, lay on her stomach beside him. Dave Frye, holding the video camera on his shoulder, started the tape as Barbara began to talk.

"I remember stretching out," she said, reaching out her arm. "That's the way I stretch. And when I stuck my hand under there"—she slid her right hand beneath the pillow under Carroll's head—"I felt something."

"Okay," Buchanan said.

"I stayed asleep," she went on. "Okay. I started pulling it out, and I pulled it out, and when I picked it up, and I don't know—"

She had removed her hand from beneath the pillow and was pointing it, forefinger out, like a pistol, at the back of Carroll's head.

"And I don't know how it was in my hand. I had no idea if I touched—I don't know. I heard the awful noise."

Barbara lifted her head and chest, arching her back, then quickly dropped back to the pillow.

"Well, wait a minute, that wasn't quite right."

She moved her hand a little deeper under the pillow.

"Okay," she said, "and then I started getting up . . ."

Again she removed her hand and pointed it, pistol-like, at the back of Carroll's head.

"That's how it was. I started getting up with it in my hand."

"Okay," Buchanan said.

She stopped again.

"Wait. I don't think this is going—he's not quite in the right position."

She repositioned Carroll, pushing his lower body away from her, tugging his shoulder toward her, bringing his head closer.

"Maybe more like that."

She tugged at the edge of the pillow under Carroll's head.

"This cover was all over the bottom," she said, indicating that the pillow was partially covered. She pulled out her hand and pointed it again at Carroll's head. "Maybe like that."

"I have it if it will help you," Buchanan said, offering the .25-caliber semiautomatic pistol that had fired the bullet that killed Russ.

"No!" she said sharply, shaking her head. "Please."

"Okay, okay," Buchanan said quickly. "All right. No problem."

" 'Cause I don't even know how it was in my hand. That part doesn't even, it doesn't even register. I don't know."

"Okay."

She sat up, looking at Buchanan.

"I didn't even—I don't know how, what position it was in under there. I just realized what it was, started to get up to get it out from under there, heard the noise. Shocked! Couldn't figure out what it was, sort of realized what had happened."

She spun around, reaching for the bedside table.

"Turned over, I got my glasses. 'Cause I'm blind. I get my glasses. I get up. I turned the light on over there. I came back in here, and I saw the pillow, and I got over him like this . . ."

She rolled back over, hovering over Carroll on her knees.

" 'Russ, Russ, Russ!' You know. Might even have turned him over."

She rolled Carroll toward her, looking at his face.

"Something like that, then turned him back over like this."

She pushed him back.

"His hand was all balled up in the stuff and I might have pulled that out," she said, speaking of the covers. "I don't know. I was just all over him and the pillow."

She sat back up.

"Oh, and when I turned the light on, told Jason, 'Call 911!' before I got back in here on him. Jason called 911, and they were here real quick."

She sat up on the bed, still on her knees, facing Buchanan.

"I don't know if that's close enough, or if that answers your questions, but that's about the best I can do."

"That's fine," Buchanan said.

The reenactment had taken exactly two minutes and thirty-eight seconds, and Buchanan was certain that he had gotten exactly what he came for. He wasn't going to tell her that, though.

That was why he had remained cool earlier, while the officers had been getting their equipment ready, and Barbara had told him in an offhand way that her first husband also had died in a gun accident. She hadn't mentioned it earlier, she said, because she didn't think it was important.

Buchanan tried to make her think that he didn't already know about Larry Ford's death and was unconcerned about it.

"I'm not looking at anything involving your first husband," he said. "I'm just trying to straighten out the one we've got right now."

As he was leaving, Barbara asked the status of the case.

Buchanan felt no need to be forthright with her. "As far as I'm concerned," he said, "it's closed."

"Closed as accidental?"

Russ and Barbara Stager's marriage was undergoing great stress when this family portrait was taken in 1984. Russ had adopted Barbara's sons, Bryan, who was 16 at the time, and Jason, who was 10, and he held the marriage together because of them. *(Olan Mills Studio)*

The house on Fox Drive was Barbara Stager's dream, but Russ Stager had second thoughts when the time came to close the deal. *(Jerry Bledsoe)*

As a high school senior, Barbara was looking forward to going to college and becoming a teacher. *(courtesy: Northern High School annual)*

Barbara dropped out of college at the end of her freshman year after becoming pregnant with her first child. She and Larry took snapshots of each other holding Bryan soon after his birth.

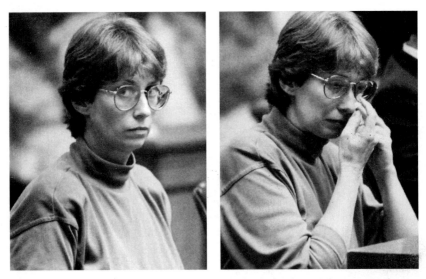

Barbara had taken on a far more matronly look for her trial in 1988, during whch she frequently broke into tears. *(John Page, Greensboro News & Record)*

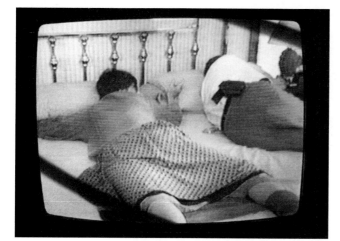

Sargeant Rick Buchanan could not believe his good fortune when Barbara agreed to reenact Russ's shooting on video-tape. The tape proved to be vital evidence in her trial. *(Joseph Rodriguez, Greensboro News & Record)*

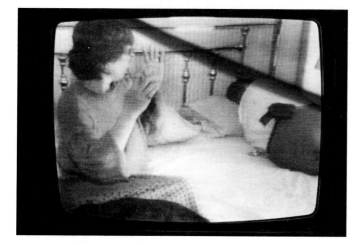

The check at the top caught the attention of Russ's former wife, Jo Lynn, and proved to be the clue that provided the motive for Russ's murder. Russ wrote the check at bottom as his weekly tithe to his church on the day before his death. The other two checks were written by Barbara to clear his accounts upon his death. *(Joseph Rodriguez, Greensboro NEWS & RECORD)*

Barbara got a friend to help her buy the .25 caliber pistol at left. He showed her how to fire it just hours before Larry was killed. Russ bought the other .25 for Barbara's protection. He had shown her how to use it only a few months before he died. *(Joseph Rodriguez, Greensboro NEWS & RECORD)*

Russ's father, Al, was concerned about Russ and Barbara's continued lavish spending, and repeatedly admonished his son about it. *(courtesy: Doris Stager)*

Larry held his troubled marriage together because of his sons. This portrait was taken shortly before his death in 1978. *(courtesy: Doris and Henry Ford)*

Larry's parents, Doris and Henry Ford, were convinced that their son had been murdered, but they couldn't get law enforcement officers to do anything about it until Russ Stager was killed. *(Vicki Buckner, Greensboro NEWS & RECORD)*

Barbara's parents, Jim and Marva Terry. Marva expected much from her daughter, and Barbara always turned to her in times of trouble. *(John Page, Greensboro NEWS & RECORD)*

Jo Lynn Snow, Russ's first wife, was certain that Russ's death was no accident because she knew something that nobody else knew: Russ feared for his life. *(Joseph Rodriguez, Greensboro NEWS & RECORD)*

Russ had dreamed of coaching at his alma mater, Durham High School, and he put all of his enthusiasm into the job. *(Joseph Rodriguez, Greensboro NEWS & RECORD)*

Russ had a boyish and magnetic personality that endeared him to almost everybody who knew him. *(courtesy: Doris Stager)*

Russ's players were devoted to him, because he involved himself in their lives. Durham High's annual paid tribute to him after his death. *(Joseph Rodriguez, Greensboro NEWS & RECORD)*

Judge J. B. Allen presided over
Barbara's trial with a firm hand,
and was never reluctant to set
new legal precedents.
(*John Page, Greensboro NEWS &
RECORD*)

District Attorney Ron
Stephens (*left*) wanted
A.D.A. Eric Evenson
(*right*) to take this case,
and it became the biggest
of Evenson's career.
(*John Page, Greensboro
NEWS & RECORD*)

Barbara's lawyer, William Cotter,
did not share Barbara's optimism
about the outcome of her trial.
(*John Page, Greensboro NEWS &
RECORD*)

After realizing that Russ's death was no accident, Sargeant Rick Buchanan faced the most difficult investigation of his career. He knew who killed Russ; his challenge was to find out why. *(Joseph Rodriguez, Greensboro NEWS & RECORD)*

Henry Ford was certain that his son's death was no accident. He knew that Larry would not have been carelessly handling a gun in bed because Larry had been trained in firearms safety. *(John Page, Greensboro NEWS & RECORD)*

Randolph County Sheriff Robert Mason was not in office when Larry Ford was killed, but he closed the case by ruling Larry's death an accident, allowing Barbara to collect additional insurance money. *(Jerry Wolford, Greensboro NEWS & RECORD)*

Russ's friend Harry Welch felt obligated to tell Russ that Barbara's big book deal was a hoax. It was one of the hardest things he'd ever had to do. *(Joseph Rodriguez, Greensboro NEWS & RECORD)*

"As far as I'm concerned."

Barbara asked if she could get a copy of his report.

Sorry, he told her, but that wasn't allowed.

"How will the insurance company know it was accidental?" she asked.

"You don't have to worry about that," Buchanan said. "I'm sure the insurance company will contact me."

Buchanan was exultant as he left Barbara's house. He thought that she might have just convicted herself of murder. He couldn't wait to get back to the office and make certain that the tape had what he thought was on it. He called Eric Evenson as soon as he got into his office to let him know that Barbara had gone for it, videotape and all. He was getting ready to watch the tape right now.

Evenson dropped what he was doing, went to tell his boss what had happened, and the two hurried to the detective bureau. Buchanan was already watching the tape when they got there. Nobody said anything as Barbara went through her act on the bed.

"Play it again," Stephens said when she had finished, and Buchanan rewound the tape and pressed the play button.

Once more the group watched closely, saying nothing.

Evenson broke the silence.

"Cold," he said.

None of them could believe that Barbara had reenacted it. How, only four days after a fatal shooting, could she climb back into the bed where her husband had died by her own hand, accidentally or not, and relive it so unemotionally? The simple fact that she climbed onto the bed was damning. But her replay of the events spoke volumes.

Barbara's uncertainty about where her hand had been and how she had been holding the gun were telling factors. Despite what he had earlier told a reporter, Buchanan knew that the pistol that had killed Russ did not have a "light trigger." The sheriff's department's weapons expert had put blanks in the pistol and beat it around trying to get it to fire accidentally and it wouldn't do it. It would fire only when deliberate pressure was put on the trigger. And a finger had to be inside the trigger guard to do that.

Not even a sleepy person would be likely to do that without realizing what was happening.

But one other fact was even more telling. In every position in which Barbara had held her hand, the pistol had been aimed so that the bullet would have passed upward through Russ's head. It was impossible for him to have suffered the wound he had from the description Barbara had given of the shooting.

Stephens and Evenson agreed that this was powerful evidence. But alone it was hardly enough. They all knew that even more incriminating evidence might await them in Randolph County.

# Chapter Twenty

On Tuesday morning, February 9, eight days after Russ's death, Eric Evenson joined Rick Buchanan and Detective Valerie McCabe for the sixty-five-mile drive to Randolph County. They went first to the county sheriff's department in Asheboro, where they met with Captain Richard Hughes and Lieutenant Tommy Julian, who pledged full cooperation with any investigation into the death of Larry Ford.

The meeting was a courtesy call, a mere formality. Neither Evenson nor Buchanan had any intention of asking for help from Randolph County officers in their investigation. Randolph County had had its chance, as far as Evenson and Buchanan were concerned, and they had blown it.

Evenson, Stephens and Buchanan knew that they would be investigating not one killing but two. One of those investigations would be centered in Randolph County. The distances and the manpower required for the second investigation would tax the resources of Durham County's detective division. The three already had agreed that they would have to call upon the greater resources of the State Bureau of Investigation, particularly for looking into Larry Ford's death.

While they were in Asheboro, Evenson and the two detectives also made a courtesy call on District Attorney Garland Yates. He had been elected after Larry Ford's death and unlike Sheriff Robert Mason, who was still in office, he was untainted by the botched investigation of the case. Stephens already had talked with Yates about the possibilities of using evidence from the Randolph County case in any trial that might result from Russ's

death. Stephens had wanted to make sure that there was cooperation and coordination between the two district attorney's offices
and that rancor and recrimination did not develop.

Before leaving Asheboro, Evenson and the two detectives had
gotten copies of the paltry records from the Larry Ford case, plus
other legal documents from the courthouse: Larry and Barbara's
separation agreement, the permit for the gun that Barbara had
bought. They did not leave town with the gun itself. Nobody at
the sheriff's department had any idea what had become of it.

The next stop was the Archdale Police Department, where
Chief Larry Allen greeted them cordially but warily, ushering
them into his meticulously neat office. He had found the report
he had written about Larry's death, along with the Polaroid snapshots he had made at the scene. He was happy to make these
available.

Buchanan, however, was not impressed. In the report he later
would write about this meeting, he noted of Allen: "He was evasive and kept stating that after his initial response he had no further contact with the case. He also kept reminding us he was
only there for two hours. The only thing he could really recall
was that there was no cleaning equipment present in the bedroom. He appeared to be a well-organized person for one who
conducted such a sloppy initial investigation. Most of the time
during the interview he remained defensive."

At five-thirty, with darkness settling, the three Durham County
officials pulled into the driveway at the mobile home of Doris
and Henry Ford in the rolling, open countryside near Colfax,
where they had moved after Larry's death. Both Doris and Henry
were now retired. Both had finished their longtime goal of hiking
the entire distance of the Appalachian Trail, a trek they knew that
Larry would have enjoyed making with them. Their other children all were married and gone, but they all still got together for
special occasions, and when they did the small mobile home
overflowed with happiness and the joyous voices of grandchildren. Always, though, there was an empty spot that Larry and his
children should have filled.

Despite their conviction that Barbara had killed their son,
they had been determined to keep the lines of communication
open with her. They continued to send gifts for birthdays and
Christmas and cards for other occasions. Doris had continued

writing long letters, and sporadically Barbara had responded. Once Bryan had replied, and Doris had written "very special to us" on the envelope and tucked it away with other family treasures. The Fords had tried to arrange visits with the boys and although Barbara had agreed to meetings on several occasions, she always had backed out at the last minute, offering excuses. Now nearly ten years had passed since they had seen their grandchildren, and they despaired that they might never see them again. They had not even heard from Barbara in a year and a half.

The arrival of Evenson, Buchanan and McCabe gave Doris and Henry an opportunity they thought they would never have: a chance to tell their suspicions about their son's death to law enforcement officers who seemed to want to do something about it. For more than two hours, the three listened as Doris and Henry told their story. Doris brought out family photos and the letters that Barbara and Bryan had written.

Evenson and Buchanan told them what they could about Russ's death and their investigation into it. They assured them that the SBI would conduct as thorough an investigation into Larry's death as possible ten years after the fact.

The Fords could hardly believe what they were hearing. At least three times they had requested that the SBI be called into their son's case. Now, through the graces of another county, and at the cost of another family's son, it finally was going to happen.

After the three law enforcement officials had left, a peace settled over Doris and Henry that they had not known in a decade. They knew that God was answering their prayers, and they were certain that soon they would have answers to all the questions that had been torturing them for so long.

Evenson was impressed by the Fords. They were warm, decent and forbearing people, he thought. They had been betrayed once by the law, and he was determined to see that it would not happen again.


On the way back to Durham that night, Buchanan thought about three calls he had received before the group left for Randolph County that morning.

The first had come from a contact Buchanan had developed at the County Health Department, a neighbor of Russ and Barbara's. She said that the funeral home had requested a dozen copies of Russ's death certificate. That usually was an indication of a lot of insurance policies.

But only twenty minutes later, another contact, this one in the clerk of court's office, had called to report that Barbara had filed for probate on Russ's estate.

She had come to the courthouse Friday afternoon, just four days after Russ's death, less than an hour after she had reenacted the shooting for Buchanan. While he had been watching the videotape in the detective division, Barbara, her mother and her brother Alton had been just upstairs submitting Russ's will, naming herself executor of the estate. On the preliminary inventory, Barbara had listed only $98,000 in life insurance. Was she trying to hide the true amount? If not, it seemed a paltry payment for murder.

If greed for insurance money was not behind Russ's death, might the motive lie in the third call Buchanan had received that morning?

An informant who wished to remain anonymous had called to say that Russ had been having an affair with a black woman, a teacher at the junior high school, where he once had been director of athletics. Barbara, the caller said, supposedly had found out about it.

Jealousy, Buchanan knew, was often reason enough for a homicide, but most of those killings came in heated moments. Rarely were they coldly calculated and executed, as the murder of Russ now appeared to be.

As he considered the possibilities, Buchanan figured he could count on one thing at least. He likely would endure many long and frustrating hours and a lot of hard work before he knew why Russ Stager had died.

# Chapter Twenty-one

In the seemingly interminable days following Russ's funeral, Doris remained in a grief-benumbed daze, a depression so deep and dark that she thought she might never emerge from it. She later would recall that she nearly lost her sanity. She didn't want to see anybody, talk to anybody, go anywhere, do anything. "I could feel myself going down, down, down," she said.

Her energy wouldn't allow her to sit still, however, and so she walked, a tiny, solitary figure stalking back and forth on the road in front of her house, bearing a burden greater than she could carry. At times she walked on past the point where the pavement ended and the houses stopped, following the dirt road downhill to a wooden bridge that crossed a creek deep in the woods, and there she yelled out her anger at God.

Why had He betrayed her? Why had He let Barbara kill her only son?

"Fortunately, God was patient with me and didn't take offense," she said later.

When she reached the point where she could bear no more, she yielded to her faith.

"I said, 'All right, God, take over. I can't handle it by myself.' "

He allowed her to understand, she later said, that He had let His only son be killed so that anyone who accepted Him could spend eternity in Heaven. He had given people free will to accept Christ, to choose right or wrong. Barbara had used her free will to murder Russ, Doris had become convinced, and she knew that Barbara would have to face judgment before God for that, but she also became determined to see that Barbara faced justice on earth as well.

Rick Buchanan did not want Barbara to know that she was being investigated, and he had advised the Stagers to keep quiet about it. He also wanted them to keep lines of communication open with Barbara so that he could know what she was doing and thinking. Doris began taking notes on every conversation and meeting that she had with Barbara so that she could be as accurate as possible in what she told Buchanan.

She first reported to him that Barbara had called her two days after the funeral, the same day that Barbara had reenacted the shooting. Barbara said that she had been to the Veterans' Administration and needed to know if Russ had been in the regular army.

"I don't think he was," Doris told her.

Barbara said she had been told at the VA that she could not draw any military benefits unless Russ had been in the regular army.

"Let me check with Al," Doris said, turning to her husband to ask him. "No, Al says he was only in the reserves and the National Guard. He has never been in the regular army."

On Monday, a week after Russ's death, Doris called Barbara to tell her that she and Al wanted Russ's Campbell College ring and the train set he'd had since he was a little boy.

During the conversation Barbara mentioned that she was remaining in her job at Duke. A woman she liked, Mrs. Watkins, would be replacing her boss, Tim, who was resigning, and she had begged her to stay.

Barbara also told Doris that she had an appointment to see a psychiatrist to help her over the trauma of Russ's death. She was sure, she said, that Doris would be glad to know that the psychiatrist was a Christian.

Doris said that she and Al would come the following night to pick up the train set and ring.

"I've got plenty of food," Barbara said. "Would y'all like to have supper with us?"

"No, thank you," Doris had said. "I'm not eating very much."

"Well, I understand if you're not comfortable."

Doris and Al drove to their son's house the following evening. Russ's Blazer was there, along with another car they didn't recognize when they pulled up the driveway, but Barbara's Mustang convertible was missing. As Doris and Al were getting out of their car, Barbara turned into the driveway behind them. She got out of her car carrying a sackful of fast-food hamburgers. It was hard for Doris to face Barbara, knowing in her heart that she had killed Russ, but she forced herself to control her rage and hide her true feelings.

The train set had been put in the garage for them, Barbara said before taking the hamburgers on inside. Doris and Al went to the garage and began loading the train set into the car. Barbara soon returned with Russ's college ring and the Masonic ring that Russ's grandmother had given him.

Barbara went back into the house, and shortly afterward Doris followed. She wanted to get Barbara alone to ask more about the psychiatrist she had mentioned so that she could pass the information to Buchanan. She found Jason sitting at the dining room table, wolfing down hamburgers with his best friend, Josh Burch. Barbara was in the living room chatting with three members of Russ's baseball team, the same three who had been at Barbara's parents' house when Doris and her family arrived on the night of the shooting to plan the funeral.

"Could I see you for a minute?" Doris asked.

Barbara left the baseball players and followed Doris to Jason's bedroom with a concerned and quizzical look upon her face, as Doris later recalled.

"Are you going to finish your education?" Doris asked.

"Yes, but I'm not going to be able to do it right now," Barbara said. "Maybe a little later on."

Was the psychiatrist Barbara had mentioned the same one Marva had offered to pay for after the financial crisis nearly six years ago?

No, Barbara told her. That was just a counselor that she had been seeing. This one was a "real psychiatrist" at Duke, Dr. Wallace. Her mother had made the arrangements and her first appointment would be on Thursday, two days hence.

Barbara seemed edgy, uncomfortable with this conversation, and when she heard Al coming into the kitchen, it gave her the excuse to break away. She returned to the living room with the baseball players. Doris followed her and said that she guessed she and Al would be going, but Barbara was busy talking and didn't respond.

"We've got to go," Doris said, trying again to get Barbara's attention, but she continued talking.

Only when she saw Doris and Al leaving did Barbara come to see them out.

She and Russ had a small television in their bedroom at the Stagers' lake cottage, Barbara said as they walked to their car. Would they mind bringing it back the next time they went to the lake? Her brother Steve was going to be staying with her to see her through this difficult period, and he could use it in his room. Al said he would get it for her.

Then Barbara mentioned, almost as an afterthought, that she'd given Russ's clothing away. "I didn't think Dad could wear them," she said, meaning Al, "so I gave them to two churches."

The Stagers went to their lake cabin on Saturday morning, February 13, to get the TV Barbara wanted. They didn't linger. Doris couldn't stand to walk into the bedroom that Russ and Barbara always used. All she could think about were the wonderful times Russ had always had at the cabin and how he never would again. She and Al returned home, and Doris stayed there while Al took the TV to Barbara and hooked it up in Bryan's bedroom, where Steve now was staying.

Doris was cleaning house that afternoon when Barbara called and said that she wanted to have a talk.

No, Doris told her, she was too upset.

"With me?" Barbara asked.

No, Doris said, only because of Russ. "If it was Bryan, you'd feel the very same way," she added.

"I'll call you tomorrow," Barbara said.

"No. My stomach is real upset."

"Do you have a virus?'

"No, it's my nerves. My stomach is bothering me day and night, and I'm having a lot of headaches."

"Well, when you feel like it," Barbara said, "call me."

That night Barbara's mother called, wanting to know how Doris and Al were doing.

On Monday, two days later, Doris worked up her nerve and called Barbara at a little after 7:00 P.M.

"Dad has gone to a deacon's meeting at church, so if you still want to talk, this would be a good time to come over," she said.

She had no idea what Barbara wanted to talk about and she didn't want Al to be there and run the risk of getting him more upset and agitating his heart condition. She mustered all her will-power to control herself as she waited for Barbara, who arrived only minutes later.

"When I called Saturday, I knew exactly what I was going to say," Barbara said after seating herself on the couch in the family room, the same place where she had sat on the last night of Russ's life, "but I don't know how to say it now."

She had been to see the psychiatrist, as scheduled, Thursday, she said, and had told him about her distress over Russ's death.

"He said my feelings were normal and to talk it out," she said.

She wanted Doris to know that she loved Russ and that living with him for nine years had been the best years of her life.

"I want you to know that it was an accident," she said, "and I want y'all to forgive me."

"Talk to God, Barbara," Doris said coolly. "He forgives."

"I do talk to Him," Barbara said. "And I go to the cemetery all the time and talk to Russ."

"Well, it won't do you any good to go out there and talk to him," Doris said.

"Well, I do."

"Barbara, Russell is in heaven, and the Bible says when you're in heaven with Christ, you don't have any more pain, and you don't have any more sorrow, and you don't have any more tears. And if my son could see me now he would have a lot of tears and he would have a lot of sorrow, so he can't hear you."

"Well, it makes me feel better to go anyway."

Barbara said she knew how much Doris and Al loved Bryan and Jason, and she wanted all of them to continue going to the lake as a family.

"It's going to take me time, Barbara. I can't stand to go there and go in Russell's bedroom. It's going to take me time. I've always put everybody else first, but this time I'm going to have to think about me."

"Would you feel more comfortable if we moved into another house?" Barbara asked. "I've been thinking about getting a condo. I can't keep up the yard at that house. But Jason wants to stay there."

That would be for her to decide, Doris said.

"I don't know if I can stand to lose y'all," Barbara said suddenly.

"Barbara, I didn't say you were going to lose us. I just said it's going to take time."

"Well, I don't know what I'm going to tell the boys why y'all aren't coming around."

"Your mother will help you."

Her parents were helping some with the bills, Barbara said.

"Well, it's good that they can help a little," Doris said.

Because Russ had been handling the money, Barbara said, she had no idea what was facing her in that regard, and the prospect of dealing with it all was almost overwhelming. They didn't have any mortgage insurance on their house, she said, and the monthly house payments would take her whole paycheck. But she thought that the life insurance Russ had with the school system and National Guard would knock down the mortgage to the point where she could handle it. "But I guess I'm going to have to sell the convertible, because it's got the biggest payment," she said.

Barbara noted that Jason had been particularly hurt by Russ's death. "He loved him so much."

"We all loved him," Doris said.

"I thought the kids at school might say cruel things to him," Barbara went on. "But everybody is being real nice."

Before she ended the conversation, Barbara offered one other observation.

"You know, this all brings back my experience with Larry."

# Chapter Twenty-two

On February 15, Barbara called Buchanan to ask why Russ's death certificate listed the cause as "pending." Hadn't he told her that the case had been closed as accidental?

Buchanan was immediately wary. Death certificates always listed the cause as pending until the autopsy was complete, he said.

"The death certificate says the autopsy *is* complete," Barbara countered.

"The autopsy is, but the final report isn't," Buchanan said.

Could she file for insurance with the death certificate as it was?

"I don't know whether the insurance company would accept it that way or not," Buchanan said. "It might be best to wait a couple of weeks until all the paperwork has been submitted."

Later, Barbara would tell her friend Brenda Monroe that this was the first indication she had that something wasn't right, that Buchanan hadn't been telling her the truth when he said he was closing the case as accidental. It was beginning to appear that once again she was going to have to endure the harassment from law enforcement officers that she had suffered after Larry's death.

The "harassment" had in fact been stepped up. Several more officers were now working on the case. Three agents of the State Bureau of Investigation joined it that very day. Two of the agents, Dave McDougald and Valerie Matthews, were still in training, Matthews just out of the academy. The third was the resident SBI agent in Durham, Steve Myers.

As it turned out, Myers was a perfect choice to investigate the

death of Larry Ford, which would be his major responsibility. He
had grown up in High Point, the son of a police officer, and
knew the area well. An SBI agent for six years, Myers, sandy-
haired and freckled, was twenty-nine, the same age Larry had
been when he was killed.

By the end of February Buchanan and the other officers were
well on course in building a case against Barbara. They had interviewed all of the emergency workers who had gone to Barbara's
house, and had begun talking to her former employers and to
friends from her past.

Bill and Carol Gordon, who had dropped Barbara from their
list of friends after her book hoax, became emotional during their
interview with detectives. When Carol's mother, Virginia, came to
tell her that Russ had been shot, Carol had blurted out, "Barbara
did it, didn't she?"

"Yes," her mother had said, "but she said it was accidental."

Carol could think only of getting to Bill to tell him, but before
she could leave for his dental office, she learned that Russ had
died.

When she got to his office, she had one of her husband's staff
members call him into his lab. He came in carrying a can of
Coke.

"What's wrong?" he asked as soon as he saw Carol's grief-
stricken face.

"Russ is dead," she said.

Bill suddenly flung the Coke can against the wall and it exploded in a spray of foam.

Carol had never heard her husband use profanity.

"Dammit," he said, "she killed him, didn't she?"

"Yes," Carol said, and they fell into each other's arms crying.

They cried again as the detectives interviewed them. They
had seen Barbara's instability early on, and since Russ's death,
they had been torturing themselves with guilt, asking themselves
over and over if they could have done something to prevent it.
One statement they made impressed the detectives so much they
put it in their reports verbatim: "Barbara Stager would do anything for money."

When the detectives tracked down Preston Adams, he, like
the Gordons, said that the first thought that had gone through his
mind when a friend called to tell him about Russ's death was that

Barbara had murdered him. He also said he was certain that he had not been Barbara's only lover in recent years. "Barbara loved men," he said, "and she liked to have a lot of them."

Barbara had told him of working briefly for a major housing-development company. The company had a house that executives used as a party spot, he said, and he was sure from the way she talked about it that she had visited there with at least one of her bosses.

When Buchanan and Myers went to talk with one of the executives of the development company, the man was extremely nervous and evasive. He claimed that he didn't recall Barbara and had no record of employing her. "Both officers believe he was being less than truthful," Buchanan later wrote in his report.

All of Russ's National Guard associates and officers were questioned, and all agreed that Russ knew too much about weapons and was too cautious with them ever to sleep with a loaded gun under his pillow.

A Pen register, an electronic device that records the numbers called and received on a telephone line, had been connected to Barbara's line, and although it had not functioned at first, by late February it was providing the officers with the numbers of many people who would have to be called and questioned.

On February 24, Buchanan and Evenson began moving the focus of the investigation to Randolph County. They went first to Greensboro to discuss the case with the district supervisor of the SBI, picked up the reports on Kay Pugh's murder in High Point, then drove to Asheboro to tell Sheriff Robert Mason of their plans.

Russ's first wife, Jo Lynn, also had been collecting information for the case at Evenson's request.

"After I spoke with you, I called Russ's mom," she wrote to him in a long letter on February 28. "I had not spoken with her in over a week, and I wanted to clarify some things she had told me. She was very distraught having just read in the Durham paper that Sergeant Buchanan had been working on another case. I had not planned on telling her anyone had called me, but after learning how upset she was, I felt she needed the reassurance your telephone call had given me. I didn't tell her who had called me, but that someone investigating the case had called. She was very relieved.

"To clarify my memory, I did ask Mrs. Stager to tell me again why it was that the children did not see their paternal grandparents, the Fords. She said that Barbara said that even Larry couldn't get along with his parents. After Larry died, the grandparents would call to see the children and then wouldn't show up. She said once they were going to take the boys camping overnight and never showed up. She said they were not dependable, that they were 'oddballs,' and that the Fords didn't care anything about the children."

Jo Lynn went over a lot of matters that she had talked about with Doris, including what Barbara's sons thought of Russ's death and whether Barbara told anyone that she actually had murdered Russ:

"Regarding his sons, Mrs. Stager feels the older one has to be suspicious. She said she was hoping Bryan would call her but that he had not. At the same time, she felt Bryan would protect his mother. Russ was extremely close to both sons.

"Mrs. Stager feels strongly that Barbara would not have told anyone. She did not have any close friends that she is aware of and agreed with me that to tell a boyfriend would only scare him off. I suspect that Barbara does have 'someone else,' but it is my opinion she has convinced that person it was an accident just as she convinced Russ [at first] that her first husband's death was an accident."

If Barbara did have someone else, the detectives so far had not found him.


The three SBI agents working on the case spent most of March delving into Larry's death. Much of that time was devoted to trying to track down the truth about Kay Pugh's murder and the rumors of Barbara's lesbian relationship with her. In the end the investigators and prosecutors would determine that their time had been wasted. The rumors were false. No connection existed between the deaths of Kay Pugh and Larry. But they did learn many other things that led them to believe that Barbara had murdered Larry.

On March 2, Myers and McDougald interviewed Carlton Stanford, who had gone with Barbara to buy the gun with which Larry was killed. Stanford told them about buying the gun and his earlier afternoon with Barbara in a Charlotte motel. Barbara had told him that she and Larry did not have a good relationship and that Larry had hit her, he said, although he'd never seen any signs of her being hit. Stanford had heard the gossip of Barbara's supposed involvement in a lesbian ring, but he couldn't believe it. Barbara had mentioned relationships with other men, he said, but she had never given any indication of sexual interest in women.

"Tell me something," Stanford said as the agents were nearing the end of their interview, "why didn't anybody come and talk to me about all of this ten years ago?"

By mid-March, the investigators knew about most of Barbara's affairs while she was married to Larry. Myers and McDougald had learned of her affair with Butch Hazelwood from Barbara's former boss, Bob Gray. Hazelwood himself had been murdered ten years after his affair with Barbara, shot in the head with a .22 pistol in his office, and the case never had been solved. Randolph County authorities suspected that his death was related to drug dealing or heavy debts.

One person the agents wanted to talk with was John Buheller, the detective who had investigated Larry's death. Buheller had left law enforcement seven years earlier, they learned, and had moved to Alamance County, where he became a truck driver. When they went to his last known address on March 24, they discovered that they had missed him by six months. The woman living at the address had lived with Buheller for several years and had a four-year-old child by him. Buheller had bought a restaurant that went under, the woman said, and had left town owing a lot of people money. She had no idea where he was. His first wife had taken out child-support warrants for him, and so had she.

Buheller had left a lot of stuff behind from his days in law enforcement, she told the officers. It was stashed in the attic. When Myers asked if they could look through it, she consented, and there they found Buheller's notes and some of the records from his investigation of the Ford case.

The day after the agents found the records, Larry Allen, the Archdale police chief, called to say that the gun with which Larry had been shot had been found in a drawer at the sheriff's department.

Back in Durham, Buchanan continued to pursue leads. He interviewed several of Russ's friends and kept track of the telephone numbers of the calls Barbara was making and receiving. He got court orders and began compiling bank records for both Russ and Barbara. He spent hours poring through them. Russ's checking account showed that he had been making regular payments to Veteran's Life Insurance Company, and Buchanan discovered that Russ had taken out a $50,000 policy with the company just a year before his death, increasing the ante on the likelihood that he had been shot for insurance money.

On March 29, five days before Easter, Buchanan got a call from a Durham lawyer, John Wainio, who said that he was calling on Barbara's behalf to find out the status of the case.

It was just a matter of getting the paperwork done, Buchanan told him.

Wainio said that Barbara had heard that the SBI had been asking questions about her in Randolph County. Did Buchanan know anything about that?

Not a thing, Buchanan said.


Barbara's former friend Carol Gordon knew that Barbara was being investigated, but as weeks passed and nothing happened, she and her husband, Bill, and their friends Harry and Terri Welch began to wonder if Barbara ever would be brought to justice.

As Easter neared and warm weather arrived, Carol was driving to her home at Croasdaile Country Club when she saw Barbara driving past the golf course toward her. Barbara was in her Mustang convertible, the top down, her hair blowing—and she was smiling broadly. Russ was dead and buried, and Barbara was tooling around in the spring sunshine, having a good time. It was more than Carol could stand, and she had to pull to the roadside and sit for a few minutes to overcome her anger and grief.

Barbara was house hunting again, and at the beginning of April she found another house that she liked only a short distance from her own, close enough so that Jason would continue to be near his friends and attend the same school. She had taken Jason to look at the house and he liked it. She told the homeowners that she was interested, but she would have to sell her own house first. Her husband had died recently, she said, without mentioning how, and she wanted to get out of the house they had shared.

She also had gotten out of the bed they had shared. In mid-March, she had spent $827 for a new king-size bed to replace the one in which Russ had been shot.

Only a few days before Easter, Barbara's friend Brenda Monroe drove to Durham for a visit. They went to the mall to do some Easter shopping, Barbara talking about her life on the way. As they were pulling into the parking lot, Barbara remarked, "I'm never getting married again, I'm a jinx."

But before Brenda could respond, Barbara said that she really didn't want to spend the rest of her life alone.

"I want somebody," she said, "somebody like Russ. No, what I want *is* Russ."


Buchanan had spent a lot of time in March trying to find out where the pistol that had killed Russ had come from. He had asked the U.S. Bureau of Alcohol, Tobacco and Firearms to trace the gun, but the trail of paperwork had ended at a Florida gun shop. He had called many area gun dealers, but none had any recollection of Russ and Barbara.

Finally, Buchanan decided to ask Barbara about it. He called her at work on April 5, two days after Easter. She and Russ had bought the gun from a friend of Russ's, Garland Wolfe, two years earlier, she said.

While she had him on the phone, Barbara said, was there anything he could do to help hurry along the paperwork that was holding up the death certificate? She was in desperate financial straits because of her huge mortgage payments, she said, and she really needed a supplemental death certificate so that she could file for insurance.

Buchanan apologized. There still were a few loose ends to tie up, he said, but he was certain that the change on the death certificate would be made soon. He did not bother to mention that the cause of death on the certificate would be changed from "pending" to "homicide."

The following week, Buchanan and Myers went to Randolph County to pick up the pistol that had killed Larry. Three days later, they interviewed Russ's friend Garland Wolfe. Russ had told him a couple of years earlier that he wanted a small handgun so that he could teach Barbara to shoot, Wolfe said. Barbara was attending night classes and she needed it for protection. Wolfe told him about a .25-caliber semiautomatic that he had, and Russ had brought Barbara to look at it. Russ had paid him for it in cash.

Wolfe acknowledged that the gun had been unregistered.

Where did he get it? Buchanan wanted to know.

He had bought it three or four years earlier for his own protection, Wolfe said. A Durham County sheriff's deputy had sold it to him.

# Chapter Twenty-three

Ron Stephens and Eric Evenson met with the officers involved in the Stager case on Friday morning, April 15, and took a careful accounting of all the evidence that had been gathered. All agreed that it was enough to ask a grand jury to indict Barbara for first-degree murder in Russ's death.

First, though, the group decided, one final attempt should be made to question Barbara and stake out her positions. After she was arrested, they would not have another chance. Before the case was taken to the grand jury, Barbara's sons also should be interviewed, and search warrants should be sought for her house and cars.

Buchanan and Myers drove to Barbara's house at five-thirty that afternoon and presented themselves unannounced. She didn't seem surprised to see them.

They just wanted to discuss a few more things about the case, Buchanan told her. "But before we do," he warned, "I'd like to advise you of your rights."

"Do I need an attorney?" she asked.

"That's entirely up to you," he said, as he recalled the conversation more than a year later. "I can't advise you one way or another."

She would go ahead with the interview without an attorney, she said, with no sign of nervousness. After all, she said, she only could tell him what she knew to be the truth.

Buchanan read Barbara's rights from a card he carried in his wallet. After that formality he asked her about the gun.

Russ had bought it for her, she said, because he was concerned about her safety when she was attending night classes. She had gone with him to buy it, and Garland Wolfe had briefly told them how the pistol worked. She knew nothing about guns, she said, and had paid little attention. Russ never showed her how to use it.

There was no routine place for keeping the gun, she said. It had remained in the console between her car seats for a long time, but it was doing her no good because she had no idea how to use it. At the end of the fall semester in 1986, Russ brought the gun into the house and stashed it in a nightstand beside their bed, she said.

Late in March 1987, some jewelry turned up missing at the house and Russ moved the gun again, but she didn't know where he kept it afterward. She did know that he had been sleeping with it under his pillow occasionally after becoming concerned about prowlers.

When Buchanan asked whether she'd ever gone to the National Guard pistol range with Russ, she acknowledged that she had. It had been a few years ago. She had fired two clips from another pistol, but she had never fired the .25 and didn't think that Russ had either. She had a tremendous fear of guns, she pointed out.

She didn't know whether Russ was careless with guns or not, she said, because she simply didn't know enough about guns to have an opinion. Russ also had told her never to point a gun at anyone unless she intended to use it, she said, and she had found that amusing, because she really didn't know how to use a gun and had no intention of pointing one at anything.

Then the first flaw in her story. Russ, she said, had talked about how he would shoot anyone who ever broke into his house, but she had found that ironic because he was such a heavy sleeper that he probably wouldn't wake up if somebody beat down the door and carted out the bed with him in it.

Buchanan was quick to note the inconsistency. Barbara had told the first emergency workers on the scene that she knew Russ had the gun under his pillow and she reached for it when she heard her son get up because she was afraid he might be awakened and think Jason a prowler and shoot him. If he was such a heavy sleeper, why would she be concerned about that?

That version also was inconsistent with the one she had told

Buchanan later on the day of the shooting and again during the taped reenactment. On the later occasions she had said that she felt something under the pillow but didn't realize at first that it was a gun.

"Have you ever bought a .25-caliber pistol before?" Buchanan asked.

"No," Barbara said. But ten years earlier her first husband had wanted her to buy a gun for protection, and she had always done what he told her. A coworker had gone with her to buy one and show her how to use it. She had fired it three or four times. She thought it was a .22. Just a little gun, she added.

She went on to recount the same story of Larry's death that she had told investigators in Randolph County at the time.

Buchanan asked about insurance and Barbara said that she thought she would be getting a little over $100,000, counting insurance they had on a truck loan, their Visa card and a charge account at a furniture store, plus about $14,000 from Russ's retirement fund.

Some time the previous year, Barbara said, Russ had to go on a secret maneuver with the National Guard and he had become concerned about what would happen if he died. He called and wanted her to come to a meeting in Raleigh about wills and death preparations. Each had made up wills on their computer, using forms supplied at the meeting, she explained, each leaving everything to the other. But she and the boys had by no means been prepared for Russ's death, she noted.

Had she and Russ had any problems?

"Only financial," she said.

The interview lasted about forty-five minutes, and as Buchanan and Myers were leaving, they noticed two new red motor scooters parked in the garage, one Barbara had bought for Jason, the other for Steve. Obviously her spending had not abated.


Buchanan went to the office on Saturday to type up a five-page application for a search warrant. For cause, he cited the similarities of Russ's and Larry's deaths, the inconsistencies in the reenactment of Russ's shooting, Barbara's subterfuge about her novel, unnamed affairs and her financial problems.

At midafternoon on Sunday, he took the warrant by the house of Superior Court Judge Thomas H. Lee for his signature.

At 7:05 A.M. on Monday, April 18, four cars pulled up to the house at 2833 Fox Drive. Buchanan, Myers, McCabe, McDougald and two uniformed deputies got out and walked briskly to the front door.

Barbara's brother Steve answered. He was alone at the house. Barbara already had left for work, Jason for school. Steve wanted to call his sister and parents, but no calls were allowed.

As McCabe wandered through Barbara's house, she was astonished by what she saw. It was as if she had walked into an article from one of those home magazines. McCabe was a mother, and when she rushed off to work in the morning, dirty dishes were sometimes left in the sink, soiled clothing often draped over chairs. Not at Barbara's house. Everything was in perfect order. Even in the closets and kitchen cabinets, everything was neatly arranged. From the interviews she had conducted with Barbara's acquaintances, McCabe had begun forming a picture of Barbara as a perfectionist and this confirmed it.

"She had to be perfect at everything she did," McCabe later recalled. "She had to be the perfect mother, the perfect housekeeper, the perfect wife. I can't imagine the kind of pressure she must have put upon herself to be that perfect."

While other officers continued the search, McCabe and McDougald took Steve aside to interview him. As could be expected, he stood by his sister. He said that he had been staying with her since Russ had died to keep her company. He didn't know whether Russ ever had taught Barbara to shoot, but he had never known her to have any association with guns. He had never seen the .25 with which Russ had been shot, but he knew that Russ had at least three other handguns and he usually kept them loaded. Barbara recently had sold the guns at a local gunshop, he said. He admitted that he had never known Russ to sleep with a gun under his pillow, but he had heard him talking about prowlers.

Steve acknowledged that Russ had died "in an odd way," but he didn't think his sister had killed him deliberately. She still cried about him, he pointed out. Russ and Barbara never argued or fought, he said, and Barbara hadn't been seeing any other men since Russ had died.

The officers spent more than two hours going through the house and Russ's Blazer. They took bank records, canceled checks, bills, insurance policies, letters, telephone bills, computer disks and personal items.

From beneath Barbara's bed, McCabe retrieved a box containing all the letters and cards the Fords had sent to Barbara and the boys over the years. In a hallway closet, Buchanan found the uncompleted manuscript of *Untimely Death* along with other writings. With it was a Doubleday letterhead taped to the top of a sheet of typing paper.

Buchanan also took the big leatherbound family Bible that Russ and the boys had given Barbara two years earlier for Mother's Day. The Bible had two brown silk markers. Buchanan noticed that one was marking a page in Deuteronomy, the other in Exodus. When he opened the Bible to those pages, he found a familiar admonition: "Thou shalt not kill."

"I thought that was significant," he said later.

Near the end of the search, McCabe and McDougald were dispatched to Jason's school to question him. He was brought to the school office, and the assistant principal and school liaison officer sat in on the interview.

On the morning of the shooting, Jason said, his alarm had gone off at six. He got up immediately, got a towel from the linen closet and went to the bathroom that was off the hallway just down from his bedroom. He had just climbed into the shower when he heard a sharp sound. He thought it was the toilet lid falling in his parents' adjoining bathroom. But his mother came running into the bathroom just as he was turning off the water to get out of the shower and told him that Russ had a gun under his pillow and it had gone off, call 911. He hadn't seen or heard his mother before she came into the bathroom, and he assumed that she was in bed until then.

Russ had taught him how to shoot the .25, he said, and had warned him against leaving a round in the chamber when he took out the clip. Russ usually kept the pistol in the unlocked nightstand beside his bed with two other handguns. He had never heard his father talk about sleeping with a gun under his pillow and didn't know whether he did or not. He had never known his mom to have anything to do with guns.

After talking with Jason, McDougald drove to Wilmington and

questioned Bryan at his university dorm. His mother was afraid of guns, Bryan said, and he didn't remember Russ ever taking her to shoot. On the morning Russ was shot, his Grandmother Terry had called and told him to come to the emergency room at Duke without telling him what had happened. Later, he said, his mother told him that she had awakened in the dark, reached out and felt something under Russ's pillow and "it just went off."

Did he remember his real father's death?

He remembered being awakened and taken across the street, he said. Later, his mother had told him that his father had been cleaning a gun and it had gone off because he had forgotten to unload it.

Both of the deaths, Bryan insisted, were just "freak accidents" and his mother certainly was not guilty of anything in either of them. He made it clear that he resented the implications of the questions that were being asked.

At two o'clock, Buchanan walked into the grand jury room at the courthouse and spent the next thirty minutes telling the jurors what he knew about Russ's death and Barbara's life. Soon after he left, the jury granted the indictment Ron Stephens sought.

Buchanan knew that Barbara likely had known since mid-morning that she was about to be arrested. He'd had her under discreet surveillance by deputies since he and the other officers had arrived at her house just in case she decided to flee.

He had decided to wait until Barbara was at home to pick her up. Shortly after four, he, Myers and McCabe climbed into his un-marked Plymouth cruiser and drove to the house on Fox Drive for the second time that day.

Barbara answered the door wearing jeans, sneakers and a hooded gray sweatshirt with a blue sailboat design on the front.

"I have a warrant for your arrest on a grand jury indictment for murder," Buchanan told her.

She burst into tears and cried out for Jason as Buchanan once again advised her of her rights and warned that it probably would be best if she didn't make any statements.

Jason also burst into tears when he came into the room and realized what was happening. Barbara cried out to him to call her parents and tell them that she was being arrested. Instead, Jason became angry, screaming at Buchanan, "I guess you think you're a big man putting handcuffs on my mama, don't you!"

The three officers led Barbara to the car, leaving Jason crying behind them. McCabe got into the back seat with Barbara, who turned to her.

"I didn't do it," she said. "I didn't kill him."

She seemed to be seething with anger. And she had a look in her eye that McCabe never would forget. The detective didn't know what to say.

"I didn't do it," Barbara kept repeating as they drove to the county jail in rush-hour traffic. It was almost as if she were trying to convince herself, McCabe thought. After all, how could a perfect wife coldly murder two husbands?

# Chapter Twenty-four

Barbara seemed such an unlikely murderer that when news of her arrest flashed on TV screens on Monday night, many people reacted with astonishment and disbelief, especially those who had seen her at church only a day earlier.

Neighbors, family members, fellow church members, friends and coworkers were shocked and angry that Barbara was in jail facing so grave a charge. How could this have happened? they asked one another as word spread. Barbara was such a good person, such a fine mother, such a strong Christian that this had to be some awful mistake. Surely a judge would realize that immediately and Barbara would be released and her name cleared.

But all of these people would only grow angrier and more disillusioned with the workings of the law as Barbara remained in jail and more and more dark revelations from her past began to work their way to the surface.

On the morning after her arrest, Barbara made her first court appearance before Judge Thomas C. Watts. At her side was John Wainio, the lawyer who had called Buchanan on Barbara's behalf a few weeks earlier. He had been summoned by her parents, but he had agreed only to see Barbara through this first appearance. He was primarily a civil trial lawyer and did not feel comfortable representing a client against such a grave criminal charge.

Barbara looked frightened and defeated as the judge asked, "Are you Barbara Terry Stager?"

"Yes, sir," she said in a small voice.

"Mrs. Stager, do you understand that you have been accused by an indictment returned by the Durham County Grand Jury as of yesterday, with the offense of murder in the first degree allegedly occurring on February first, 1988?"

"Yes, sir."

"First-degree murder is a felony offense under the laws of the state of North Carolina, commonly referred to as a capital crime, that is, a crime for which the punishment upon conviction is death or life imprisonment.

"I tell you those things not to frighten you, ma'am, but because I have a duty to explain the charges against you, and it is my duty to tell you the maximum possible punishment which could be imposed for the crime which has been alleged.

"Have you been furnished, Mrs. Stager, a copy of the bill of indictment and the other paperwork in this case?"

"I think that's what I have here."

Asked if she had counsel, Barbara said that she had retained another local lawyer, David Rudolph, but Wainio interrupted to say that wasn't so, that her parents were just talking with Rudolph.

"We ought to probably just leave it at this point where I'm representing her for the purpose of this, and we'll certainly work that out as quickly as possible."

Wainio, who had talked with Barbara only for a short time that morning before coming to court, brought up a matter of vital interest to Barbara:

"Your Honor, there is no bond set."

Barbara was a surgical nurse at Duke, he mistakenly pointed out. She needed to continue with her work, to be with her young son.

"Her parents are here, ready, willing and able to, of course, assist her and to assure that she's going to be back."

Barbara had known about the investigation for two months, he said, and if she had intended to flee, she would have done so already.

"What's the state's position?" the judge asked.

Eric Evenson rose to say that no bond should be set, the charge was too serious.

"Mr. Evenson, do you have any information that she had been charged with any other criminal offenses?"

"Your Honor, I know there are some worthless check charges. But quite honestly, there's more to this than just that. And we would like the opportunity to present some of that at a bond hearing. There's some evidence that may tend to show that this is the second husband that's been killed mysteriously while she was in the house. She's been charged in this particular crime, but there have been no charges filed in the first matter."

Wainio was immediately on his feet, protesting angrily. "Your Honor, that is an inappropriate allegation. That was an incident that occurred over ten years ago. There was never any charges, never any allegation or anything suspicious at the time. We think this matter ought to stand on its own."

Judge Watts brought a quick end to the wrangling. Bond, he said, would be $250,000.

Barbara turned to her parents with a helpless look. She knew that they didn't have the resources to meet such a bond and would have a hard time coming up with it.


Reporters hurried from the courtroom as Barbara was being taken back to the jail on the top floor of the courthouse. By noon, people throughout central North Carolina would know that Barbara had another husband who had died "mysteriously."

Wednesday morning's *Durham Herald* not only made Evenson's allegation front-page news, it reported the effect of that news. Russ's friend Mike Wood, who had taken over as coach of his baseball team, said that the team was stunned. "You can see it in their eyes," he said. "They don't really know what to think." The players not only admired Russ but loved him, Wood said, and so did he.

"He was like a brother to me. It hurt so bad when he died. It was like someone dropped a bomb on me. I want you to be sure to print one thing. Russ Stager was one of the best people I've ever known."

As people in Durham were reading this story and hearing broadcasts about the court hearing, reporters were busy digging for new material.

Thursday's *Raleigh News and Observer* quoted medical examiner Dr. Thomas B. Clark about Russ's shooting: "We did not find the circumstances of the death and the autopsy findings to be consistent with an accidental death."

That set off more news stories.

By Friday, four days after Barbara's arrest, several newspapers and radio and television stations were reporting that Larry Ford had died, like Russ, from a .25-caliber bullet wound while alone with Barbara.

The weekend brought a respite to the news stories about Barbara, but Monday morning's *News and Observer* kicked off a new barrage. Lynn Haessly had gone to the courthouse and gotten a copy of the search warrant Buchanan had typed up.

"COURT RECORDS SAY MRS. STAGER UNFAITHFUL TO SPOUSES," said that morning's headline.

That story was more than Greta Burch could take. Greta, a high school senior, lived near Barbara, who had worked with her father, a doctor at the Duke University Medical Center. Her mother had tried to help Barbara after Russ's death. Her brother Josh was Jason's best friend. She and Bryan were very close. They had carpooled to high school. She had driven to Wilmington to visit Bryan the day before Barbara was arrested.

On the day Barbara's affair was revealed in the news, Greta wrote a letter to the editor of the *Herald*. It appeared the following morning.

It all started on Feb. 1. What seemed to be a tragic accident is now a travesty. What we hear from the media and law officers is totally one-sided. If we believe what has been reported and her indictment, the death of Russell Stager was not accidental and Mrs. Barbara Stager willingly murdered her husband.

When Russell Stager died, we all suffered, but none of us can say that we suffered as much as Barbara Stager. She has carried public accusation, her own guilt at the accident, her loneliness in the same bed, the burden of handling financial matters, being there for two sons and now arrest.

The newspaper reports that possible motives include other lovers and life insurance. I am so angry at the course this incident has taken.

As an 18-year-old, I looked up to Mr. and Mrs. Stager as having the neatest, most beautiful relationship a married couple could have. The accusation of Barbara having an affair cuts like a knife. I saw those two together every Friday night at the movies and Saturdays at the mall, at home watching movies, working out and just standing by each other. When could they have even thought about affairs?

Not only were Barbara's parents unable to come up with the money and property to post her bond, they also were keenly aware that their daughter's and their own financial situations would not allow her to hire an attorney. The expense would be immense.

They conferred with John Wainio about this, and he presented an alternative. Barbara could declare herself indigent and get a court-appointed attorney. He would do what he could to see that she got the best attorney possible. He already had one in mind: William Cotter.

Cotter had a reputation as a scrapper, a wiry opponent, qualities he had picked up while growing up in South Boston, Massachusetts, and during six years he had spent as an Army airborne officer. Cotter had served a combat tour in Vietnam before leaving the army for college and, eventually, Duke University Law School. Many lawyers shied from capital cases, but Cotter, a Red Sox fan, applied a baseball analogy: "You either step up to the plate and take the big cuts, or you don't." Consequently, some of the hardest murder pitches had come his way. He had just finished the grueling retrial of a high school student who had been accused of raping a nurse and stabbing her seventy-nine times, a case into which he had put many long hours, only to strike out. Already he was into another case in which his client was charged with killing a pizza-shop manager and a convenience-store clerk during robberies. He had no time for another big case right now. And that was what he told Wainio.

As the case continued to dominate the news, though, Cotter began to feel that Barbara was already being convicted in the press, and the compulsion that always brought him to the defense of underdogs caused him to call Wainio and tell him that he had changed his mind.

Wainio filed an indigency claim with the court, asking that

lawyers be appointed to defend Barbara at public expense. The claim was heard on April 26 by Judge Thomas H. Lee, who had authorized the search of Barbara's house. Barbara listed debts of more than $150,000, including the $92,000 mortgage on her house. Her assets were far less. Her salary at Duke was only $900 a month, she claimed, although she had listed it as $1,430 when making application for a loan a few months earlier. Judge Lee noted that it was unusual for someone who owned property to be indigent, but he granted the claim and appointed William Cotter to represent her.

North Carolina law requires that two lawyers represent anybody charged with a capital offense, and Lee appointed Richard Glaser, a thirty-three-year-old former assistant U.S. attorney in West Virginia, to work with Cotter on the case. Glaser never had tried a capital case but had handled appeals in such cases.

Immediately after their appointment, Cotter and Glaser took the elevator to the jail on the top floor of the courthouse to meet their new client. Barbara was waiting for them in a small interview room, wearing the bright orange coveralls that all prisoners were issued. She cried as she told her attorneys that she was not guilty of murdering her husband.

After his mother had been in jail two weeks, Jason, a seventh-grader, got fed up with the unrelenting barrage of news reports about her. He sent a letter to the editor of the *Herald*. It was published on Wednesday morning, May 4, under the headline "MOTHER WAS FALSELY ACCUSED OF MURDER."

> I am writing on behalf of my mother, Barbara Stager, who has been falsely accused of murdering my father, Russell Stager.
>
> My mom has always been very considerate of our feelings, very loving and very understanding. She listened to our problems, talked to us about them and gave us wonderful advice.
>
> She is a mother who had a good meal prepared at meal time, looked after our health and physical needs, who saw that we went to church and did all the things that helped us to grow up to be well-rounded and respectable individuals.
>
> Our dad, Russ Stager, spent every possible minute with us and our mother. We saw our parents together and knew them

as any kids know their parents. When our father died, we all suffered, but now we are glad he doesn't know the badness of the people who are accusing his wife and our mother of such awful things.

This whole deal is very unbelievable. The outrageousness of these accusations is pitiful on the behalf of the law enforcement. Also, the news media and reporters seem to have no sensitivity. They call on the phone, crowd around us at court hearings and ask the same questions over and over again.

They have twisted this whole story around so much that it seems like a totally different story than what really happened on Feb. 1. The accusations that have been made make our parents' life and our mother's life sound like an unbelievable soap opera.

Our hearts have been broken by this ordeal. We love her and miss her very much. Friends, neighbors and relatives have all been very supportive with their prayers, visits, calls and letters, and we appreciate this, but the hurt in our hearts and minds won't go away.


Barbara was very proud of Jason's letter. She showed it off to her cellmates, telling them that Jason had written it by himself and without prompting.


The following day, Barbara and her family were back in court, this time with the support of many friends, as Cotter sought to get her bond reduced to $50,000 so that she could be released from jail.

Cotter had brought numerous witnesses to speak to Barbara's character, and after several had given their testimonials, Barbara's mother, Marva, told Judge Wiley F. Bowen that she and her husband, whom she called Norman, had been married for forty-one years. Their roots in Durham County, she said, were deep. She pointed out that she had two brothers and a sister, and her husband had two brothers and seven sisters, all of whom had remained in the county. Of Barbara's thirteen first cousins, eleven still lived in Durham County, she said.

"I believe the only asset of any real value that you and your husband have is your house, is that correct?" Cotter asked.

"Yes, sir."

And were they ready to put up their house to make Barbara's bond? They were, Marva said.

Cotter noted that half a dozen others were in the courtroom willing to attest to Barbara's good character and their certainty that she would return to stand trial if released on bond. The judge indicated that it wouldn't be necessary to hear them.

Evenson opposed Cotter's request with the same argument he had used earlier before another judge.

"I think the court needs to be aware of the fact that the state will offer evidence that tends to show that the defendant in this case committed two killings, both involving her husbands, both while they were lying in bed, with a .25-caliber pistol. . . . We feel when a person commits two such crimes that there's a safety factor."

Cotter was angry. He did not like Evenson and had told him so. The two had clashed many times over small cases, and Cotter thought that this was a cheap shot, typical of the way Evenson worked.

"Your Honor, the biggest problem I can see with this case already is the reckless attitude with which some people are treating it, and specifically the district attorney. To say that she committed two such crimes is appalling at this stage, and I suspect it's just for the ears of the press, because she has never been charged with anything other than this murder, this killing, in Durham County. . . . He's got no business saying that she committed two of these crimes. She has never been charged with anything in Randolph County."

Cotter went on to point out that Barbara had two children who needed her, and that Barbara's arrest had created many hardships for her. Her younger son was having to stay with her parents. The Duke University Medical Center had suspended her from her job until the charge had been settled. She had no mortgage insurance and couldn't make her house payments.

"She is going to have to go and find a job when she gets out," he said.

Barbara would not flee if granted a bond reduction, Cotter assured the judge. "This is where her church is. This is where her friends are. This is where she was raised. This lady literally has no other place to go."

The judge was quick in his decision.
"The motion," he said, "is denied."


That was Barbara's worst day since her arrest. She had cried after bond was denied the first time and again when she learned that she wouldn't be able to hire the lawyer she wanted. Now she returned to her bunk in Cell Block Three in the women's wing of the jail and sobbed inconsolably. Several cellmates attempted to comfort her without success and left her to cry out her disappointment.

Barbara was the only white person in the women's wing of the jail. She was older than the other prisoners, most of whom were awaiting trial on minor charges or serving short sentences. Her cellmates found her quiet and reticent at first, but gradually they drew her out, and Barbara became almost motherly to several, offering advice and consolation whenever they sought it.

Barbara ate little, often offering her food to others, her cellmates later would recall. She rarely ventured from her cell, except for visits, or when the telephone was brought around. She got lots of mail and spent much of her time in her bunk writing letters and reading romance novels.

Her conversations were mostly about her children and family. She never could have killed her husband, she told one cellmate; she loved him too much.

She was allowed visits only on Saturday with family members and her minister, separated by a sheet of unbreakable glass, and she cried after every visit.

Some of her cellmates were amazed when they learned that Barbara was charged with murder. She just didn't seem like the type, they said. She was too nice a person.

She was such a nice person that the other inmates always turned off the TV in the cell block when the news came on because they knew that Barbara got upset when she heard the reports about herself. Later, not one would say an unkind thing about her.


Two weeks after Judge Bowen denied a reduction of Barbara's bond, a group of family and friends came again to the courthouse. Her parents, an aunt and uncle and Barbara's friends and neighbors, Dr. Warner Burch and his wife, Vivian, put up the deeds to their houses as collateral for Barbara's bond, and she was freed to leave with them.

She moved in with her parents, who already had rented her house on Fox Drive to keep up the mortgage payments.

After Barbara's release from jail, her family and a group of close friends joined in a supportive circle around her. Among the friends who rallied to her side were Vivian Burch, her daughter, Greta, her brother Steve's girlfriend, Astrid Keizer, and Ginger Payne, another high school student whom Barbara had befriended at church.

But the three friends who would spend the most time with Barbara in the year that would elapse before her trial were Joan Towner, Carol Galloway and Sherry Sims.

Joan Towner met Barbara at Sunday school about two weeks after Russ's death. Joan had been living in Durham for nearly a year and had made no friends since her arrival. Her husband, Norm, was about to undergo surgery, and her son, who was only a year older than Bryan, was in the Navy overseas.

Joan's husband was confined at home after his surgery, and Barbara brought them meals and videotapes. She also began writing regularly to Joan's son, who was homesick. As a result, Joan and Barbara had become close friends. Joan could not imagine a more giving and loving person than Barbara.

Carol Galloway had known Russ since he was married to Jo Lynn. After Russ married Barbara, they had moved into the same subdivision, Heather Glen, where Carol lived with her husband, Ralph, both of whom were also in their second marriages. Carol and Ralph knew Russ and Barbara through church and neighborhood encounters, but it really wasn't until after Russ was killed that Carol got close to Barbara.

"We kind of took it on ourselves to help Barbara any way we could during the time of Russ's death," Carol later said. "We would invite Barbara over to our house for dinner, Barbara and Jason. During that time our friendship really began to blossom."

Sherry Sims had known Russ and his family since she had started attending Grey Stone Baptist Church when she was thirteen. After she had grown up and married, her husband played with Russ on the church softball team. She first met Barbara at

one of those games. Barbara, she thought, was sweet and atten-
tive. "She made me feel real comfortable," Sherry recalled years
later. "She's a little reserved, but once you get to know her, she's
outgoing, she's funny."

Sherry had lost touch with Barbara and Russ after they left
Grey Stone, and later when she left Grey Stone herself for Homestead Heights, she was pleasantly surprised when Barbara and
Russ had joined the church. Russ and Barbara were just as popular at Homestead as they had been at other churches they had
attended. People wanted to be around them. They quickly became a force in the congregation.

Sherry would see them occasionally at church and chat for a
few moments, but did not become closer to Barbara until Russ's
death. She was talking on the phone to a friend when her friend
mentioned that Barbara had accidentally shot and killed Russ.
Sherry couldn't believe it. She had just seen them at church. Later,
she would try to explain what that news did to her.

"I couldn't eat. I couldn't sleep. I was miserable. I felt so bad
for her. I couldn't imagine what she was going through. To me,
the guilt I would feel would be tremendous, the regret. I kept
thinking this must be horrible for her. I felt like God was telling
me she was going to need my help."

Sherry went to the funeral home to see Barbara on Tuesday
night after the shooting. People were lined up out the door. Then
Sherry spotted Barbara, who had stepped outside to get some air,
but people were crowding around her even there. Barbara, Sherry
would recall, was crying and shaking when she got to her.

"She hugged me real tight, and I told her I would be there for
her and I would just help her any way I could."

The following week, Sherry called Barbara and went to visit
her. After that they got together at least once a week, sometimes
just for lunch, sometimes for an afternoon. "She accepted me,"
Sherry said. "She grew to trust me pretty quick, and I trust her,
too. The Lord's hand was in it."

Sherry was aware that Barbara also had lost her first husband
in a gun accident, and to her mind that made Russ's similar death
all the worse. "The thought never occurred to me that this was
anything but an accident, a horrible accident, a freak accident,
something that wouldn't happen in a million years that just happened to happen to her."

When Barbara was arrested, Sherry couldn't believe it.

"I was appalled," she said much later. "And I'm still appalled."

Sherry immediately began writing to Barbara in jail. After a week, Barbara answered, and they began exchanging letters regularly. In her first letters, Barbara expressed disbelief at her situation and uncertainty about her future.

"I'm innocent," she wrote. "Pray for me. I didn't do it."

Sherry replied that she never had any doubt of her innocence. She sent scripture and encouraged Barbara to keep her faith. God would take care of things.

"She started writing back for me to keep *my* faith, take care of *myself*," Sherry recalled. "She's a very encouraging person. She's so concerned for other people."

Barbara returned to church as soon as she was released from jail. Some of her family and friends were concerned about the reception she might receive, but everybody was friendly and supportive, and Barbara threw herself back into church activities, working with young people, cooking for the sick and delivering meals to their homes.

"The thing that helped Barbara the most was helping other people," Sherry Sims said. "She's such a good person. If you know her, you love her. She goes out of her way to do things for you. It's just so many little things she does that make people love her."

Barbara filled her time doing things for her parents, her brothers, her numerous aunts and uncles, her friends. Steve had moved into a small house of his own, and Barbara cleaned floors and varnished furniture for him. Barbara often baby-sat Carol and Ralph Galloway's two-year-old son, Matt.

"My son and Barbara just kind of took to each other like glue," Carol later recalled. "It got to the point where there were times when Matt would rather be with Barbara than he would with me."

Barbara saw Carol at least three or four times a week, sometimes more. Carol frequently invited Barbara and Jason for supper. Often Barbara would come in the afternoon just to pick up Matt and take him to the park, or to McDonald's. Matt was always excited about her coming. Barbara became such a part of the Galloway household that Carol gave her a key to the house so that she could come and go as she pleased.

Barbara's lawyers had recommended that she keep as low a profile as possible, stay out of the public eye, avoid shopping for anything that might be deemed extravagant, by all means not be seen alone with a man. At times Barbara resented the restrictions. "It was like she had to stop living to keep people from thinking she wasn't grieving," said Sherry Sims, who saw Barbara as often as Carol did.

As the date of Barbara's trial neared, her friends had to admire the way she faced it. Often she was more supportive to her friends and family than they could be to her.

"She tried to stay positive, keep negative thoughts out, to encourage us," Sherry said. "I'm sure she was frightened and worried some of the time, but in her mind and her heart she's innocent and she just couldn't believe that a jury would think she was guilty."

That was a refrain that Barbara kept repeating to all of her friends and family: "How could a jury find me guilty of something I didn't do?"

# Chapter Twenty-five

Barbara was scheduled to appear in court again on June 6 for arraignment, but her lawyers, William Cotter and Richard Glaser, won a postponement until June 27. On June 24, however, Cotter and Glaser filed a written plea of not guilty and waived arraignment so that Barbara would not have to appear.

At the same time, the lawyers filed a flurry of motions, asking that the case be dismissed on various grounds, that the trial be moved because of the intense news coverage and that all evidence connected to Larry Ford's death be suppressed in any trial that ensued. If the latter motion was not granted, the lawyers wanted a gag order to stop prosecutors from talking about the case.

On September 1, lawyers for both sides appeared before Judge Anthony M. Brannon, who was considered to be an expert on the rules of evidence, for a hearing to determine whether the trial should be moved from Durham County. Cotter and Glaser put up several witnesses, most of them friends of Barbara's, to offer their opinions that Barbara could not get a fair trial in the county.

Judge Brannon agreed. He did not issue a ruling until early in January 1989, though, when he ordered that Barbara's trial be moved from Durham County to Sanford in Lee County, forty-five miles away. Cotter had requested it be held in Charlotte, one hundred and forty miles to the southwest, the state's largest city, where few people likely would have heard of Barbara Stager. Jurors there were also more apt to be sophisticated and not as likely to favor the death penalty.

By contrast, Lee was one of the state's less populous and prosperous counties, and Sanford was a working-class town of fewer than 17,000 people. The county's sustenance came from farming, processing poultry and manufacturing bricks, perfume, car parts and electronic equipment. Its people were largely conservative and God-fearing, people who believed in an eye for an eye.

Cotter had mixed reactions, pleased that the trial was being moved, disappointed that it would be in Lee County instead of a bigger city. But his disappointment was minor compared to the discouragement he felt at another ruling the judge made at the same time. Brannon denied Cotter's motion to prevent any evidence of Larry Ford's death from being introduced at Barbara's trial. In effect, Cotter knew, he would now have to defend against two murders instead of the one for which Barbara had been charged. And he knew that the chances of doing so successfully were very slim.

As if that weren't enough, more bad news was on its way. Early in February, Richard Glaser, who had done much of the preparatory work on Barbara's case, told Cotter that he had received a job offer from the U.S. Attorney's Office in Greensboro, and he felt that he had to take it. He withdrew from the case on February 15.

Not until more than a month later was Eddie Falcone appointed to assist Cotter in the Stager case. Age thirty-six, he mainly had handled domestic and traffic cases. He had never defended a client in a capital case. That didn't really matter, however, because it was too late for him to get to learn enough about the case to have much effect.

Cotter assigned him to conduct the sentencing phase, a stage of the trial with which Barbara, despite Cotter's foreboding, had become more and more convinced that she would not have to be bothered.

That was not Evenson's feeling. He was pleased with the change in court venue. He thought that coldly executing a husband while he slept would not sit well with the people of Lee

County. He had enough evidence to prove that Barbara had done exactly that. And now he thought that he would be able to show why.

Evenson had put more hours into the Stager case than any other, had spent so many evenings and weekends working on it that he worried about neglecting his family. Detective Rick Buchanan, who had continued his investigation on into the fall, had done the same, causing his wife to begin referring to Barbara as "the other woman" in his life. Despite all their work, though, one crucial aspect had eluded them: a solid motive.

Although Buchanan and his officers had spent many weeks tracking down rumors, all had proved to be just gossip. Buchanan had not turned up any evidence that Barbara had been having an affair at the time of Russ's death, so she likely hadn't shot him to be with somebody else. The anonymous tip Buchanan had received about Russ's affair had proven false as well, ruling out jealousy. And Russ's life insurance seemed unlikely to offer the sole incentive for his murder. Something else must have prodded Barbara to act, Evenson and Buchanan thought, and if they couldn't find it, they feared that a jury might be willing to accept her story of an accident.

During the long months of investigation, thousands of pages of documents had accumulated, and Evenson and Buchanan sifted through them time and again looking for some overlooked clue that might lead them to a more substantial motive than Russ's insurance. As fall of 1988 had arrived they decided to ask for help from people who knew Russ better, who might be able to spot something that they had missed: Russ's mother and his former wife, Jo Lynn. Buchanan delivered boxes of documents—interviews, financial records, cancelled checks—to the Stager house, and although some of the material was startling and painful to her, Doris spent hour after hour poring through it, filling legal pads with notes. Jo Lynn came at night and on weekends to help her, and they sent pages of observations and suggestions to Evenson.

Late in October, Jo Lynn had been closed up in one of Doris's bedrooms, going through cancelled checks and other material, when something unusual caught her eye. One check on Russ's account was numbered far out of sequence with the others. It was dated December 28, 1987, made payable to Barbara, but the signature did not look like the others on Russ's checks.

"Look at this," Jo Lynn said, going into another room where Doris was working.

Doris agreed that something was fishy about the check. She searched a Mother's Day card that Russ had sent her to compare signatures. Russ clearly had not signed the check. Apparently Barbara had written the check to herself from Russ's account just thirty-five days before his death. Why? Had Russ known about it? Was this somehow significant?

They thought it notable enough that they made it the lead item on the list they sent to Evenson on October 17. Unbeknownst to them, that check was the little thing that Evenson knew had been lying there right before his eyes all along. It brought about a whole new phase of the investigation that continued through January, producing the evidence that he and Buchanan had been seeking for so long. By the first anniversary of Russ's death, they had no doubt that when the trial began on May 1, they would be able to show, step by step, exactly what had led to Russ's murder.

For all their hard work, though, neither could have imagined that before the trial began, they would get help from a source they couldn't have dreamed possible.


On Tuesday evening, April 18, 1989, less than two weeks before the trial was to begin, Rick Buchanan got a call at home from a Durham police officer named Ralph Mack.

A woman he knew had given him something that she thought might be significant to the Stager case, Mack said. Could he bring it over?

By all means, said Buchanan.

Mack arrived at 8:37 carrying a tiny audiotape cassette. It was a minicassette, made in Mexico, with a faded green label that bore the Realistic brand.

Buchanan should listen to the tape, Mack told him. It could be very important.

When Eric Evenson walked into the courthouse the next morning, Detective Valerie McCabe was waiting with a smile on her face. "Wait until you see what Ricky's got," she said, but she wouldn't tell him what it was.

Evenson went straight to the detective division, where Buchanan and several other officers were listening to the tape. Nobody said anything as Evenson joined them, listening intently to the voice coming from the machine. It took Evenson only a few moments to realize what he was hearing.

"It was like, this is just unreal, it's too hard to believe," he recalled later.

Evenson hurried upstairs to tell Ron Stephens what Buchanan had turned up.

Under a process called discovery, North Carolina law requires the state to let the defense examine any physical evidence before the start of a trial, and Stephens did not want to risk a judge ruling that he had delayed something so important that had cropped up so late.

"We've got to get it to Cotter," Stephens said.

The tape set off a whole new round of last-minute investigation and legal research for both sides.

Eight days after he got the tape, Buchanan asked Doris and Al Stager to come to the district attorney's office. He had something that he wanted to see if they could identify. He took them into the law library and seated them at a table. He took a seat on the other side behind a small tape recorder.

"I have a tape," he said. "Listen to the tape. See if you can identify the voice."

Doris's and Al's expression revealed that they recognized the voice immediately, but they listened intently to the entire recording before speaking, their initial shock at what they were hearing turning to sorrow by the time the voice had stopped. Doris broke the silence that followed.

"That's Russell," she said.

# PART FIVE

# Judgment

# Chapter Twenty-six

The Lee County courthouse is a two-story brick structure of neoclassical design built shortly after the turn of the century. Porticoes on the east and west sides of the building are each supported by six Ionic columns painted to match the locally made burgundy brick. Inside, old men sit passing time on benches along the broad tiled hallways leading to the double staircase in the lobby that offers access to the second floor with its spacious single courtroom.

The charming exterior is deceiving, however. In the recent past the creaky old courtroom was renovated at minimal expense. The balcony, once the only place in the courtroom for black spectators, has been hidden behind a cheap drop ceiling with fluorescent lights. The walls are covered with imitation pine paneling, the walkways between the hard wooden benches topped with durable green carpeting of the sort found on miniature golf courses. The stern countenances of past judges scowl from dark portraits along the courtroom walls, as if their dignity has been offended by this cut-rate setting.

The courtroom had often been the scene of drama but never of the spectacle that Barbara Stager's trial promised. Rarely were reporters, photographers and TV camera crews from the state's largest cities drawn here. County officials knew that they would be coming in large numbers for this trial, though, and shortly before it was to begin they sent cleaning crews in to put the best face on the old building.

Few reporters and photographers were present, however, when the trial opened on Monday, May 1, 1989, though Judge

J. B. Allen, who believed in wide public access to trials, already had ruled that cameras, audio recorders and video recorders would be allowed in the courtroom, ensuring that Barbara's every display of emotion during the trial would be on front pages each morning and TV screens each night. But the early proceedings were too dull to attract many news people.

Instead, the courtroom was crowded with more than a hundred Lee County citizens who had been summoned for the purpose of choosing twelve who would decide Barbara's fate.

Choosing those twelve was delayed while Barbara's lawyer, William Cotter, put up a wall of motions. Barbara sat listening patiently in a pale green dress as Cotter fought to have her charges dismissed or her trial postponed.

"I am not prepared to try this case," he told the judge, citing as reasons the sudden last-minute appearance of a mysterious audiotape and the departure of Richard Glaser, the second lawyer originally appointed to defend Barbara.

The tape had been a devastating blow to Cotter's defense. His first reaction after listening to it was that his case suddenly had gone from bad to hopeless. Although Barbara remained sublimely confident even after learning of the tape, he was certain that if jurors were allowed to hear it, along with evidence about Larry's shooting, she didn't stand a chance.

"It was so damaging that it actually was exhilarating in a very strange way," he later recalled. "It made me say, 'Okay, Cotter, you've got to do something with this, let's get going.' "

Judge Allen was not sympathetic. Now fifty-one, Allen had been a probation officer, prosecutor and District Court judge before his election to the Superior Court bench two and a half years earlier. A burly man with a deep, stentorian voice, he was a commanding and intimidating presence. His silver hair fell in a dip across his forehead, and he stared down from the bench through wire-rimmed glasses with a pensive expression. He had no patience with lawyers' excuses, and he was ready to get on with the trial.

He already had denied several of Cotter's motions, and now he denied this one. But Cotter was ready with more. Among them was another request that the state be ordered not to bring up anything about Barbara's previous marriage or her character.

"We didn't even want the name of James Larry Ford to come up in this trial," he said.

"Are you asking me to order that the state be prevented from presenting any evidence of any crimes, wrongs or acts that are not directly related to the death of Allison Russell Stager III?" the judge asked.

"That's correct," Cotter said. "What concerns me is the prosecution's opening statement about what it is they are going to prove in their case."

Allen decided to reserve decision on that until after the jury had been picked.

Although he was getting nowhere, Cotter, who would grow to like and respect Allen as the trial wore on despite an avalanche of rulings against him, wouldn't give up. "Your Honor, one last motion," he interjected.

"All right," the judge said wearily.

"I am going to renew my motion to continue and ask for one week."

"All right. The motion is denied. Now, Counsel, I am prepared for the state and for the defendant to bring in the first panel and commence jury selection."

The jury would be chosen from panels of a dozen citizens, many of whom were reluctant to serve. The first to be called was a housewife of Japanese descent, and Evenson quickly made clear the line of questioning he would be following.

"How do you feel about capital punishment? Are you opposed to it, or do you feel like it is a necessary law?"

"I am opposed to it," the woman said. "I don't believe in it."

"Okay, that's fine. Is that based on some moral or religious belief that you have or just a general feeling that you have?"

"Just a general feeling."

"You feel strongly about that?"

"Well, I guess so. I never have faced to ask me like that question, but I generally, I don't like to be having capital punishment in the United States."

The judge intervened to excuse her, explaining that her views would impair her ability to serve.

The second prospective witness was as clear on his position as the first had been. "I feel like I like it," he replied when Evenson asked his feelings about capital punishment.

This was a gun-owning fundamentalist. If you murder, he said, you should die. The prosecution was happy with him.

Would he always vote for death after convicting a defendant of first-degree murder? Cotter asked.

"Yes, sir."

He too was excused.

By the end of the day only two jurors had been accepted. By the end of the second day, half the jury had been seated. Not until the fourth day, after eighty-three people had been questioned, was the fourth and final alternate chosen, a man who said he found the death penalty an "unfortunate necessity." Asked if he could sentence somebody to death, he responded, "I think I could do it but it would be rather hard to live with."

The final makeup of the jury was nine men and three women, all white. Most were married and had children. Their jobs included carpenter, telephone worker, salesman, assembly-line worker, media technician, nursing instructor. Most were church-goers, with Baptists being predominant. Barbara, with her own strong Baptist background, knew that such a jury likely would be strongly conservative, not reluctant to impose a death penalty. But she could not accept, friends later said, that people such as these possibly could believe that she would deliberately kill somebody.

The Fords and Stagers never had met, but the parents of Barbara's two husbands recognized one another instinctively as they arrived at court for the opening of testimony on Monday, May 8. The two mothers met in warm embrace.

The Fords and Stagers took front-row seats, just behind the table where the prosecutors sat, separated from them by a wooden rail. They were joined by the Stagers' daughter, Cindy; Russ's first wife, Jo Lynn; the Fords' son Ronnie and their granddaughter Dana who was living with them temporarily.

Across the aisle, seated behind Barbara and her two defense attorneys, were her parents, her sons and her minister. Behind them were a group of close friends and supporters.

Reporters and photographers had turned out in force, as expected, and halfway back on the defense side of the courtroom, a TV camera had been mounted.

Before court was called to order, Barbara remained with her family and friends, chatting and laughing, never acknowledging her former in-laws across the way. Her brown hair had been cut short, and all hint of blond was gone. She wore big wire-frame glasses, a bulky turtleneck blouse with a single strand of pearls and tiny earrings. On her left hand were the diamond engagement ring and wedding band that Russ had given her.

After the jury had been impaneled and sent to the jury room, Cotter again asked that his motion be heard to deny admission of any evidence of Larry's death. He was particularly concerned that the state might bring it up in opening remarks. He didn't want any mention of the recently found audiotape either.

"Does the state intend to make an opening statement?" the judge inquired.

"If Your Honor please, because the jury selection has taken basically a week, we're ready to go ahead and proceed with evidence," said Eric Evenson, who didn't like giving the opposition an outline of the case he planned to present. "We're not going to make one at this time."

That being the case, Cotter told the judge, he wouldn't make one either. "But we reserve the right to do so at another time," he said.

The judge delayed hearing Cotter's motion until the matter came up in the course of the trial.

A technician set up a recorder to play the tape of Jason's call to 911, and after the jury had returned, the state's first witness, dispatcher Barbara Parson, told them about the call and the actions she had taken.

As the tape was being played, Jason, seated in the front row beside his brother, broke into tears at the sound of his trembling voice pleading for help.

Doug Griffin, who had been first to reach the house that morning, told about his arrival.

"Did you see any blood on the lady at all?" Evenson asked.

His reason for asking this would become apparent when the videotape of the reenactment was shown later. In it Barbara described crying out to Russ and rolling him over and back after she realized he had been shot, something Evenson was convinced never happened. If so, Barbara should have had blood on the flannel shirt she was wearing that morning.

"No," said Griffin. "I did not notice any, no."

Russ, however, was bleeding profusely, Griffin noted a few minutes later. "It wasn't spurting," he said, "It was oozing . . . coming from his nose and mouth and running down the side of his face . . . in his hair, all around the back left side of his head."

James Wingate, the fire department captain, related that Barbara had told him the shooting was an accident soon after he arrived in the room. He, too, said that he had not noticed any blood on Barbara.

"Did you later in fact find out there was blood on the front of Mrs. Stager's shirt?" Cotter asked on cross-examination.

"No, sir, I did not."

"Did you look for blood?"

"No."

"That really wasn't your function, was it?"

"We were concentrating on him very hard at that time and really didn't pay that much attention to her," Wingate said.

Clark Green, the first deputy on the scene, told of questioning Barbara with Deputy Paul Hornbuckle.

"As you were talking to her, observing her, did you form an opinion about her emotional condition?" Evenson asked.

"Yes, sir."

Cotter objected to this line of questioning, and the judge sustained.

"Did you watch her demeanor?" Evenson pressed on. "Would you describe—was she crying?"

"Objection to the leading," said Cotter.

"Overruled. You may answer that."

"I didn't see her cry," Green said. "She seemed concerned and shaken, but she wasn't crying. She was calm."

Deputy Paul Hornbuckle testified next, telling of removing the cocked and loaded pistol from the bed, of being asked to remove Barbara from the room and of questioning her afterward.

"Was she saying anything before you started questioning her?" Evenson asked.

"Yes, sir. She was stating, 'I kept telling him about those damn guns.' "

When Cotter cross-examined Hornbuckle, he tried to show that Barbara wasn't unemotional and composed that morning.

"Isn't it a fact that either you or Deputy Green or both of you told Mrs. Stager to calm down so she could answer the questions?"

"Yes, sir, that is correct. We were asked to take her out of the room while they were still administering aid."

"But you told her on more than one occasion to calm down so she could answer your questions?"

"Yes, sir."

Kevin Wilson, the director of emergency training in the county, followed Hornbuckle to the stand and said that Barbara had been so loud in the room that he and other emergency workers couldn't hear one another.

"Okay, you say this was a distraction?" Evenson said.

"Yes, sir."

"Was she repeating this over and over?"

"It was more of a chant, best way I could describe it."

Evenson asked him to demonstrate Barbara's chanting, and he attempted it, mimicking her words. " 'I'm scared of guns. Guns are not safe. My God, I wish we didn't have them.' "

Wilson told of getting Russ into the ambulance and then going back to see if he could help Barbara by taking her to the hospital or going to get Russ's parents. After telling of Barbara's quick and cold rejection of his offer of help, Wilson said, "I backed up and just did not say anything else."

It took him ten or fifteen seconds to regain his composure, he said. "It sort of startled me. I guess that's the only way to describe it."

It was then, Wilson said, that he went to Doug Griffin and told him to document the events of the morning, only facts, no opinions. "Before you talk to anybody, before you eat breakfast or anything," he recalled telling him.

"Let me ask you," Evenson said in closing, "do you remember her ever asking, 'Is he going to make it?' "

"I don't recall that being asked of me, no, sir."

After Phyllis Cagle, the now-retired secretary to the principal at Durham High School, testified that Barbara had calmly called her on the morning of the shooting to report that Russ was "sick" and wouldn't be at school, Evenson turned to the judge and said, "Your Honor, at this time we would call Mrs. Doris Stager."

The time had come to show the jurors how differently Russ's mother had reacted.

Wearing a bright red suit, Doris strode to the stand, looking nervous but purposeful. After identifying herself and answering a few background questions, she was brought to the events of the day before Russ's death.

"He went to church and he ushered and they was supposed to have come home and eat with us in the middle of the day," she said. "We love to have them over on Sunday. As many times as they could come, they would come and the day before, he had called and said, 'Mother, instead of us eating in the middle of the day, how about us eating at night?' "

She went on to tell of the supper and of Barbara going to sit near Russ. "She sat on the floor beside him and she reached up and held his hand, and as she did she looked at me. And Russ was sitting over to the opposite side of the chair with that hand over there and he didn't respond. By that, I mean usually he would have come over and kind of acknowledged, but he just sat there like this." She demonstrated the way he was sitting, indifferent to Barbara's obvious attentions, which Doris had come to believe to be a devious move to impress her.

Evenson next led Doris through the events of the morning of the shooting. Her words came in a gush and she fidgeted, wringing her hands as she told of arriving at the hospital and her experiences there.

Later, as she spoke of making funeral plans at the Terry house, Doris had a slip of the tongue that caused her to grasp her head with both hands, as if in horror at her own words.

"Al said he would like for Russ to be born," she said, then caught herself, "to be buried, to be buried, to be buried in our family plot . . ."

The judge interrupted to declare the lunch recess, and when court resumed Doris again took the stand to continue her story of Russ's death and its aftermath. At the funeral home on Tuesday morning, she said, Barbara had brought up the matter of Social Security benefits with the funeral home director.

"What did she say about Social Security in specific detail?" Evenson asked. "Drawing what kind of Social Security?"

"She was talking about drawing Social Security for the boys."

"On both boys?"

"Yes, sir."

Doris went on to describe her later, much longer conversation with Barbara about their strained relationship before Evenson brought an end to his questions.

Doris, he knew, had been a strong witness, holding the rapt attention of the jurors, who seemed obviously sympathetic to this tiny mother who had lost her son. Cotter could risk no cross-examination.

"No questions," he said.

As Doris left the jury stand, Barbara averted her eyes.

# Chapter Twenty-seven

Evenson continued building his case with Durham County Medical Examiner Franklin Honkanen. He told about examining Russ on the morning of the shooting and finding him brain-dead. When he went to the hospital's counseling room to talk with Barbara, she told him of waking, stretching, feeling something hard under her husband's pillow. She pulled it out, realized it was a gun, started to get out of bed with it.

"She was backing off the bed and the gun went off and hit him," Honkanen said. "I asked her if she knew approximately how far away she was at the time and if she could describe how the gun discharged. She said she didn't know how the gun went off, but it was in her hand and she thought she was somewhere at the edge of the bed, about three or four feet, maybe five feet away at most."

From her description, he said, he thought that "she was not holding the gun up but dragging it across the bed."

He had expressed his condolences, he said, and asked if she could recall any other details, but she couldn't. She had been "very upset and seemed very shaken" but had a good command of the facts when he had talked with her, Honkanen said.

"Now, before you ended your conversation, did she make one other statement to you?" Evenson said.

"Yes, when I was expressing my condolences and asking her if she could continue talking about it, she said she thought it was just a terrible accident and it was just something she was going to have to live with and she really hadn't grasped the fact that he was going to die."

"Said it was just something she was going to have to live with?" Evenson said for emphasis.

"Yes."

Detective Rick Buchanan took the stand in midafternoon. He first heard of the shooting when Honkannen called him, he said, and he told of going to the Terry house later that afternoon, where Barbara's father showed him the bedding.

"What did you tell them at the time?" Evenson asked.

"I told them as far as I was concerned, everything appeared to be accidental and I had no need for it and to clean the bedding would be fine."

Evenson led Buchanan to February 5, the day he and other officers had gone to Barbara's house in the hope of getting her to reenact the shooting.

"At this particular point, what was your posture regarding your investigation?" asked Evenson.

"Publicly it was listed as an accidental shooting. However, we were doing a more in-depth investigation."

The videotape of the reenactment was introduced, and Barbara cried as it was being played. After the tape had ended, the attorneys gathered at the bench. The jury was sent out and District Attorney Ron Stephens moved that the tape be played again, because the volume had been too low at the beginning. Cotter objected strenuously.

"It's just like asking a question, getting an answer and asking it again," he said. "It is just repeating what their evidence is."

The judge played the tape again for his own benefit before ruling that he would allow it to be played again only if the jury requested it.

After returning, the jury got to hear only one question (Did Buchanan have a conversation with Barbara at the time the tape was made?) before the judge intervened and sent them out again.

"I understand at this time the state by examination of this witness intends to bring in some evidence as to a prior husband?" the judge asked Evenson.

"Your Honor, that's not exactly what we're attempting to do."

There was no intention to introduce evidence of another shooting, Evenson explained, merely to show what Barbara had told the detectives.

"Is there going to be an objection?" the judge asked Cotter.

"I don't know. I haven't heard the exact question. I haven't heard the exact answer."

Evenson was instructed to continue his questioning out of the jury's hearing, and he asked if Barbara had made mention of a prior husband's death.

"Prior to the filming she stated she had not mentioned to me about her first husband being killed because she did not think it was important," Buchanan said.

"Is that all she said?"

"Yes."

After hearing Buchanan, Cotter renewed the motion he had filed before the trial asking that any evidence of Larry's death be denied admission.

"Do I understand that the state later on in the trial is going to attempt to offer more evidence as to the death of James Larry Ford but at this point this is all the state intends to go into?" the judge asked.

"That's correct, Your Honor," said Evenson.

Larry's death had been more than ten years earlier, Cotter reminded, and introducing it now would only be prejudicial.

The judge ruled that he would allow Buchanan to tell the jury what Barbara had said "over the strong objection of the defendant."

The jury returned and Buchanan continued his testimony, telling of Barbara's mentioning Larry's death and asking if she could get a copy of his report so that she could file for insurance. He went on to tell of other contacts with Barbara, stressing her concern about insurance, much to the satisfaction of the prosecutors.

Late in the afternoon, as Buchanan got to the search of Barbara's house, Evenson had a big cardboard box delivered to the witness stand. In it was the evidence that had been seized in the search. Cotter objected, and the judge asked the jury to leave. Cotter was concerned again about prejudicial evidence making its way to the jury.

Evenson said that he only wanted to have the evidence marked, not introduced at this time.

"How are you going to be prejudiced marking this and the jury not even seeing it?" the judge asked.

"I don't know," Cotter said. "He won't tell me."

"You tell me how you could be, any reason at all."

"I don't know. I don't know what they have in mind with it."

It was now 4:40. Everybody was growing weary from the long day of testimony and haggling, and Evenson suggested that the jury be released for the day. The judge called the jury back and let them go.

The first day of testimony came to a close with Buchanan identifying all of the many planned exhibits seized from Barbara's house, each marked and accepted by the court over Cotter's unrelenting objections.


The second day of testimony would see twenty-one witnesses take the stand. Buchanan returned to start the day's testimony, identifying the items that had been marked the day before and telling the jury where he had found each, as they were allowed into evidence. The jurors did not yet understand the significance of any of them, but Evenson would make sure they did by the end of the trial.

After all of it had been introduced, he had no more questions for Buchanan, and the detective braced himself for Cotter's cross-examination.

Cotter reminded Buchanan that on the day of the shooting, he had told Barbara's father that he considered Russ's death an accident.

"Were you being truthful with him?" he demanded.

"At that time, yes, sir."

"Did your feelings about whether or not this was an accident change between February first and February third?"

"No, sir. I was still trying to substantiate the accidental shooting."

He hadn't changed his mind, yet he had gone back to retrieve the bedding, Cotter said. "So by February third there was some reason for the examination?"

"I had received some additional information about the case."

"And you became suspicious?"

"Yes, sir, there was a little doubt."

Yet Buchanan had established a rapport with Barbara that was "fairly friendly," Cotter brought out, and every time he talked with her he had let her think he was looking at the shoot-

ing as an accident. He even had been quoted in the press as calling it an accident.

"And the entire time you were misleading her and the general
public by saying this was an accident, isn't that true?"

"To the best of my knowledge," Buchanan replied, "I am
under no legal or moral obligation to inform her of the status of
a criminal investigation."

"I understand that," Cotter said. "My question was—"

"In a sense," said Buchanan interrupting, "to her and to the
public it would be misleading."

"Well, not 'in a sense.' It would be flat misleading, right?"

Cotter moved on to Buchanan warning Barbara of her rights
before she talked with him on April 15.

"Isn't it true that she asked, 'Do I need a lawyer?' "

"I do not recall if she asked that or not. She may have."

"And you said that she did not?"

"No, sir."

"What did you say?"

"I never tell anyone they do not need a lawyer."

"What did you tell her?"

"I tell them it's their choice. It's up to them whether or not
they want to have an attorney."

Cotter and Buchanan liked each other and enjoyed sparring
in court. Buchanan took no offense at Cotter's effort to cast doubt
on his truthfulness and thought the jurors would be able to see
that in making those statements he simply was being a prudent
detective.

Evenson had a few more questions before Buchanan stepped
down, reemphasizing that Barbara had been told about her
rights.

"And she voluntarily gave the information?"

"That's correct."


Dr. Tom Clark, the state medical examiner who had performed the autopsy on Russ, used diagrams to show how the
bullet had entered the back of Russ's head, puncturing his skull
just to the right of midline at eartop level, passing through his
brain and fracturing his skull over his left eye before bouncing
back into his brain where Clark had found it.

"This causes bleeding," Dr. Clark told the jurors. "It causes swelling. It disrupts vital pathways that are essential to maintaining life."

With such an injury, Dr. Clark explained, the brain swells but has no place to go. At the back of the skull is a small hole where the spinal column connects. The areas of the brain that control respiration and other vital functions are just above that hole. That part of the brain gets squeezed into the hole by swelling and cut off from oxygen. The consequence is inescapable.

As Dr. Clark described Russ's injuries, Al Stager put his arm around his wife's shoulders and pulled her closer.

Not only did Dr. Clark draw the jurors a vivid picture of the injury that had killed Russ, he also clearly showed that the angle of the shot was downward. Every juror already had seen the videotape in which Barbara had shown how the shooting happened, and never could the angle have been downward.

Risking no further emphasis of this, Cotter had no questions and the morning recess was called.

Sergeant A. C. Webster, the Durham County Sheriff's Department firearms instructor and range director, came to the stand to tell the jurors of testing the pistol that killed Russ. He had tried to determine if it would jam, if it were prone to accidental discharges and in which direction it ejected shell casings. He fired eight rounds from a magazine, he said, and the pistol didn't jam. He beat it on a mat to see if it would discharge accidentally, but it didn't.

The shell casings, he said, ejected to the right and rear of the shooter, even when he fired the pistol on its side, as Barbara would have had to have fired it in her version of the shooting. The jurors already had heard several witnesses say that the shell casing was lying only inches from the pistol, near Russ's head, which would have meant that the casing ejected to the front and left if Barbara's version were true.

A telling flaw in her story was then revealed. The pistol had one unusual characteristic, Webster said. The safety was difficult to get to and to turn off. He demonstrated from the stand.

"It is hard for me to do it here," he said. "You have to come back and get your fingernail on it and get it down."

"But it does work?" Evenson asked.

"Yes, sir, it does work."

Evenson had people lined up to say how safety-conscious Russ had been, and he hoped the jurors would see that he would not likely have been sleeping with a pistol under his pillow and the safety off.

"So you're saying it is difficult to take the safety off," said Cotter, trying to dampen the impact.

"Yes, sir."

"So if a person wanted to have this gun ready to fire, they probably would have the safety off, wouldn't they?"

"It would kind of depend on the situation, I would imagine."

"No, no. My question is regardless of the situation, if a person wanted to have this gun ready to fire, they would have the safety off, wouldn't they?"

"Yes, sir."

"Because it might be difficult to get to the safety in time to fire as fast as they might want to fire, isn't that true?"

"Yes, sir."

After the lunch break, another firearms expert, Eugene Bishop of the SBI, showed the jurors how the pistol worked. He found it to have an erratic ejection pattern, he said. Eight times out of ten it ejected to the right and rear. But sometimes the casing hit the shooter in the face and at other times it went to the left, but always to the rear. The shell would travel two to six feet. In trigger-pull tests, he had found that it took four to four and a half pounds of pressure to make the hammer fall and cause the shell to fire.

"Could a child pull that trigger?" Cotter asked, on stronger ground here.

"It depends on the age, sir."

"A young child."

"How young?"

"Could a three- or four-year-old pull that trigger?"

"Possibly."

It also would be possible for someone to try to put the safety on and not get it all the way in place, leaving it off but thinking it was on, Bishop acknowledged.

"And that could happen pretty easily, couldn't it?" said Cotter.

"Yes, sir."

"It is not a very safe gun, is it?"

"If it is treated like a normal gun, it is a safe gun, yes, sir."

"It is not a safe gun to have under someone's pillow, is it?"

"Objection," said Stephens.

"I will let him give his answer to that," said the judge.

"Sir, I would not sleep with a gun under my pillow," Bishop said.

An SBI forensic chemist, Mike Creasy, told of examining the bedding and finding no sign that a weapon had been fired near it. He acknowledged that the bedding had been cleaned before he got it, and that would have removed any gunpowder or soot.

"I would still expect to find singe marks or actual damage to the fabric if a gun were discharged close to it," he said.

"Can you give the jury some idea about distances?" Evenson asked.

"With this particular type of gun, I would say it would be probably within six inches or less. It does not have a large flash to it."

On cross, Cotter made it clear that the singe marks would occur only on something that was directly in front of the muzzle when the pistol was fired. If Barbara had been holding the pistol above the sheets when it fired, no damage or residue would appear below.

"If you're six inches below, no, sir, it would not."

As for Barbara's supposed ignorance of guns, Sandra Biddle, wife of Russ's friend and fellow coach John, told jurors of a trip the two couples had made to Myrtle Beach, South Carolina, only a few months before Russ's death.

"She told me Russ was teaching her how to shoot a small handgun for protection," she said.

Gilly Boaz, a fellow member of the National Guard pistol team with whom Russ frequently practiced off-duty, was brought to the stand for two reasons. First he described the elaborate safety procedures that Russ had followed on the firing range. He also revealed that Russ had attended a military pistol coaching course so that he could teach others.

"Safety was a number-one item there," Boaz said.

Boaz also told of Russ bringing Barbara once to an indoor pistol range near Raleigh where they sometimes practiced. Russ showed her how to fire a .22 target pistol, he said.

"The clearest picture in my mind is of her standing there at the firing line and Russ instructing her how to use that pistol."

"Did she fire?" Evenson asked.

"Yes."

"How did she do?"

"She hit the paper, which is no small feat."

"Did she appear to be comfortable with it?"

"No, she did not."

Boaz said that the National Guard allowed pistol team members to check out .22 target pistols for extended periods and .45 match pistols usually for a week or less.

"Anything improper about him checking those pistols out?" Evenson asked.

"No, absolutely not."

On cross-examination, though, Cotter deflated the safety-conscious issue with ease.

"It takes a great deal of effort and a great deal of training to know a lot about a handgun, does it not?" Cotter asked Boaz.

"To know a lot, I would think so."

"And Russ Stager had a lot of training, didn't he?"

"More than most."

"How many guns do you have in your home now?"

"I have one."

"Where do you keep it?"

"I keep it under my bed."

"Is it loaded?"

"Yes, sir, it is."

"Why do you keep it loaded?"

"As a matter of expediency. It is hard to load a gun at night in the dark."

The gun was a Smith and Wesson Model 686, Boaz said, and it had no safety.

"It has no safety? You keep it under your bed ready to fire?" Cotter asked incredulously.

"Yes, sir, I do."

"And you know a lot about handguns, don't you?"

Cotter was grateful for little victories such as this one. He had had few such moments to relish so far. His objections had been constantly overruled by the judge, and he had been able to do little to keep the state from showing that Russ's death had been no accident and that Barbara's version of events was highly questionable. Moreover, he knew that the worst was yet to come.

# Chapter Twenty-eight

Evenson began laying out the motive for Russ's murder on Tuesday afternoon, when he presented a series of witnesses who revealed pieces of Barbara's tangled financial problems. All of it would become powerful ammunition when he tied it up for the jury in his final summation.

Teresa Long, a branch manager for First Union Bank, told of Barbara coming alone to the bank in January 1987 to get a $3,000 ninety-day loan to pay back a loan from a relative and pay off her First Advance card, which allowed her to get cash advances to a set limit. Barbara agreed not to use her First Advance card during the term of the loan, Long said. She also requested that any notices about the loan be sent to a different address than her home.

"She didn't want somebody at home finding out about it," Long said.

After Long moved to another branch, she received a call from loan officer Rob Willingham in July saying that Barbara wanted to renew the loan and increase its amount.

"I told him Barbara had not lived up to our verbal agreement not to use the First Advance and I would not increase the loan amount," Long said.

Willingham followed to tell that he had renewed the note for another ninety days after Barbara paid the interest. Later he renewed the note again, after once more denying Barbara's request to increase the amount, he said. The loan was paid off in October. Not until Wednesday did the jurors hear how Barbara eventually paid the note.

Eunice Peterson, manager of the Duke University Medical Center branch of Wachovia Bank, where Barbara had done her banking in recent years, said that Barbara had come to her on August 5, 1987, to ask for a $5,000 loan to pay off a ninety-day note at another bank and to pay her son's college tuition.

Barbara came alone, she said, and took the note home for Russ to sign. The loan was granted, with Barbara to pay back the money in forty-two monthly installments of $144.62 beginning on September 21.

Evenson asked why she had allowed Barbara to take the note home when policy required both spouses to sign in her presence.

"People I know and trust, you know, I felt were fine, I let them take the application home to the spouse to sign simply because it is difficult for employees' spouses to get to Duke and park in the deck and pay for parking."

Barbara had the loan for only two months before she returned asking for more money, Peterson said, telling her that she needed extra money to pay for braces for her younger son and to finance a study trip to Europe for herself. Again Peterson allowed her to take the note home for her husband's signature.

"I knew Mr. Stager was a teacher, and I knew it was difficult for him to leave and I knew Barbara and felt good about her taking it home," she explained.

This time Barbara wanted $10,000. When she returned with the note, the section requesting optional life insurance had been filled out, Peterson said.

Evenson asked who was insured.

"Russ's name is on that line."

"Okay, so that provides for what in the event of his death?"

"It pays off the loan."

"Okay," he added for emphasis, "in event of his death, is that correct?"

"Right."

The loan was secured by a lien on Russ's Blazer, Peterson said, and it was to be paid back in installments of $303.98 drafted monthly from Barbara's checking account. But when the first payment came due, there wasn't enough money in the account to pay it. Peterson said she called Barbara about it, and Barbara told her that she would make the payment soon.

When the second payment also came up short, Peterson testified, she called Barbara again.

"I told her that I would have to call Mr. Stager and see if I
could get the payment and she told me not to," Peterson said.
"She said that they were having problems and that there was,
you know, some other person involved, female involved, and
she would prefer I not call him and I did not."

Barbara, she said, had sounded "slightly upset."

The first two payments were finally made late by Barbara, and
by the time the third payment was due, Peterson had been promoted to branch manager and no longer was personally handling
Barbara's account.

The third payment was due January 28, 1988, and on February 1, a subordinate came to her, Peterson said, and told her that
that payment, too, had been returned for insufficient funds.

"I told her to call Barbara about the payment . . . and if we
couldn't get Barbara we were going to call Mr. Stager. And before
we did that, someone called us from downtown, or we just got
news, that Mr. Stager had died."

Evenson pointed out that Russ's signature on the loan application and car lien had been notarized by a bank employee.

"You asked her to notarize the signature, is that correct?"

"Right."

"Was Russ Stager in the bank at that time?"

"No, he wasn't. When Barbara brought it back, like I said,
Barbara was a nice person, I had no reason to believe that Russ
had not signed this, so I asked my employee to notarize this,
which was not an unusual request."

Cotter got Peterson to read the monthly incomes of Barbara
and Russ from the loan application, $2,800 for Russ, exactly half
that amount for Barbara.

"It is true, isn't it, that the person who is going to be insured
on any note is going to be the person with the greater income?"
he asked.

"No, that's left up to the customer."

Cotter finally got her to admit that it made sense to insure the
one with the greater income. "I mean, that would be the normal
way of doing it, wouldn't it?"

"Uh-huh, the usual way."

Still piecing together motive, Evenson brought to the stand a former bank teller who identified the $500 check drawn on Russ's credit union account that had caught the attention of his former wife and mother when they had sifted through the investigative files searching for clues. Barbara had deposited the check into her account on January 7, 1988, the teller said. Evenson wanted the jurors to see that this had been Barbara's desperate means of making the overdue monthly payment on the $10,000 loan that Russ knew nothing about. It was this check that had actually led to Russ's murder on February 1, Evenson believed, for soon after that date, he would have received his monthly statement containing the cancelled check. That surely would have led him to discover Barbara's new indebtedness. And that, Evenson was convinced, likely would have brought about a confrontation that would have been the death blow to Barbara's marriage. With Russ out of the way, the debt would be paid and Barbara would have a whole new pile of insurance money to begin spending.

To prove his theory, Evenson continued his parade of damning witnesses.

An insurance company official described two life insurance policies Russ had bought by mail, one for $50,000 only a year before his death, another for $23,000 eleven months before that. Barbara, he said, was the beneficiary of both.

Cotter objected to this testimony as irrelevant, but was overruled. He did bring out on cross examination, however, that Barbara also bought a $50,000 policy from the company, naming Russ as beneficiary.

Doris Stager returned to the stand to identify signatures of Russ and Barbara from cards, checks and other sources, the first of a series of witnesses who would demonstrate Barbara's guile. The next person called was Claire Clayton, the deputy clerk of court in Durham County.

Barbara had brought Russ's will to her office at midafternoon, four days after his death, she said. "She came in. She had a lady and a gentleman with her and they were the witnesses on the will and they signed before me that this was their handwriting on this will."

She identified the witnesses as Barbara's mother, brother and sister-in-law, and Evenson brought out that they had signed a sworn oath that they had witnessed Russ signing the will.

When his turn came, Cotter got Clayton to say that there was nothing unusual about the will, that most husbands leave every-thing to their wives, that insurance was not really affected by the will and that the house was owned jointly by Barbara and Russ.

"And isn't it true that by that kind of ownership, when one spouse dies, the house automatically goes to the other spouse?" he asked.

"That's correct."

"And it has nothing to do with the will?"

"No."

"So the insurance and the house were not affected by that will whatsoever, were they?"

"No."

A recess was called, and when court resumed, Clayton re-turned to the stand for more questioning by Cotter, who brought out that without the house and insurance, the entire worth of Russ's estate, according to the estimates Barbara had filed, was only $14,500.

Evenson cut to the heart of the matter with his next witness. When Durward Matheny, the SBI's supervisor of questioned doc-uments, took the stand, he identified three checks supposedly signed by Russ: a $1,500 check on his First Union account and a $175 check on his credit union account that were deposited in Barbara's account after his death, and also the $500 check on his credit union account that Barbara had put into her account in early January 1988.

None actually bore Russ's signature, Matheny said. The signa-tures had "enough similarity" to Barbara's, he said, "to warrant a degree of belief that she could have been the author."

The same was true, he noted, for a National Guard paycheck bearing Russ's purported endorsement that also was deposited after his death.

As to the signature on the October bank note for $10,000: "I could not identify him or eliminate him as being the author," Matheny testified, "mainly because this was a copy. It was very dark and hard to see, and we do not like to make identifications from copies." There were, however, "numerous differences" from his known signature.

The signature on the car lien that Barbara had brought to the bank along with the note definitely was not Russ's, Matheny said.

When Evenson brought out the will, Matheny left the stand to demonstrate his testimony with charts of the enlarged signature from the will, plus enlargements of the known signatures of both Russ and Barbara.

"It is my opinion that this is a simulation attempt of his signature," Matheny said of the signature on the will. "The very first thing I noticed was the letter A, which is a higher skill than Russell Stager had."

Everybody has a set writing skill, he explained. The level of skill can go down, but never up.

Using a pointer, Matheny noted the differences in the signature. "On the letter R and the letter S, if you will observe, it is very shaky. It was written very slowly and unnaturally. Russell Stager had a very casual handwriting style, but it flowed. There was no interruption. It was very smooth throughout."

Russ's Ls, he noted, were always very small. "Notice how tall and slender these Ls are on this particular document," he said, using the pointer to sweep along the letters.

"Each time he wrote the word Stager," Matheny said, pointing to the A in Russ's known signature, "it looks almost like a zero instead of an A. If you look closely, this looks very much like an A." The A also was unnatural, crammed against the G in the signature on the will, Matheny noted, and the Ss were closed in. "He left his Ss open."

There also were shoulders, marks broadening the top of the R, in his first name in the will, but Russ never put shoulders on the R.

"Someone was looking, or had a signature of his, and they were able to make this reproduction," he said.

"Who do you think wrote A. Russell Stager on that will?" Cotter asked as his first question.

"I have no idea," said Matheny. "In other words, it's a simulation. I do not know who simulated it."

"But you're absolutely sure that it's simulated?"

"Yes, sir. I have no doubt whatsoever."

Cotter brought up the $1,500 check.

"So you think it was written by Barbara? You think Russell Stager was written by his wife, Barbara?"

"I do."

This signature, Cotter brought out, was unlike the signature on the will. It was not a copy.

"There was no effort to simulate? This is Barbara Stager writing her husband's name on a check, is that correct?"

"That's correct."

The same was true, Cotter noted, for the other checks.

"It's all clearly her handwriting?"

"That's correct."

Cotter also got Matheny to admit that he had no idea who had written the signature on the bank note.

"The only thing I can say about it is in my opinion that is not his signature."

Later, Evenson would call Oma Smith, once a friend of Barbara and her mother, to testify about Russ's will. Smith and her husband, a Baptist minister, had visited Barbara's family on the day of the shooting. She now worked at the Fuquay School of Business at Duke University, but she once had worked at the medical center with Barbara. It was there, she said, that Barbara had come to see her about Russ's will.

"Barbara brought this in and asked if I would notarize it since I knew Russ's handwriting," she said. "I had typed a paper previously for him, and she said, 'You know his handwriting,' and she said, 'We're going to have a will made up later by a lawyer,' but in the meantime he travels with the National Guard and, you know, going to drill and whatever, and in the event something happened to him, and would I mind doing it for him, and I said I would be glad to."

She had asked Barbara where she wanted her to notarize it, she said, and Barbara replied that it didn't matter.

"I said, 'I'll put it underneath' [the signature], because there was no other names on the paper."

"No witnesses?" Evenson asked.

"No witnesses. No witnesses were in the room with us either."

"Do you remember when she brought it in?"

Smith thought that it was in the month of March, adding, "It has been a couple of years."

Cotter swooped in on this vagueness. "Isn't it a fact that this was done on February 5, 1988?"

"No. No, it was not."

"Four days after Russ died?"

"No," Smith said adamantly.

"Are you absolutely sure of that?"

"I'm positive."

"And isn't it a fact that these names," he indicated the witnesses, Barbara's mother, brother and sister-in-law, "already appeared on this will?"

"No, they were not. There were no names on that will and no one else was there. It was us."

As Smith came down from the stand, Barbara turned toward her family, silently mouthing, "Can you believe that?"

# Chapter Twenty-nine

Judge Allen had been alerted that a crucial point in the trial would be coming after lunch Wednesday, the third day of testimony, and when court reconvened, he called the attorneys to the bench for a brief conference, then asked the jury to leave the courtroom.

The prosecution wanted to introduce the evidence about Larry Ford, which had been mentioned earlier before the jury by Rick Buchanan.

"And you object?" the judge said to Cotter.

"Yes."

The judge decided to hear some of the testimony without the presence of the jury before allowing arguments about the admission of the evidence, and Robert Perry, one of the emergency medical technicians who had answered Barbara's call for help more than eleven years earlier, came to the stand.

He told of arriving at the house that night and Barbara meeting him at the kitchen door and saying, "He's upstairs. He has been shot and I think he's dead." Larry Ford was on the bed, he said, and he hurried to examine him.

"What was his condition?" Evenson asked.

"Well, you could tell from the looks of the skin that he was already dead."

After Perry had related what Barbara had told him about the shooting, Evenson brought out the photos taken of Larry and the room that night and got Perry to identify them. When describing the photo that showed the pistol clip on the bed, Perry said, "We turned the cover back and the clip was under the covers, as if he had been covered up. The clip was under the covers with him."

Perry told of calling his supervisor, Eddie Hoover. Asked why, he said, "It showed the possibilities of being suspicious."

Evenson asked about Barbara's reactions that night.

"She wasn't overly concerned," Perry said. "It seemed like she should be more upset in the situation."

Barbara's attitude was one reason he had become suspicious, Perry said. Another was the pistol.

"My wife owns a .25. It won't fire with the clip out of the gun, and I didn't expect that gun to fire with the clip out either. The clip being out of the gun and under the blanket, it just didn't ring true."

Had he discussed his suspicions with anyone? Evenson asked.

Only with his partner, Jim Owen. "Me and Jim, after we left the scene, discussed that things just didn't go together."

Cotter's first question was whether Perry had made any notes about the call that night.

Only the notations on the official records about the times he had responded, arrived and left the scene, Perry said.

"So you didn't write anything down other than the fact that you responded?"

"No. Some calls stick with you and that one did."

Quizzed about Barbara's demeanor, Perry responded, "Demeanor?"

"Yeah. How did she act?"

"Matter-of-factly, and you expect anybody in that situation to be very upset."

Did she cry, show any remorse, any signs of being upset at all? Cotter wanted to know.

"I don't really remember her being upset. Her demeanor didn't fit the situation."

"She didn't cry at all?"

"No."

How much of Larry's body was covered when Perry entered the room? Cotter wanted to know.

"About to the nipple line," Perry said.

"So it did not cover the wound?"

"I'm not real sure about covering the wound or not."

"Any damage to any of the bedsheets?"

"No. We checked that."

"No indication that the bullet went through any of the bed-clothes?"

"No."

"Did you see the wound before removing the bedclothes?"

"I can't exactly remember."

"So, actually, you don't know where those covers were, do you?"

"It has been a long time," Perry said, then remembered. "It was above the wound."

"How do you remember that?"

"Because of the indication of blood on the corner of the blanket."

Perry acknowledged that he and others who had been at Barbara's house that night had returned there with Durham County authorities to go over the details of the shooting.

When had that been? Cotter asked. After Barbara's indictment?

"I don't remember if it was at that time or not," Perry said, "but they indicated that the Durham case depended on the Randolph case."

"Who told you that?"

"I'm not real sure," Perry said, and Cotter had no more questions for him.

"All right," the judge said to Cotter. "And you object to this coming before the jury?"

"Absolutely."

"I will hear counsel on both sides," Allen said.

Cotter had his argument ready. "The state is trying to show she killed her first husband," he said. "It's what they want to show you, and it's what they want to show the jury."

That evidence, he claimed, was irrelevant, prejudicial and had no probative value.

Evenson's argument was more telling. He brought up nineteenth-century jurist John Henry Wigmore to defend his position.

"The argument here is purely from the point of view of the doctrine of chances, the instinctive recognition of that logical process which eliminates the element of innocent intent by multiplying instances of the same result."

He quoted from a ruling by Wigmore:

If A while hunting with B hears the bullet from B's gun whistling past his head, he is willing to accept B's bad aim or B's accidental tripping as a conceivable explanation. But if shortly afterwards the same thing happens again, and if on the third occasion A receives B's bullet in his body, the immediate inference (i.e., as a probability, perhaps not a certainty) is that B shot at A deliberately; because the chances of an inadvertent shooting on three successive similar occasions are extremely small.

"Your Honor, also we have prepared a list of similarities in this case," he said, handing up the list that he had collected over the months. The similarities numbered thirty-four and were listed in two columns, one marked "Ford," the other "Stager."

After Evenson went through the similarities, he acknowledged that while the evidence of Larry's death was prejudicial, the probative value of it outweighed the prejudice.

Finally, Judge Allen ruled that the evidence would be prejudicial but not unfairly so, and its probative value would outweigh any prejudice.

"After considering this matter, the Court does conclude that this evidence should be allowed for the purpose of showing any proof of intent, any plan, any preparation or the absence of accident in the shooting of Mr. Stager, and over the strong objections of the defendant, the Court is going to rule that it can be admitted."

Evenson brought Robert Perry back, and went through his earlier testimony for the jury. Perry also told of going back downstairs to tell Barbara that Larry was dead and to ask her what had happened. "She said something to the effect that he had bought the gun for her protection," he said.

He went on to tell of calling his supervisor, Eddie Hoover, to the scene, and of Hoover asking him and his partner, Jim Owen, to help bag Larry's hands so they would be protected for gunshot residue tests.

"When was it that you were interviewed about what happened in that particular room?" Evenson asked, hoping to emphasize how inadequate the Randolph County investigation had been.

"The first time was approximately six to nine months ago," Perry said.

"The very first time?" Evenson asked incredulously.

"Yes, sir."

Perry's partner that night, Jim Owen, told of meeting Barbara at the carport door. "And she was, you know, wasn't exactly very upset about the whole situation," he said. "That's what stuck in my mind.

"I recollect her saying to us that he had shot hisself cleaning the gun and that she was pretty sure, thought he was dead."

"Is this before you even went to see him?"

"This was before Robert and I went upstairs."

Owen went on to tell of examining Larry, turning him over to look for an exit wound, finding the clip under the cover.

"The whole situation was just very unusual," he said.

Later, at home, Owen told the jury, he talked with his wife about what had happened that night and drew a diagram of the room where Larry had died.

"The whole situation just bothered me a lot, and I felt like something should have been done," he said. "Mrs. Ford's reaction bothered me quite a bit."

"You were concerned about what you saw that evening?" Cotter asked when his turn came.

Owen nodded.

"Is that correct?"

"Yes, sir."

"Did you not write any notes down?"

"Excuse me?"

"You did not write any notes down?"

"I did at the time."

"You did write notes?" Cotter seemed surprised.

"Yes, sir."

Where were they? Cotter wanted to know, but Owen said that he had not been able to find them. They were on the back of the diagram he had drawn while talking with his wife.

Had he told Deputy Larry Allen, the first officer on the scene, about his concerns? Cotter asked.

"No, sir. I assumed that the sheriff's department would do their job."

"And did Mr. Allen not do his job?"

"I don't know. I know that another gentleman had taken over, a detective."

"Did he do his job?"

"I think not."


When court opened on Thursday morning, the state called Larry Allen. He told of spending ten minutes in the room with Larry's body before going downstairs to talk with Barbara and one of her neighbors.

"She told me she had been watching a movie on TV. I can't remember the name of it. *Having Your Baby,* or something." He went on to give Barbara's version of the evening.

"She said she heard a noise like a lamp fell off of a table or something. She went to the bedroom and looked and she saw her husband bleeding on the bed and appeared he had been shot."

Eddie Hoover, the former director of Randolph County's emergency services, now a police officer, would prove to be a more significant witness. First he told of being taken to see Larry's body by Jim Owen. "On the way, Owen said he had doubts that it was a suicide," Hoover said.

He told of taking measurements and filling out a medical examiner's worksheet. Then Evenson asked if he knew which way the shell casing ejected from the pistol with which Larry had been shot.

"Do you know anything about weapons?" Evenson asked him.

"Not that much," he said, going on to tell of helping Allen look for the empty shell casing.

First they searched the bed, but it wasn't there. "We moved things around and more or less disarranged the room." Then Allen put a shell into the gun and ejected it, he said. The shell went to the right and back.

After more searching, the empty casing was found on the floor between some tennis shoes, Hoover said, and he pointed out the location on the room diagram.

"At that point, we all looked at each other in amazement," he said, because if Larry had fired the shot that killed him, the shell shouldn't have been there.

After Hoover told of taping plastic bags around Larry's hands so gunshot residue tests could be performed to determine if Larry had fired the weapon, Evenson asked, "Was any such test done on Barbara Ford at the scene?"

"I can't recall any, no."

Next, Larry's mother, Doris Ford, walked resolutely to the stand.

She had arrived at her son's house that night at the same time as Barbara's parents, who had come from Durham, a much greater distance, she said. "Both sets of parents went in about the same time and we went into the living room. Her parents were one on each side of her and we were just so upset and you really just walk around. You don't know whether to go in the kitchen, upstairs or . . . we were just upset."

She talked of her son's funeral. "He was buried—would you believe the name of the church has left me . . ."

"Is it Cedarcrest?" Evenson offered.

That was it, she said, and she told of coming back to the house after returning to the grave to see the flowers and of Barbara beginning to give Larry's clothing away. As she told about the clothing, Doris shook with sobs.

"You had two grandsons by Larry, did you not?" Evenson asked.

"Right."

"When is the last time you saw in person, Barbara Ford, Barbara Stager?"

Cotter objected to the relevance of the question.

"You can connect this some way?" the judge asked Evenson, who changed his question.

"How long did she stay in the area?"

"That, sir, I don't know," Doris Ford said. "Bryan completed the rest of the school year, which may have possibly been the end of May or June."

"Is that the last time you saw him?" Evenson asked.

"Object. Irrelevant."

"I withdraw that question," Evenson said, but he knew that the jury no doubt understood what he was getting at, that the Fords had been denied access to their grandchildren.

"I have no further questions," he told the judge.

Cotter had none either, and Larry's father, Henry, came to the stand to tell about his son's military training.

"And did you ever have an occasion to see him handle a firearm of any nature?" Evenson asked.

"Yes, I did. I taught him to hunt squirrels."

"And did he know how to load a gun?"

"Yes, sir."

"And did you ever see him handle it?"

"Yes, sir. And clean it."

"Did he ever own a firearm?"

"Not to my knowledge."

Before the lunch recess, officials of three different insurance companies came to the stand to tell of the life insurance Barbara had received from Larry's death, one of them reading a letter Barbara had written just two days after Larry's funeral, trying to collect.

After lunch, the deputy clerk of court from Randolph County testified about Larry's will and the disposition of his estate.

Seeking to defuse the issue of Russ Stager's name being forged, Cotter asked if there ever had been any question about the authenticity of Larry's signature on the will.

"Not to my knowledge," she said.

"Who told you that was his signature?" Evenson asked on redirect.

"There were three witnesses that came in, a Mary W. Terry, a James N. Terry and a Marva R. Terry came in and verified it was his signature."

"And that was in 1978?" Evenson said, certain that the jury would see the similarity to Russ's death.

"Yes, sir."

Cotter had some more questions as well, getting her to say that she had turned the will over to the Durham County Sheriff's Department on April 26, 1988, only a few days after Barbara's arrest.

"So they had it over a year?"

"Yes, sir."

"To do with as they please?"

"Right."

Evenson came right back with another blow.

Michael Creasy from the SBI's crime lab was called back to

the stand to identify the pistol that had been the instrument of Larry's death and the handwipe kit that he had received from John Buheller. The tests sent by Buheller, he said, had revealed that no gunshot residue was found on Larry's hands.

Creasy said that he had fired the same pistol four times himself, once with his hand bent as it would have to be to fire the pistol at himself, and each time the gun had left what he called "significantly high" concentrations of residue.

Cotter had only one question:

"Your results are only as good as what was sent to you?"

"Correct, sir."

Evenson came back to get Creasy to explain that the chemicals in gunshot residue do not break down and will not evaporate. The greatest loss of residue from those who had fired a weapon usually came when they had been handcuffed behind their backs or had washed their hands, Creasy said. On a dead person the residue would remain until it was removed.

The next question to tackle was the possibility of the gun firing after being dropped. SBI firearms expert Eugene Bishop returned to the stand to tell of tests he had conducted on the gun that had been found beside Larry's bed. Using live rounds from which he had removed the projectile, he loaded the pistol and dropped it onto the floor from different heights to see if it would fire. Dropped from a foot in height, it didn't fire, he said. Neither did it fire from two feet, three feet, four feet, five feet. Dropped from six feet, it fired twice.

What if it had been dropped onto a carpeted floor from a height of less than five feet? Evenson asked.

"Sir, it did not fire when I dropped it on a tile floor, so in my opinion, it would not fire on a carpeted floor."

Evenson was pleased as Bishop left the stand, certain that he had shown the jurors that Larry's death could have been neither suicide nor accident. They could only conclude, he thought, that Barbara had gotten away with murder once and had convinced herself that she could do it again.

# Chapter Thirty

J udge Allen and the attorneys for both sides were well aware that the second of the two most contentious points of the trial would come on Friday, the fifth day of testimony, but the day began peaceably with the jurors examining physical evidence, Barbara's lawyer, Bill Cotter, objecting only to the evidence having to do with Larry's death.

The morning passed slowly as the jurors, in groups of four, closely examined the photos of Larry's body, the pistol, the box it had come in, his will, insurance policies and other items. As they passed the evidence from hand to hand, Evenson sat idly fingering the two pistols that had killed Larry and Russ. He twirled one, brought the barrel to his nose and sniffed. Later, as the jurors examined the pistols, the click of the safety on the gun that had killed Russ could be heard throughout the courtroom as they repeatedly pressed it off and on.

When the jurors were finished with the evidence, the lawyers huddled once more at the bench, mapping the plan for the battle that was to come. This day would decide whether the jurors would get to hear the tape recording that had been discovered just before the trial began.

The jury was sent out so the lawyers could argue, and Ron Stephens told the judge that he anticipated calling seven or eight witnesses about the tape. It was nearly eleven-thirty, he noted, and since the jury would not be involved in the maneuvering to come, perhaps the judge would want to release them for an early lunch.

That done, Cotter moved to sequester all the state's witnesses if the tape were to be played, so that they would not be influenced by the testimony of one another. Stephens countered with a similar motion for defense witnesses, and both were allowed.

After the witnesses had departed the courtroom, the judge declared that he would hear the witnesses about the tape, listen to the tape, then decide whether or not the jury would be allowed to hear it.

Frederick Evans, a lanky young black man who had played football and baseball for Russ at Durham High School, came to the stand and said that he had known Russ for four or five years.

Was he close to him? Evenson asked.

"About as close as any other student. He was easy to get along with."

"Did you find something there at the school?" Evenson asked.

"Yeah, I did," Evans replied, going on to say that it was during basketball practice the previous December.

"I was cleaning, getting the uniforms out of the dryer, and I walked downstairs and saw a tape up under one of the stalls of the bleachers in the locker room. . . . I knew my mom had a cassette that would play it, so I picked it up and took it home and gave it to her."

It was early in the morning when he found the tape, he recalled. He had some orange juice and wanted ice for it, so he had gone to the locker room to get it. That was when he saw the tape.

Where was the tape in relation to the coaches' offices? Evenson asked.

"The baseball coach's office is inside the locker room."

"Would you say fifteen or twenty feet?"

"Yes."

"A little longer than a free throw?"

"Yeah."

After finding the tape, Evans said, he had carried it upstairs, put it in his book bag and taken it home. Evenson handed him the tape, and he identified it as the one he had found.

Nobody had listened to the tape right away, Evans said, because the batteries in his mother's tape player were dead.

"It just sat there for a while and then one day my little brother took batteries and put them in there, and I guess he was just curious to listen to it."

"Did you hear it?" Evenson asked.

"Part of it. It was shocking to hear his voice."

"Whose voice did you hear?"

"Coach Stager."

"How did that make you feel?"

"It was shocking. Funny feeling on the inside."

After hearing it, he said, he had talked with his mother, trying to decide whether they should tell someone about it.

"We decided we would give it to one of her friends."

"Was that a police officer?"

"Yes."

On cross, Cotter tried to get Evans to pinpoint the time he had found the tape. It was during the holidays, Evans said. School was out. The basketball team was practicing for a Christmas tournament. Nobody was in any of the coaches' offices.

Cotter asked if the tape was difficult to see.

"Not really, because it was kind of leaning up against, leaning up against the table."

Hoping to indicate that the tape could have been planted, Cotter got Evans to demonstrate how it was leaning, then he backed up from the witness stand to get Evans to tell him how far the tape was from the office that Russ once had occupied.

Durham Police Officer Ralph Mack next testified that he had received a call from a man who worked with Linda Evans. Then she had come on the line and said that she had something she needed him to listen to. He had gone to her place of work about an hour later, he said, and she showed him a tape player with the tape in it.

"We sat there and listened to it together, and when it was over, she said, 'Someone needs this, because it could be some evidence.' Well, to be quite frank, I had forgotten about this particular incident and didn't even know if the trial had been held."

He took the tape, he said, went to the sheriff's office, called Detective Buchanan at home, then took the tape to his house.

Cotter had no questions.

Rick Buchanan followed Mack to the stand and told of making copies of the tape and providing one for Cotter. He said he had played the tape for Russ's family so that they could identify the voice.

To ensure authenticity, Mike Robertson, an SBI crime lab audio and video technician, testified that the tape showed no signs of tampering. The case never had been opened, there were no breaks in the tape, no splices or alterations of any kind.

The tape was a minicassette, not a microcassette, he said, and they were rare. Few were made anymore. Radio Shack had ceased production in the spring of 1987.

"Your Honor," Evenson said, after Robertson had identified the tape, "we would like to offer the tape at this time, and we would like to have it played."

"How long is it?" the judge asked.

"The entire tape is slightly over thirty minutes," Evenson said. "The voice portion is nine minutes and some few seconds."

The voice portion could be played, the judge said. Robertson inserted it into the tape player, and for the first time publicly, Russ's voice began telling of some of his concerns in the final days of his life.

"The last few nights, during sleep, Barbara has woke me up to give me some kind of medication. I have not taken it. Last night she woke me up and gave me what she said was two aspirin, but this was like four-thirty in the morning. She stood there to see if I took it. I did not take it. I placed it under the bed. She came back to check and make sure I had taken it, saying she wanted something to drink from what I was drinking.

"This morning—she normally is up and gone by seven—today at seven she was still in bed. She said that she was going to go to work at eight. Before I got up she was over around there on the side, acts like she was looking for what I supposedly took last night.

"Now this was the night of January the twenty-eighth, a Thursday night. So she stayed there looking to see if I had taken the stuff this morning. I got it out of there, although she was very . . . looking very close to see if I was trying to retrieve it.

"She made the comment that, 'You didn't take that . . . those aspirins that I gave you.' I said, 'Yeah, I did.'

"Well, I took the two capsules to Eckerd's Pharmacy at Forest Hills, and they said that it was sleeping pills. Now, if I was already asleep at four-thirty in the morning, *why* would somebody wake me up to give me two sleeping pills?

"Also at one time a few years ago I had to get a post office box because a lot of the mail coming to the house—bills and stuff—seemed to be disappearing when she got home first. Now I've only got one key to this post office box. For the last couple of weeks, every time I've turned around, she'd taken the key off the key ring and supposedly gone to check the mail herself.

"Now, a couple of months—December and January—I haven't even gotten the bill from Visa which she says she's called them and they said there's just been an, uh, misunderstanding. I don't understand myself why a person wouldn't send the bill if they had been sending it for a year every month and not missing—why all of a sudden they would miss. Here my question is, why every time I turn around she is taking that key and running over there to check the post office box unless there's something in there she's trying to hide, 'cause that's the reason I got the post office box to start off with, so I would make sure I got all the mail and nothing got misplaced or destroyed.

"Years ago, her grandmother died. On the day of the funeral she supposedly had to go somewhere to do something. I took one of the cars to wash it. When I was coming back through after washing the car and getting it filled up, I saw our other car sitting at the county stadium out there in the parking lot all by itself, nobody around. So I went across to the armory and sat in that parking lot waiting to see who came up.

"She came up with some guy. I couldn't see great, but I did see that they were in the car making out and stuff like this. When I went over there in my car, he took off and then she tried to put it off on me that uh, uh, I wasn't giving her affection and all this kind of stuff. Now that's pretty strange, to be doing it on the day that they're gonna put your grandmother in the ground, in my opinion.

"Barbara's second husband—the first one—I don't know what happened, but according to his parents there was some foul play going on. He supposedly accidentally shot himself in their bedroom with a pistol. Now, I have no idea what really went on, what really happened. She was there when it happened and so were the boys. My question is *did* her husband, Larry Ford, accidentally shoot himself?"

There was a brief break in the recording, a sudden loud squawk, as if the person speaking had been taping over music and had paused, backed up to listen, then advanced the tape a bit past the point where he had stopped talking. The voice returned in midsentence.

". . . I'm just being paranoid about all this stuff. Sometimes I wonder.

"When we lived on Falkirk Drive, numerous times policemen were coming over there supposedly to serve some kind of warrant on her for some bill she didn't pay. Now that's, uh, pretty tough considering that you're hiding that from your husband and everything, which it would be hard to hide from the law.

"She also took money from WTIK when she worked there and didn't do with it what she was supposed to do with it. It was like payment, but she never did the work, which I had to turn around and try and reimburse them for some of that.

"Also, at, uh, I think its, uh, one of the banks here in town that we tried to get a loan from knew her and because of that wouldn't even give us the loan, wouldn't give me the reason why but would not give us the loan. The bank was NCNB over on, uh, Duke Street. I still to this day don't know the reason, what she had done when she supposedly had worked there for a short time. But her parents were sitting right in there with me and they wouldn't give us any . . . any answer why.

"Also at CCB and First Union at one time she had flip-flopped some money that she supposedly had covered in the bank. But what she was doing was taking . . . writing a check from one bank, taking the money out of the other bank to cover that and vice versa, which obviously did not work.

"Uh, jiggling this money back and forth was done for some car payments which really weren't being made, and I had to come up with the money to pay the car off because the bank was ready to raise all kinds of cain.

"She supposedly signed my name on one of the bank cards . . . but really was not my name. . . ."

Another brief squawk followed before the voice returned.

"Back to Wednesday night, January the twenty-seventh. Barbara had given me something that was supposedly for sinuses and some, uh, and some aspirin that supposedly was Nuprin and about, uh, five that morning I woke up and I was feeling terrible. I was hurting real bad around my eyes, under my eyes, my temple and I really wonder if what she gave me was sinus medicine and Nuprin. She also . . . I also had a real bad case of the cotton-mouth. Even after all this, when she woke up and saw I was in pain, she actually tried to give me some more stuff, which I wouldn't take.

"What I would really . . . I really hope that I'm being paranoid about all this stuff that's going on, but I really wonder."

Another quick break.

"This is, uh, Russ Stager, uh, this is January 29, 1988, ten min-utes of two."

Nobody in the silent courtroom had to be told that three days later at that hour Russ would be dead with a bullet in his head.

Only shuffling could be heard as Robertson stopped the tape with more music playing. Judge Allen broke the spell that the haunting recorded voice had cast over the old courtroom, noting that it was well past time for the lunch break. Court would be re-cessed, he said, until two o'clock.

# Chapter Thirty-one

Testimony resumed with the jury still out and Cotter cross-examining Mike Robertson, who admitted that there was no way to tell if Russ had made the entire recording at one sitting. "I count eleven pauses that appear to be caused by manual function, either with the pause button or cutting it completely off and back on," he said.

Could the recording have been made over a period of months? Cotter asked.

"No way of telling," said Robertson. "I can't put a chronology on the tape. It's a voice recording. It's a free-air–type recording. It's not a patch-cord recording."

Cotter brought up background sounds that he had interpreted as pages being turned.

"There are points where I think he backs up, listens and then talks again," said Robertson. That would explain the music between voice segments.

Cotter got Robertson to play the tape again, listening for the background noise.

"I hear the noise you're talking about," Robertson said. "I don't know. The click is the pause switch on the tape recorder."

"But do you hear the other?" Cotter got him to play a section of the tape again. "Could that be a page turning from a notebook or pad?"

"I really don't know."

Cotter requested that more of the tape be replayed, interrupting to say, "Do you hear that noise?"

"I heard the noise you're talking about, but I can't tell you what it is."

Every move near the recorder would be picked up, Robertson pointed out, "a button on a coat brushing a tabletop."

The tape played on, until Cotter again called to stop it.

"Now, does that sound like a page turning? Does that sound like possibly not knowing what the next word is and turning the page and deciding what the next word is?"

Now Cotter's strategy was obvious. He wanted to make it appear that someone was impersonating Russ's voice and reading from a script, a plot possibly concocted by the police or prosecutors.

"I don't think I'm qualified to make that assumption," Robertson said.

When Cotter had finished, Evenson began calling witnesses to corroborate the information on the tape. Preston Adams admitted that he had been at Durham County Stadium with Barbara. Harry Welch confirmed that Barbara once had worked for him and had left owing his radio station money that she had been advanced against commissions.

Once again, though, Evenson knew who would make the strongest impression. "Doris Stager," he called, and once more Russ's mother made her resolute way to the stand.

"Would you tell the judge whose voice that is?"

"That is my son, Russell Stager."

Evenson then asked about the family meeting Doris had organized when Barbara and Russ found themselves in deep financial trouble.

"I said, 'Son, call Mr. and Mrs. Terry,' " she said, going on to tell about the gathering she had arranged to deal with the problem and of getting the post office box for his bills. She said, too, that Russ had told her about the incident at the stadium.

Evenson also called Russ's father to identify his son's voice and talk about the financial problems.

"Barbara had gotten them in debt," Al said. Russ had told him about all the overdue notices that kept coming and of giving Barbara money to pay bills, then discovering that she hadn't paid them. "He found bills under the chairs and in certain places and became real disturbed," Al said. But he never mentioned anything about officers coming to serve warrants on Barbara, he added.

"Call Cindy Thomas," Evenson said after Al had stepped down. Russ's sister had heard the tape for the first time only a short time earlier.

"It was Russ," she said firmly, and Cotter chose not to challenge her on it.

"Yes, it was Russell Stager," Jo Lynn Snow told Evenson, as if to say he had been her husband, she should know. She went on to inform them that Russ had spoken to her twice of his fears for his life.

Court recessed for the weekend after Jo Lynn left the stand, and on Monday morning, with the jury still out, Cotter began putting on witnesses to question the authenticity of the tape. Bryan Stager, the tall, thin, serious-looking son of Larry Ford, came to the stand to say he had known Russ as his father and had lived with him for ten years. He also had heard the tape that had been played in court Friday.

"In your opinion, is that your father's voice?" Cotter asked.

"No, sir."

"No further questions," said Cotter.

"Is that the only time you have heard that tape?" Evenson asked, his voice soft and gentle.

"No, sir." He had heard it at Cotter's office with his mother, brother and his mother's family, he said.

"And after you listened to it, did anybody say anything?"

"They just said it wasn't my dad."

"Who said that?"

"Everybody."

"Who said it first?"

"I can't recall."

"Was it you?"

"I don't think it was me, but I knew it wasn't him from the first couple of sentences."

"Was it your mom who said, 'That's not Russ?' "

"I can't recall who said it first."

"Has your mom also told you that wasn't him?"

"Well, we have all—we all know it's not him."

"Do you have any idea who it might be?"

"No, sir."

"Do you have any idea who might have all that information?"

"No, sir."

"I believe that's all I have."

Cotter had more questions of his witness, though.

"When was the first time you heard that, the very first time?"

"In your car."

"Was that Friday morning?"

"Yes, sir."

"Who was in the car besides you and me?"

"My brother Jason."

"And did I ask you before I asked Jason whether or not that was his voice?"

"Yes, sir."

"What did you say?"

"I said no, it wasn't."

Cotter went on to get Bryan to explain that he'd heard the tape for the second time in court, and for the third time at Cotter's office.

"And you still determined that was not your dad's voice?"

"Yes, sir."

The judge wanted to know how much of the tape Bryan had heard in Cotter's car—only a part of it—and when he had heard it at Cotter's office—just the day before.

"How soon after you started hearing that voice the first time in my car did you conclude it was not your father?" Cotter asked.

"Probably after the first couple of words."

Keith Belcher, Barbara's second cousin, said he had heard the tape on the TV news at home on Friday night.

"I picked up the telephone and called my mother," he said.

"What did you tell her?" Cotter asked.

"That I did not believe it was Russ's voice."

Bryant Webster, a student at the University of North Carolina at Chapel Hill, had been in Russ's and Barbara's Sunday school class and knew Russ's voice. He was not related to Barbara, he said, and had not heard the tape before it was played in court on Friday.

"I do not believe to the best of my knowledge that that is his voice on the tape," he said.

* * *

Judge Allen had been reading cases for three weeks in preparation for the lawyers' arguments over the tape, and he was ready to fend with them. Cotter maintained that the authenticity of the tape was in doubt, that it was hearsay and irrelevant, that it had cropped up so late that he hadn't had time to defend adequately against it. Evenson admitted that the tape was hearsay but countered that it was extremely relevant to show Russ's state of mind. He was willing to exempt parts of the tape that would reflect unfairly on Barbara's character—the affair, the money owed the radio station—but the rest should be admitted as an exception under the hearsay rules, he argued.

The judge wanted time to think about his decision and declared a twenty-minute recess. He returned looking solemn. He never had been a waffler, and he didn't fear being overturned by a higher court. He knew that he already had broken new legal ground in this trial by allowing the evidence of Larry Ford's death and he was not hesitant to do it again. Nobody had to guess that he had made up his mind. He spoke in a measured tone.

"In considering all of the evidence and arguments of counsel, the Court . . . finds as a fact that the voice on the tape is in fact the deceased, Russell Stager."

The tape, he said, would be allowed.

When the jury had returned, Fred Evans, the basketball player who had found the tape, again took the stand to tell his story to the jury. His mother followed to tell of the call she had received from her son after he heard the tape. He was upset, she said.

"I asked him, 'Do you know who he is?' and he told me. I asked him was he sure, and he told me he was."

After Officer Ralph Mack told of relaying the tape to Buchanan, Buchanan related how he had taken it to the SBI lab for tests, then got it back two days later and played it for the Stagers.

Mike Robertson, the SBI lab technician, again went through his testimony, and while he remained on the stand, the lawyers huddled before Judge Allen. Again the jury was sent out, and Evenson told the judge that he would ask that only the first section of the tape be played, only the parts about the sleeping pills and the bills.

The jury returned unaware of what they were about to hear, but when the tape began, none betrayed surprise that the voice they were hearing had to be that of the man whose death had brought them all together.

When the voice had been stopped by Robertson, as directed, the judge declared a recess for lunch.

After lunch, Russ's friend and fellow coach, Mike Wood, was sworn in. Soon after Russ's death, he said, he had cleaned out Russ's desk in the locker room office they had shared so that his belongings could be taken to Barbara. But one of the desk drawers was stuck and he couldn't get it open. A week or so later, he said, he forced the drawer open and a tape recorder slid to the front. It was gray, he said, with a clear face, a handle on the side.

"It was about that big," he said, gesturing with meaty hands, "played little minicassettes."

Just before the trial began, he said, Evenson had called him, told him about the tape and asked him to look for the recorder.

"I couldn't locate it in the office anywhere," he said.

Evenson had one more question. Did he recognize the voice on the tape that had been played just before lunch?

"That was Russ's voice."

Russ's sister, mother and father came to the stand one after the other to identify the voice as Russ's. After Al Stager had confirmed the voice, Evenson proceeded to nail down the source of the sleeping pills. He asked Al if he took any medications. Heart medicine, he said, and Dalmane for sleep, thirty-milligram tablets.

On one occasion during the previous year, he said, he had just gotten home from work and was looking through the day's mail when Barbara's car pulled into the driveway. She got out and came inside.

"We got to talking and she mentioned that she was having a little problem sleeping, wanted to know if I had any sleeping medication. And I said, 'The only thing I have is Dalmane, it's strong,' and she wanted some, so I said, 'Well, how many do you want?' And she said either two or three. I know I gave her at least two, but I told her that you ought to only just take one, because they are very high potent. They really put you to sleep."

Did he remember when that was?

"It must have been around the twenty-sixth or twenty-seventh of January."

Cotter tried to counter this as best he could. "Mr. Stager, do you know if any Dalmane was found in your son's body?"

"No, I don't."

"I have no further questions."

"You may step down," said the judge.

"That's the evidence for the state," Evenson said.

"The state rests?" asked the judge, his voice showing slight surprise.

"Yes, sir."

It was 2:09 P.M., May 15. The prosecutors had gotten in part of the tape of Russ's voice. They had gotten in Larry's death. They hoped that the jurors would put the two together and see what they had seen after hearing the tape: that in a small but telling way, it confirmed that Barbara had murdered Larry, too. The jurors had seen the photos of Larry's body on his bed. It appeared that he had been trying to get up when he was shot. Surely he had been awakened by some noise and had seen Barbara, or at least her silhouette, standing before him with a gun aimed at his heart. That must have haunted her, and that would explain why she had given Russ sleeping pills in the days before he was shot. She didn't want to risk him waking up and seeing her ultimate betrayal. That would explain, too, why Russ ultimately had been shot in the back of the head.

The prosecutors were satisfied, even though there was much that the jurors didn't know. Because the state was restricted from presenting any evidence adversely reflecting on her character, the jurors had heard nothing of Barbara's affairs, the warrants for bad checks, the job she had lost for mishandling money, the rumors and charges of a lesbian love triangle that had abounded after the death of her friend Kay Pugh. They knew nothing of the suspicions of Larry's parents and their long, futile struggle to see that something was done about their son's death.

The evidence of Barbara's tangled financial affairs in the year preceding Russ's death might have seemed less than clear. Had the jurors absorbed it? Did they understand? Would it be enough to show motivation? Evenson would have to depend on his final argument to make sure that they did.

"I would like to be heard," Cotter said.

When the jurors had filed out, Cotter entered a motion that the charges against Barbara be dismissed.

"There is nothing in the state's evidence that is inconsistent with what Barbara Stager demonstrated to the police on video," he said. "There is nothing inconsistent with what she told the police officers and what they have is a lot of other evidence about other circumstances that don't relate to this case, and I would ask Your Honor to dismiss it at this point."

The state offered no response.

"The defendant's motion to dismiss is denied," the judge quickly ruled, and ordered the jurors back.

# Chapter Thirty-two

Cotter wanted to make an opening statement, and the judge reminded the jurors that it was their duty to be open-minded at this point. What they were about to hear was not evidence.

The issue at stake, Cotter said, was what had happened on the morning of February 1, 1988, nothing more. The defense would show that Barbara had little knowledge of guns and was afraid of them, that Russ liked guns very much and slept with them, that he had four other loaded pistols in a nightstand by the bed.

"The evidence will show that this couple had money troubles from the day they got married until the day that Russell Stager died, that this was not something that just flared up toward February 1, 1988.

"They were both irresponsible about spending money and they were used to balancing money and doing different things to keep afloat."

About the financial matters after Russ's death, Cotter said, "The evidence will show Barbara was kind of in a daze. She didn't participate much in getting all of this stuff together."

Bryant Webster returned to the stand to say the voice on the tape was not Russ's. Likewise, Keith Belcher, Barbara's cousin, said that he had played softball with Russ each summer, and the voice on the tape wasn't Russ's.

After Barbara's son Bryan took the stand again, he said he had no doubt that the voice was not Russ's.

"You called him Dad?" Evenson asked when his turn came.

"Yes, sir."

"He adopted you as his own son, didn't he?"

"Yes, sir."

"He got you into the National Guard to help you pay for your college, didn't he?"

"It was sort of a joint decision."

"You wanted to take karate and he went with you?"

"Yes, sir."

"And he bought you a Volkswagen?"

"Yes, sir."

"And he bought you a truck?"

"Yes, sir."

"And he spent a lot of time with you, didn't he?"

"Pretty much, yes, sir."

"Went skiing with you?"

Bryan acknowledged with a nod.

"Took you squirrel hunting?"

"Yes, sir, one or two times."

"And he taught your Sunday school class, didn't he?"

"Yes, sir, he did."

"And you recall at one point when you were up for an award, I believe it was soldier of the month or something like that?"

"Yes, sir."

"And he talked proudly about you, he was beaming when you got that?"

"Yes, sir."

"Bryan, you know that's your dad, don't you, on the tape?" Evenson said softly.

"It's not him. It's not his voice."

"But you know it really is, don't you?"

"No, sir. It's not his voice."

Rebuffed, Evenson went on to ask about things Bryan had told the SBI agent who had talked with him after his mother's arrest. Did he remember saying that he didn't know that Russ had a .25-caliber pistol?

"I didn't know exactly what kind of guns he had."

Did he remember telling him he didn't recall his parents expressing any fear of prowlers?

"I was at school at the time, so I never really heard. I didn't really know anything about any prowlers."

"And were you told that Mr. Ford was cleaning the gun and it went off because he had forgot to unload it, did you tell them that?"

"That's what I always thought. I never knew exactly what happened."

"Never knew what happened," Evenson repeated. "Do you remember who told you that? Did your mom tell you that?"

"She may have. It might have been my uncle. I'm not sure."

"Okay, well, it certainly wasn't Mr. and Mrs. Ford, was it?"

"No, sir."

"The reason is you haven't seen them."

"That's right."

"This is the first time you have seen them in almost ten years, isn't it?"

"Yes, sir."

"Did you want to go see them?"

"They didn't make hardly any contact with us."

"Is that what you think?"

"I don't think that," Bryan replied adamantly. "I *know* that."

"How do you know that they made no contact?"

"The only contact we ever got from them was an occasional Christmas card, and that's it."

"Did you think that was a little odd?"

"Yes, sir."

"Did you ever want to drive up there after you got your license and see your grandparents?"

"I did, but I wasn't going to go up there uninvited."

"And did your mom ever talk to you about the Fords?"

"Occasionally, well, yes, sir."

"Did she tell you that they didn't want to see you?"

"No, sir."

Why hadn't he ever mentioned the Fords to the Stagers? Evenson asked.

"I don't know."

Was it true that the Stagers didn't even know the Fords' first names?

"I don't know what they know."

"Well, did you ever tell them about your grandparents?"

"No, sir."

Evenson brought up Bryan's and Jason's visits with the Monroes in Randolph County. Did Bryan ever think about dropping by to see his grandparents on one of those trips?

"Not really," he said.

On redirect, Cotter got Bryan to recall a meeting he had had with his mother and Russ.

"They had gone to this National Guard thing. It was them and Jason. I guess I was at school and I had come home, I guess the next weekend. They called me and Jason back to their room and said something to the effect that they had made out wills and they wanted to know what articles of jewelry and stuff like watches we would want if they were to die."

"Did you make a comment to them about that?"

"Yes, sir."

"What did you say?"

"I said it was kind of morbid for them to be doing that."

Did he remember the cars his mom and stepfather had?

"There was no way I could remember all of them, but I remember some of them."

"Approximately how many new cars did they have?"

"Around twenty."

"Tell me some of them."

"Cadillac. Mercedes. Mazda RX7. 280Z." Each, except for the 280Z, he failed to mention, had been his mother's car. "There were two boats also. Oldsmobile Royale. Broncos. Two of those. Cutlass Supreme. 228 Firebird. The Volkswagen I had, and the truck. Blazer. That's about all." Then he remembered the Mustang convertible his mother had been driving when Russ had died.

During a break after Bryan's testimony, his grandfather spotted him standing alone, tall and slim, looking so much like his father, the son Henry Ford had lost.

Henry approached him. "Bryan, when this is over, I want you to come and see us," he said. "Find out who we are."

"I don't know why you're doing what you're doing," Bryan replied, and walked away.

Cotter called Linwood Tew, one of the owners of Clements Funeral Home, which had handled Russ's funeral.

He had talked with Barbara on Tuesday, Tew said, the day before Russ's body had been sent for autopsy after it had been cleaned and embalmed. He had found nothing unusual about Barbara's demeanor or concerns, he said.

"I went over with her some of the things as far as benefits she may be eligible for, such as Social Security. And being in the military, there may be some military benefits available. She would need death certificates. Just basic information that we do for most all families."

Barbara's close friend Carol Galloway said that she had known Russ for a year or so before she met Barbara and had played golf with him. She and Barbara hadn't become close until Barbara and Russ joined their church, Homestead Heights, about a year before Russ's death, she said.

"I will ask you is that Russ Stager's voice?" Cotter said of the tape.

"In my opinion, it is not."

Was she sure?

"Absolutely."

Cotter took her through her actions after she had learned of Russ's death. She had gone to see Barbara at her parents' house, she said.

"What was she like? What was she acting like?"

"She was very emotional, very upset. It took probably forty-five minutes before we could even talk to her."

When she had asked what she could do, Carol said, Barbara had told her that the funeral home needed Russ's dress uniform. She offered to fetch it from Barbara's house. While she and her husband were looking for the uniform, she said, she noticed soiled towels and clothing and decided to take them home and wash them for Barbara.

"I'd picked up a red flannel, red plaid flannel nightshirt, or shirt, man's shirt, actually, that was covered in blood down the front and the insides of both arms. The sleeves had been rolled up, so it was probably this length," she said, demonstrating on her own arm, "and there was blood in this area right here."

Where would the length of the shirt reach on a woman Barbara's size? Cotter asked.

"Four or five inches below the waist."

Carol said that she had put the shirt into a laundry basket with towels and other items, and taken it home and washed it.

On Wednesday night after the funeral, she called Barbara and told her about the clothes.

"She told me that was the shirt she had on that morning, and she would just as soon not ever see it again. I was standing in the kitchen at the time. I walked into the laundry room, picked it up and threw it in the garbage can."

Cotter asked what she had found in the closet in Barbara's bedroom. Clothing, she said, mostly Russ's.

"On one side and a half of the other side were all men's clothes, and only one half of one side contained women's clothes and they were—do I go further?"

"Sure."

"They were quite expensive clothing. My husband and I both commented on the fact that there were a lot of clothes there, and I primarily buy my husband's clothes, so I am aware of the cost of men's clothes."

"Why is that important?" Evenson asked of her testimony about Russ's expensive clothing.

"It was important I think at the time we mentioned it, because of the fact that we knew Russ was a teacher and didn't work in a coat and tie, as my husband works in his business, so therefore we noted there was a lot of suits and a lot of expensive clothing."

"You're not trying to tell this jury that she didn't have nice clothes?"

"No, oh, no."

"As a matter of fact, she had real nice clothes and a lot of jewelry, didn't she?"

"I wouldn't say she had a lot of jewelry, no."

"Wasn't it true that just about every time you saw her, she had a new outfit on?"

"No, sir, it wasn't."

"She was well dressed, wasn't she?"

"I wouldn't say she was more well dressed than anybody else is."

Had she shopped with her? Evenson asked. No. Seen her use her credit card? No.

Had Barbara been in a room away from the coffin at the funeral home on the night before Russ's funeral?

"There was such a mob of people there that night that it's kind of hard to tell who was where," she said.

Did Barbara talk with anybody?

"As coherently as anybody could talk. At one point, she almost passed out and we had to take her out to an area where she could get some air. I never left her side that night."

Following a fifteen-minute recess, Cotter called Barbara's friend and former neighbor from Randolph County, Brenda Monroe, who recalled the activities at Barbara's house on the night Larry was killed.

Soon after she got to the house, she said, Barbara asked her to call her parents and the Fords to tell them of the death.

"I did call the Terrys, but I just didn't feel like I could call the Fords, and so I told them that we had called our pastor and to just wait and let him do that."

"Is that why they were called significantly later than the Terrys?"

"Yes."

How had Barbara acted? Cotter asked.

"She was upset. I was sitting beside her on the sofa, and I could feel her body shaking. She was trembling. I gave her a Valium."

The Valium, she said, had come from their pastor.

Cotter asked Monroe to describe Barbara's demeanor during the time she and the boys had stayed with them after Larry's death.

"Well, there was times when she broke down. Some days were better than others. We spent a lot of time entertaining the kids. I didn't discuss the thing much with her. We just tried to change the subject."

"Did she express any sorrow or sadness?" Cotter asked.

"Yes, she did. She said she missed Larry and that she didn't know what they were going to do without him."

"Did she cry?"

"Yes, she did."

"Were there times when she would cry a lot?"

"There was times when she cried, you know. I don't know what you mean by a lot."

Brenda said that her understanding of Larry's death was that the gun had been dropped and went off. She was there, she said, when Buheller had come to the house to discuss the shooting with Barbara.

"That was what with me standing listening, that's what I got had happened," she said. "He was commenting something about the cartridge went under the bed, you know. That was discussed. I do remember that."

Evenson went swiftly on the attack.

"Did she tell you that she went upstairs and she found Larry in the bed gurgling?"

"Yes, it was a gurgling noise."

"Did she tell you she called her mother first?"

"She had already called her mother when I called her mother, but Mrs. Terry didn't know then that Larry was dead."

"So she called Mrs. Terry first, and Mrs. Terry said, 'Hey, you need to call an ambulance,' is that what happened?"

"I don't know. I think she did call. I believe she did say she called her mother first, but I'm not sure."

Did she remember Barbara and the Terrys staying in a separate room at the funeral home, while the Fords were in the room with the coffin?

"No."

"You didn't notice that?"

"No, I didn't."

Barbara's sister-in-law, Mary Terry, an accountant and mother of two, said that she frequently had seen Barbara and Russ at family Sunday dinners at her in-laws' house. They also had gone to Duke football games with Russ and Barbara and often to their house to watch sporting events on cable TV.

The voice on the tape, she said, was not Russ's.

Had Mary helped Barbara settle affairs after Russ's death? Cotter asked.

"The day before, I asked her if she needed any help going through her paperwork. So we planned a time to meet, and we did that on Thursday after his death."

Barbara had been out and had just gotten home, Mary said. There was little conversation. "It was more like staring at the wall."

She asked Barbara if there were any insurance policies or notes that they could go through.

"She said, 'Yeah, it's around here somewhere. I'll have to go look for it.'"

Barbara went to the bedroom and came back with an expandable file, went through a drawer in the kitchen and found some things. It took her nearly twenty minutes to come up with the stuff, Mary claimed.

"She just set it there on the chair, and I took the papers out and just went through them and I tried to account for everything I could," Mary said.

She finally found several insurance policies, but some had old dates and she wasn't sure if they were valid, she said. Some turned out not to be.

"Did she know the status of her insurance?" Cotter asked.

"I don't think so. I would question her about different things . . . I would have to ask her two or three times just to get the information yes or no, if she knew anything about it. Most of the time I got a no. I just had to keep reading the policies until I could find something."

Was she the person who had come up with the $98,000 figure that had been put on documents at the office of the clerk of court? Cotter asked.

"It was around that amount, yes."

"That was your best guess at the time?"

She nodded.

"Did you find his or her will in that folder?" Cotter asked.

"I didn't see hers, but his was there."

After Larry's death, Mary said, she and her son had stayed for several days with Barbara "to have somebody there." Barbara had needed somebody to witness Larry's signature on his will, she said, and she had done so, using a letter about business that Larry had sent her to verify the signature.

Had she witnessed Russ's will as well?

She had witnessed the signature only, she said.

"I took the note payment from the Mustang, which was in his name only. I had that paper there and it was the same signature and that's all I did." Her husband also had signed it, she acknowledged.

"Was it notarized when you and Al signed it?"

"It was not."

Cotter then assaulted the question of debt head-on, trying to show that Russ was just as responsible. Mary recalled an occasion when Barbara had called to borrow $200 from her brother to pay an insurance bill. She and Al were thinking about buying a new house then, and only a few weeks later, they had gone looking at houses with Russ and Barbara. "Russ was driving and we were just driving around."

Russ mentioned that he and Barbara had just joined Croasdaile Country Club, she said.

"When I heard that, I got really hot, because here it was we were loaning our money out for someone to join a country club. We just brushed it off as a lesson learned, but it just really surprised us."

Cotter asked about the cars Russ and Barbara had owned.

"It started off, I think, with a Cadillac, and it went to a BMW, no Mercedes, not BMW. Then it went to . . . they sold the Mercedes—I remember having a conversation with Barbara that it paid for a station wagon, a boat, and, I'm thinking, a motorcycle. And then next thing I knew there were two Jeeps, one right after the other, because it seems like one was green and one was blue, and then I kind of lost track. I know there was a 280Z. There was an RX7. These are two-seater jobs, which we thought kind of strange, the four of them, you know, having a two-seater."

"Were they pretty free spenders?"

"Well, we couldn't keep up with them, so we just stopped trying, you know. There was no way."

"But you all made at least as much money as they did, didn't you?"

"I think so. I'm pretty sure we did. I never could understand how they could manage their money."

"Were they both equally spending money?"

"It appeared to me like they were. They had just as nice clothes as the other."

"Did you know whether or not they had Rolex watches?"

"Yeah, when they got those, I remember Barbara coming and saying, 'Look what Russ got me.' It was a joint thing. I know he loved fine things and so did she."

The final point to be made concerned the couple's marital status. Mary had last seen Russ on Sunday, the week before he died, she said.

"Anything unusual about the way he acted?"

"No," she said, going on to add that she actually was "kind of envious" of Barbara and Russ. "Because it really seemed like they got along great, I thought."

Evenson was once again quick to attack.

"You say as far as you were concerned, they looked like they got along great?"

"I thought they did. They always seemed happy together. Half the time I saw them, they were holding hands. He always called her honey."

"So he treated her nice?"

"Yeah, and vice versa. She always cooked him his favorite meal."

"In all appearances he loved her, is that correct?"

"Both ways."

"But it did appear he loved her, didn't it?"

"It appeared both ways."

"You're not answering my question, are you, ma'am?"

"Yes."

Evenson then challenged her on Russ's will. Oma Smith had testified that she had notarized Russ's will more than a year before his death, yet Mary had said the will had no seal. Would she say that Mrs. Smith was mistaken?

"I would."

"She would be lying about that?"

"Right, because the seal was not there."

Mary said that she didn't remember the will being dated, either.

"Any idea who would put that date on there after you went ahead and put your name on it?"

"I don't remember the date being there," Mary said.

Barbara's brother Alton followed his wife to the stand. He first declared that the voice on the tape was not Russ's, and Cotter got to the meat of the matter. Alton had gone to his sister's house with his brother Steve after the shooting and found numerous weapons in the bedroom.

"I know very little about any type of gun," he said, but he recalled a pump shotgun in the corner, two military pistols in the nightstand, "a cowboy revolver-style gun" and another small revolver.

"We could see the bullet in it," he said of one of the revolvers, "so him and myself took it out on the deck, which was just behind their bedroom, and my brother unloaded the shells out of that gun. The rest of them we wrapped in blankets. I know that sounds silly, but we wrapped them up in blankets because we didn't know if they were loaded or not."

They put the guns in the back of his car, he said, then checked Russ's Blazer. "There was another loaded pistol in the glove compartment."

Alton also recalled seeing several "Bowie-type" knives—"big meat-cutting–type knives mixed around in his dresser drawer."

He had told Detective Buchanan and Russ's sister about the weapons, Alton said. Cindy said she didn't want any of them, and Buchanan had told him they could be sold. National Guard officials had come to claim the military weapons, he said, and had unloaded the others.

Satisfied this point had been driven home, Cotter brought up Russ's will, knowing that if he didn't let Alton attempt to explain why he had witnessed Russ's forged signature, Evenson would make the matter look even worse.

"I was just floating around the house and I was asked to sign his signature," he said. There had been another document with Russ's signature on it. "I looked at that versus what was on the will and signed it stating that was his signature."

He had gone to the courthouse with his sister and mother, he said, because both were upset.

He was surprised, he said, when he got to the clerk's office and saw that the will had been notarized.

"I was really upset. I thought I had done the wrong thing. It scared me. I asked my mother, I said, 'When did you get it notarized?' and she said she knew somebody who had notarized it. I have been trembling ever since because it scared me that I had signed it and it was not notarized and all of a sudden it became notarized. That's all I was asked to do, just to verify that it looked like his signature."

On cross-examination, Evenson asked if Alton had based his opinion about Russ's voice on the tape from listening to the entire tape.

"Yes."

"Pretty shocking, some of the stuff on there, isn't it?"

"It's very shocking knowing both parties."

"As far as you know, Russ loved Barbara, is that true?"

"That's true."

"And he was an honest guy, wasn't he?"

"As far as I know."

"Nice guy?"

"Yeah."

"I believe you have in essence been through this twice, haven't you?"

"No, I have never testified."

"What I'm talking about, you have witnessed two wills?"

"I don't remember witnessing Larry's."

Evenson quickly moved to undercut the credibility of the witness. He got Alton to acknowledge that he had been to notary school, and Evenson handed him the affidavit he had signed when he had accompanied his sister to the office of the clerk of court with Russ's will.

"That is your signature, isn't it?"

"Yes, it is."

Evenson asked him to read item number three on the document, which swore that the attesting witness on the will had signed at the request of and in the presence of the deceased.

"Is that true?" Evenson asked.

"I don't understand what it's saying."

"You don't understand?" Evenson said, making no attempt to hide his contempt.

"You tell me, no."

"When you signed that, what did you think you were signing?"

"I had no idea."

"You just signed your name?"

Alton was clearly uncomfortable. "Well, no. Let's see if I can. I really don't know. It has been what? A year or so."

"Well, you take your time, and when you're ready, just let us know," Evenson said disdainfully.

Alton pondered the document. "Okay, I signed the paper as subscribed witness. That's what I signed."

"So in essence, did you see Russ sign that will?"

"No, I did not."

"But you signed your name and you took an oath on the Bible that you saw him sign that name, didn't you?"

"No, I did not. Not that I saw him sign, that that was his signature."

"Did she tell you it was his signature?" Evenson asked, nodding toward Barbara.

"Yes."

"She did?"

"Uh-huh."

"I have no further questions."

Cotter returned to safe ground with the next witness. Barbara's younger brother Steve was able to describe exactly the weapons he and Alton had found in Russ's bedroom: two military .45-caliber pistols, a .38 revolver, a .357 Magnum. The pistol found in the Blazer, he said, was a 9mm Browning semiautomatic. All were loaded, he said, and he had unloaded only one of the revolvers.

"Did Russ and you ever talk about guns?" Cotter asked.

"Yes, we did."

"Was he a gun collector?"

"I would say yes."

"Has she told you she was scared of guns?" Evenson asked, sweeping his hand toward Barbara at the defense table.

"I believe so."

"Terrified?"

"I don't know if she said she was terrified."

Did he tell investigators that Barbara had taken Russ's guns to a Durham gun shop and sold them?

"I can't remember what I told the investigators," Steve said.

"Is that possible?"

"It is possible. I believe she took them and sold them."

Had he told the investigators that he had never known Russ to sleep with a gun under his pillow?

"I don't remember."

"Did you tell the investigators that he had died in an odd way?"

"No," Steve said adamantly.


Barbara's mother, Marva, looking cool and reserved, followed her two sons to the stand. Cotter asked how she had come to sign Russ's will.

"Well, I went over to Barbara's to be with them, and Al and Mary were there. They had, I think, just witnessed Russ's signature and Barbara, well, some of them, indicated that it needed the third witness, and I witnessed that was his signature. Should I go on and tell about—"

"Tell anything you want about the will," Cotter said.

"Barbara called Oma Smith and asked to bring it over. She said yes, come on."

She had gone with her daughter, she said, and waited in the car while Barbara took it into the school of business at Duke where Oma Smith worked.

"I drove Barbara because she was in no condition to drive around herself."

Barbara had returned with the will notarized, she said, and they had taken it to the courthouse.

"As far as you were concerned, were you doing anything wrong about that will?" Cotter asked.

"No, not that I know."

Cotter then reemphasized Russ's free-spending ways. "Did Barbara and Russ have money problems?"

"From the day they got married," Marva said. "Well, beginning, I would say, very soon, maybe within the first month. Cars, golf clubs, diamonds, watches, just about anything you can name, boats."

Were they equally responsible for all the spending? Cotter asked.

"Well, I never knew that Barbara had any interest in boats," she said. "She never owned a diamond before. A lot of the stuff, she never had any interest in, I will say that."

Was she responsible for it at all?

"Partly, yes."

Was it a problem? Cotter wanted to know.

"Continually. Continually."

"Was that Russ Stager's voice?" Cotter asked.

"No," Marva said with an odd little smile. "Not the Russ Stager I knew."

Evenson would get little from her in cross-examination.

"How is she partly responsible for the financial trouble?" he started.

"Well, most families, both spend the money and that happened here."

"What was she spending it on?"

"Well, I don't know that anybody can answer that question. I would say she bought clothes and she bought maybe—whatever a woman usually spends the money on."

How did she come to know about the trouble? Evenson asked.

"Most people were familiar with it, I think. You could hardly know that people could buy a car every four or six weeks and not be in financial trouble."

Evenson led her through the troubles that caused Doris Stager to call a gathering to try to deal with Russ and Barbara's financial problems.

"We had a family meeting. The blame was put on Barbara at that point, so James and I said we would pay for her to get some help with managing her finances. The Stagers should have done the same thing for Russ, but they didn't. He was as much to blame, or more, than Barbara was. So we did that. She did get some help and we paid for it."

She and her husband also had gone to a bank with Barbara and Russ to see about getting a loan, but the bank wouldn't give it to them, she said.

"They were refused a loan, but I do not know the reason why."

Did she recall a name being mentioned when the bank turned down the loan? Evenson wanted to know. "Did they mention your daughter's name?"

"Well, I don't recall that. That's as much as I know about the bank situation."

After Barbara's arrest, Marva said, she had gone to her daughter's house with Richard Glaser, the lawyer who had been assigned to the case with Cotter, and when they came out, a man from the bank was waiting to tell them that he was going to take Russ's Blazer and Bryan's truck unless the loans on them were paid in full that day.

"I said, well, I would not like for Bryan to lose his truck," Marva recalled, "for somebody to go down to Wilmington and take his vehicle away from him, I will get the money." She paid off the truck, she said, but the bank took the Blazer.

She hadn't known of Barbara's troubles at the radio station until Russ told her, Marva said.

"So she did have some problems there?" Evenson said.

"Apparently, from what Russ said."

"Did you receive a phone call from your daughter when Larry Ford was shot?"

"I did. She told me that Larry had been hurt and she was afraid he was dying, and she was just so upset that I knew she did not have a good sense about her. And I said, 'Well, have you called the police and the rescue squad and whoever else you're supposed to call?' She said no. I said, 'You better hang up and do that.' "

"Is that when he was still gasping or gurgling?"

"I do not know."

"And you were long distance, is that correct?"

"That's correct."

"In Durham. She called you from Trinity."

"Right."

When the Fords and Terrys were together following Larry's death, were there times when Barbara would start to say something and she would stop her? Evenson inquired of Marva.

"What is this now?" Marva said.

Evenson made the question clearer.

"No," she said. "That's not true. No. No, it isn't."

"And did you grab her there in the funeral home and take her out at one point?"

"Possibly. I don't remember that, but I might have."

Did she and her husband take the bedding from Russ and Barbara's bed on the day Russ was shot?

"We did."

"Was it right after he died?"

"It was, yeah. Right after, or right before. I'm not sure. Maybe it was right after."

Frustrated, Evenson zeroed in on Marva's partiality.

"You did witness that will?"

"I did."

"Did Barbara tell you it was Russ's signature?"

"I knew it was."

"You're sure of that?"

"Mmmm-huh."

So the experts who had said the signature was forged were mistaken?

"In my opinion, they are."

"Was Mrs. Smith mistaken?"

"Absolutely, she is."

"She's lying about that?"

"She certainly did."

"She's lying?"

Marva nodded.

"She really hadn't seen Russ sign his name, as she had sworn, had she?"

"Well, to be frank with you, I'm like my son. I didn't read the document at the courthouse. I witnessed his signature."

This wasn't the first time she had done this, was it? Evenson asked.

"Well, this was the second time we have been through something like this."

Evenson had no more questions, and Cotter asked for a bench conference. It was only four-thirty, but things had moved along quicker than Cotter had thought. He had no more witnesses.

In response to a question from the judge, Cotter said that he might, or might not, have more, but he didn't want to make that decision until the following day.


Overnight, Cotter decided that he had to do at least two more things before resting his case.

First he wanted to attempt to plant doubt in the jurors' minds about Barbara's forgeries, and he had only one way of doing that. He called SBI handwriting expert Durward Matheny back to the stand to show that Larry Ford's will was authentic. If she had killed both husbands in such similar ways, wouldn't she have forged Larry's will as well?

Under Cotter's questioning, Matheny noted the Larry's will was dated 1975 but the only certified signatures of Larry's that he had to compare with the one on the will were prior to 1960. Still, his conclusion was favorable to Barbara.

"Based on those signatures, I said there was a degree of belief that he was the author of that signature."

Next Cotter had to deal with a problem he had seen developing as Evenson had cross-examined the witnesses who said that the voice on the audiotape was not Russ's. He realized that on rebuttal the prosecutors were going to ask the judge to let the jurors hear the unplayed portions of the tape, and if he did—and it seemed likely that he would—it would appear that Cotter had been trying to keep damaging information hidden. He decided to cut the state off before it could make its move and introduce the remainder of the tape himself. To set it up, he called a surprising witness: Doris Stager.

"Were you and Russ very close?" he asked.

"Very close."

"Did he confide in you?"

"Yes, sir. Even as a child, I was the one that always took him to his ball games, picked him up, made him study, go over multiplication tables, went to school with him.

"His daddy told him several things. One was if you get a spanking in school, when you get home you're going to get another one, and for years later, I did not know that my son had gotten a spanking.

"My son came to me. We were that close. My son's makeup and my makeup were more alike. The little things didn't bother us; we could work the little things out. And then when the big things came, that bothered. My daughter's temperament is more like her father."

Cotter had listened patiently as she had nervously gushed out her answer. "So he would confide in you?" he said, jumping in. "That was my question."

"I'm sorry. He would confide in me before he would anyone else."

Had she helped him at one time to get a post office box?

"I gave him the money. I suggested it."

Then Cotter asked a surprising question. Had Russ ever made a statement to her about finding Barbara's car at county stadium?

He had, Doris acknowledged.

Had he mentioned trying to borrow money and being refused?

That, too.

"That's all the questions I have," Cotter said. "Thank you, ma'am."

Evenson was taken aback by Cotter's question about the incident at the stadium. Cotter had to have a reason for bringing up a matter so detrimental to his client, and that reason only could be that he intended to try to let the jurors hear the unplayed portion of the tape to try to make it look as if the state had been trying to hide something, leaving the jurors to wonder perhaps if there was more that they still hadn't heard. Still, he had to seize the opening Cotter had handed him.

"Well, he has asked you about it. What did he tell you about the situation with the car, coming upon a car?"

"He told me that he came by county stadium and his car was sitting up there and he discovered Barbara and another man was in the car and when he drove up, the man got out of there in a hurry. And I can add something that I don't think I'm supposed to say anything prejudicial that he then said."

"Just hold it right there," Evenson said, going on to ask how the situation had come about that Russ had gone to the bank for a loan that he couldn't get.

Doris told about all the bills Russ had discovered, bills that he thought had been paid. "Russ told me he had found them hidden under a chair in his family room. That was on Falkirk. And he said that morning he was sitting there in the chair crying and Barbara came down there and said, 'You're spying on me,' and turned around and went back upstairs."

She went on to tell the jurors about the family gathering she had organized to deal with the problem, and how when Russ and Barbara had gone to the bank for a bill-consolidation loan, the loan officer had asked Barbara if she had been Barbara Ford.

Cotter objected, and the judge sustained.

"Did they get the loan?" Evenson asked.

"No, sir."

Cotter again called Mike Robertson, the SBI audio expert, to the stand and asked if there had been more on the tape than had been played, confirming Evenson's suspicion.

That was the case, Robertson acknowledged.

Cotter then moved that the part of the tape the jurors hadn't heard be played as well.

"I'm not inclined to do that," the judge told him after sending the jury out. "I'm inclined to order Mr. Robertson to play the entire tape. State?"

"Well, if he wants the tape to be played, he has the right to ask it to be played," Evenson asked. "I question his motivation. I'm not going to put any ideas in his head, but he's trying to telegraph to the jury something that really isn't what happened."

"I assure Mr. Evenson he will not put any ideas in my head," Cotter snapped.

Evenson said that it would be fine with the state if the entire tape were played, but he would object if only the unplayed parts were played.

The judge ruled that the whole tape could be played, but Cotter said that if the part already played were replayed, it would be over his objection. A long discussion and bench conferences ensued. Finally the judge granted Cotter's request to play the previously unplayed parts of Russ's voice.

After those parts were played for the jury, Cotter called Buchanan back to the stand and carried him through all of the things Barbara had told him in his interviews. He also brought out the *National Guard Guide to Family Readiness* that Buchanan had seized from Barbara's house and got him to read from the section on preparing wills and planning estates, attempting to show that Barbara had simply followed the advice given there.

Finally, Cotter got back to the tape.

"There's another voice on that tape that people can identify, is there not?"

"Not to my knowledge."

"You don't know?"

"No, sir."

"You really don't know?"

"I do not know."

Evenson got Buchanan to again go over the part of his interview with Barbara in which he had questioned her about the insurance benefits she would receive from Russ's death.

"But does she make any reference to the $50,000 term policy that was taken out by mail one year prior?"

"No, sir."

After Buchanan had stepped down, the judge called a fifteen-minute morning recess. "Call your next witness," he said after reconvening court.

"That's the evidence for the defendant," Cotter said.

"The defense rests?"

It was 11:10 A.M., May 16.

"That's right."

Although reporters and other spectators had speculated—and hoped—that Barbara might take the stand in her own defense, that had never really been a consideration for Cotter. He knew that the state had evidence of sexual affairs, lying, mishandling money. If Barbara took the stand, the prosecutors could question her about all of that, and if she denied it, they could bring in rebuttal witnesses. That would be devastating. Cotter couldn't even put up witnesses to say that Barbara was not the type of person who would commit murder without opening up the character issue. Cotter had felt severely restricted and was frustrated by it, he later said, yet he had no other choice.

"Rebuttal evidence for the state?" the judge asked.

Evenson called Russ's old friend Harry Welch back to the stand and Cotter asked to be heard.

Once again he renewed his motion to dismiss the charges. That denied, he objected to Welch being allowed to testify, claiming there was nothing that his additional testimony could rebut. It would corroborate what was on the tape that the jury hadn't heard when Welch had testified the first time, Evenson argued, and the judge allowed the testimony.

Evenson took Welch back through the meeting at Shoney's with Russ when he had told him that Barbara wasn't working at the radio station, as Russ had thought, and hadn't been for months.

"He got very emotional and teary-eyed," Welch said, "and he asked me, he said, 'Well, what has she been doing?' and I told him I did not know."

Evenson showed Welch the promissory note that Barbara had signed agreeing to pay back money she had been advanced against commissions she never earned, and he identified it.

Cotter had only one question: "And this occurred in 1982?"

"Yes, sir."

"That's the evidence," Evenson said.

"The state rests?"

"Yes, sir."

"Further evidence for the defendant?"

"No, Your Honor."

"Defense rests?"

"That's correct."

It was 11:29. The judge again asked the jurors to leave, and after denying Cotter's renewed motion to dismiss the charges, he conferred with the lawyers about the order for the afternoon. Final arguments would begin at one-thirty. The state would have the first and last. The defense would offer a single one between.

With the case now resting on the final arguments, reporters and others who had sat through the whole trial thought that Cotter had done little damage to the state's powerful case. Even Cotter himself looked worried.

But one person remained sublimely confident that the state's case would fail. No matter what the jurors had seen and heard, Barbara simply couldn't believe that they would think that she was a murderer.

# Chapter Thirty-three

Ron Stephens began the state's final arguments by telling the jurors that this was a tragic case and that they had to be totally objective in judging it, basing their decision solely on the evidence. It was not, he reminded them, a personality contest between lawyers.

"Mr. Cotter may contend to you that this is a conspiracy on the part of the state and police officers against Barbara Stager," he said. "I contend to you that you are the sole finders of facts in this case."

They should look closely, he reminded them, at the physical evidence, the more than one hundred exhibits that had been offered for their examination.

The pistol that killed Russ, he said, ejected its shell to the right and rear, but where had the shell been? Under Russ's pillow—with the pistol nearby.

"A staged situation," he said. "Physical evidence doesn't lie. Does not lie. Staged situation."

Then there was motive, he said. The state didn't have to show motive to prove murder, but he and Evenson had taken that extra step to show just why Russ had died. "We would contend that Barbara Stager tried to solve her money problems . . . by the death of Russ Stager. One hundred and sixty-five thousand cash alone just from life insurance. This is the lady who said, 'Well, I guess I'll just have to learn to live with it and go on about my life.' "

Why had the state brought the death of Barbara's first husband into this case? "To show intent," he said. "A plan, a scheme, and to show lack of accident." The state did not have to prove that she had killed Larry, too, he said, but simply had to show the similarities in the two deaths to demonstrate intent.

"You make your own assessment about what happened in the death of Larry Ford in 1978," he said, but he left no doubt of his own conviction.

"Randolph County just blew it," he said, "botched it, and maybe y'all'll decide that Barbara Stager hoped that Durham County was about to do the same thing."

Consider Deputy Allen's investigation of Larry's murder, Stephens said. "Decides it's an accident and he is back on patrol, forty-five minutes, cleared this one up, didn't talk to anyone around there, nothing, pretty much accepted the word of Barbara Stager."

After the hand wipings led to the body being exhumed, he said, "They decide, well, he must have dropped the gun, case closed and that's it."

Yet Larry had been shot straight on, he reminded. "He would have to be laying down on top of the gun trying to pick it up at the time it hit the floor for it to be anywhere close. But, hey, closed case, hey, no problem.

"Larry bled to death," he went on to note. "There was no effort to keep him from bleeding to death. Just let him bleed to death while she called mama."

And just look at all the similarities between the deaths of Larry and Russ. Could they all be truly coincidental?

He picked up the pistol that had been the instrument of Russ's death. "Do you know what that is?" he asked, pointing out the curving steel that protruded from beneath the gun. "That is a trigger guard." He held the pistol out sideways, demonstrating. "If it's laying down, I would contend you have to go to a lot of trouble to get that finger inside that trigger guard and around that trigger to be able to pull it for four and a half pounds' worth to shoot somebody with it, because that's what that trigger guard is all about."

He reached for the safety, fumbling to push it to show how difficult it was to take off, so that the weapon would fire. As many witnesses had testified, Russ was very safety-conscious, he noted. Would he really sleep with a loaded pistol under the pillow with the safety off?

Finally, he said, give close attention to the tape in which Russ told about his concerns about Barbara only three days before his death. And that was Russ's voice, he said, no doubt about it, no matter what Barbara's witnesses had said.

"They could not accept that that was Russ Stager's voice if they watched Russ Stager make the tape, because you think about it. If you accepted that that was Russ Stager's voice, then you would also have to accept that Barbara Stager, this mother, this daughter, this sister, this sister-in-law, this friend, this neighbor, is a cold-blooded murderer, and that is a fact that some people will not and just cannot accept.

"Does it not amaze you that this woman who sat in this courtroom, who has cried off and on during the course of this last week and a half, that this woman shed so few tears for the two men in her life that said until death do us part?

"She's guilty of first-degree murder," he said, and returned to his place at the prosecution table, leaving the floor to William Cotter.


"Mr. Stephens ended with that tape and I guess I will start with that tape," Cotter said, after thanking the jurors for their service and attentiveness. He reminded them of how the tape supposedly had been found, and just as Stephens and Evenson had suspected, he tried to make the jurors believe the tape was a planted fake.

"I can't believe that Mr. Evans had anything to do with that tape, but maybe Mr. Evans was not the one who was supposed to find it during Christmas vacation when students would not be in school.

"It's a mysterious thing, and when you play it, you don't know what people are going to say. You get mighty nervous."

Yet everybody he had played it for, nine or ten people, had immediately said that it wasn't Russ, and the jurors had heard from all of them.

"Do you think Bryan Stager was lying?" Cotter asked. "Well, he has reason to lie. That's his mother that's on trial for her life. I suppose if you're ever going to lie, that might be the one time, but he's also talking about his father and he also clearly said that's not his father's voice.

"Why would Carol Galloway lie? She knew Russ Stager first. She knew him better."

It was only natural, he said, that Russ's parents would say that it was his voice. "They want it to be his voice. They want Barbara Stager to be guilty of killing him because they honestly think she killed him. They are emotionally involved in it."

Acknowledging that some of the information on the tape could be verified, Cotter noted that it was he who had made that information available to the jury. "They played you the parts they wanted to play and they had no more evidence. They rested. I said, 'Okay, let's play the rest of the tape.' "

It was he, he said, who had put Doris Stager on the stand to say that she knew about not getting the loan, knew about the man at the stadium. Noting that the audio equipment was set up in the courtroom, Cotter said that the state no doubt would play the tape again in Evenson's final argument.

"Probably be helpful," he said, but the tape "just doesn't fit. It doesn't make sense that he would make a tape three days before he died."

He got the transcript and read the part in which Russ had wondered about Larry's death.

"It doesn't even sound like a normal way to speak. If he is wondering and worrying and concerned about that, why didn't he tell somebody? Why did he go home and sleep in a room with five loaded pistols?"

Then, almost as if he suspected the jurors might be thinking that he was grabbing at straws, he said, "Ladies and gentlemen, I can't tell you that a lot of this makes sense, because a lot of this does not make sense. It's not his voice."

Why hadn't the state put up others to swear that it was his voice? he asked. The EMT who knew him, the school secretary, the National Guard members?

"They are required to put on good solid evidence. Where are all of those people that were familiar with Russell Stager? Where are the rest of the coaches, the teachers? This is a serious case. Don't you think if they had these people who could say, yeah, that's his voice, they would be up here?

"I don't know. I just don't know about this tape. I think that tape is more problematic than anything else about this case. I think it's more problematic than where the cartridge was under the pillow."

Which brought him to the physical evidence and Barbara's version of what had happened. "Nothing she has said or nothing she has demonstrated is inconsistent with any of the physical evidence."

He picked up the pistol from the evidence table. "I assume she had the gun like this," he said, holding it out as Barbara had shown on the tape. "You could do this or this or that," he said, turning the pistol, "or this, and come up like that.

"If it's coming out of the bed like this, then that cartridge could have come out and just as easy hit her or that nightshirt or something and bounced back just as easily as it could have gone over her shoulder. Now if she were staging it, she wouldn't put the cartridge under the pillow, because that doesn't make sense. She could have knocked that cartridge with her knee when she was coming back to the bed to Russ."

As to the angle of the shot, Cotter said, Russ's head might have been deeper into the pillow, at a different angle than Barbara had shown the officers in the videotaping. "Barbara didn't know where Russ's head was at," he said. "The lights were out, she had no glasses. Nothing inconsistent about it."

About the location of the gun on the bed, Cotter said, "She dropped the gun and what happened to the gun after that, I don't know."

Having disposed of this matter, Cotter met the issue of Larry's death head-on.

"One of the ways they want to convince you that she killed Russ Stager is by taking something that happened ten years before, which there is no evidence of. If circumstantial evidence is so important, why didn't they take it and charge her in the death of Larry Ford? They want to give you bits and pieces and say, by the way, folks, really what are the odds of a woman whose husband is accidentally shot by a small handgun, a .25, ten years later having a second husband shot by a small handgun, a .25?

"Well, at first, your impression of that might not be very good. There's another way of looking at it, and the other way is if you flip a coin and nine times it comes up heads, the tenth time, the odds of it coming up heads are still fifty percent. Another way to look at it is, what are the odds of a person whose first husband dies of an accidental gunshot wound and then marries a person who is a member of a unit of the National Guard pistol team, who is a pistol aficionado, just nuts about having guns around? Well, actually, the odds are better because she's in a pool with men who have an excessive interest in handguns and it's more likely than the average person that her husband would die of an accidental gunshot wound."

The state wanted the jurors to believe the investigation of Larry's death was botched, he said, yet they wanted them to accept that the handwipe tests showing that Larry hadn't fired the gun that killed him were accurate.

"They can't have it both ways," he said. "Is this a sloppy investigation, or is it not? I don't know what Detective Buheller did. It was such a sloppy investigation he might not have done the right thing. Yet they say this part was well done."

Evenson had made a big deal, he said, out of all the similarities, yet there weren't as many as there might seem.

"Again, if they have any evidence that she killed Larry Ford, their duty is to charge her and she has never been charged. It's not fair. It's just flat not fair for you to convict Barbara Stager of murder because of anything that took place concerning Larry Ford."

He did know, however, that he had to answer the question: How could Larry have dropped the gun and still have been shot at a straight angle?

"If it fell and he was reaching for it, then it could have very easily gone off like that. That was a malfunction of the gun. That gun was not supposed to hit the floor and go off. Mr. Bishop acknowledged that was a malfunction. If the gun will malfunction twice at six feet, it will malfunction sometimes at two, three, four, five feet. The fact that it didn't when he dropped it doesn't mean anything. It's pure speculation, because we don't know."

Barbara, Cotter reminded, was not required to prove her innocence; she was presumed innocent, and the state had to prove her guilt beyond a reasonable doubt.

"Ladies and gentlemen, if you vote for first-degree murder, then you must decide that the state has proved to you beyond a reasonable doubt, then the only two possible punishments are life in prison and the death penalty. That's it. There is no option and you would decide that."

Don't be swayed by any other juror's position, he pleaded. "If you're not convinced beyond a reasonable doubt, it's your duty—and you said you would do your duty, that's why you're on the jury—to vote for not guilty."

# Chapter Thirty-four

A big easel was set up before the jury box. On it was a thick pad of oversized newsprint on which Eric Evenson had written key points to explain and emphasize the case he had spent so long developing.

"Ladies and gentlemen," he began, "there has been a tremendous amount of evidence presented in this case and just because there has been doesn't mean it's a complicated case. As a matter of fact, it's not. It's a very simple case, and for that reason I want to highlight some things that you have heard and maybe didn't catch. . . . Maybe as all the documentary evidence was going by, you said to yourself, well, there does seem to be something there and it doesn't seem to be absolutely legitimate, but I'm not sure how it all fits together. So these are some highlights that maybe will help you get a grasp on what's going on in this case.

"The first thing I decided to put up here on this chart is on January 10, 1987. I think this is significant."

That was the date, as the chart showed, that both Russ and Barbara had mailed in applications for $50,000 in term life insurance.

"Three days after that, as you will recall—this is all unrefuted, it's not refuted on cross examination—Barbara Stager goes to First Union Bank in Durham. She's alone."

That was when she got a loan for $3,000 to pay off a First Advance account and, supposedly, a relative.

"She tells Teresa Long, don't send any bills or notices to my house, there's someone there that I don't want to know about this loan. Now, who's she talking about? Is she talking about Jason? Is she talking about Bryan? Absolutely not. You know who she's talking about. She's talking about Russ Stager."

This, he noted, was a ninety-day note. On April 13, she would have to pay back $3,123.

Three weeks later, Barbara and Russ go to the same bank and borrow $4,500 to buy a truck for Bryan, this to be paid back in forty-two monthly payments. Their monthly payments increase.

On April 13, Evenson pointed out on his chart, Barbara returned to the bank, unable to pay the ninety-day note. She paid the interest and rolled it over for another ninety days. Russ still did not know. On July 13, the note is due again, and once more she can't pay. She not only wants to roll the note over again, she wants to borrow more money. Moreover, the bank discovers that she had broken her verbal agreement not to use her First Advance card, which already has more debt. She is allowed to roll over the original note but is denied additional money.

Three weeks pass, Evenson shows on his charts, and Barbara goes to another bank, Wachovia at Duke University Medical Center. She borrows $5,000, saying she needs it to pay off a ninety-day note and to pay college tuition for her son. She must repay it in forty-two payments of $144.62.

"Do you think that Russ Stager really knew about this loan when the reason for this loan was to pay off the ninety-day note? I would submit to you that he didn't know because she's alone on this one."

But the ninety-day note was not paid, and on October 13, it was due again. "So where does she go?" Evenson asked. Back to Wachovia, where she already owes $5,000 in addition to the earlier note. This time, she wants $10,000 to pay off both loans, buy braces for Jason and pay for a study trip to Europe.

"Did she tell the bank the truth that time?" Evenson asked. "She's alone on this one. She says, 'Look, can I take it home and get my husband's signature?' " She returned with the note signed, Evenson pointed out, the block checked to take out life insurance on Russ, plus the application for the lien on Russ's Blazer, which would provide the collateral, it too bearing Russ's signature, later to be found a forgery.

After the two earlier loans were paid, Evenson told the jurors, Barbara now had an extra $1,175. But she also had payments of

$303.98 per month for forty-two months to be deducted from her checking account.

Russ doesn't know about this, Evenson pointed out, and her salary is not enough to make these payments. But despite all the money she has received from banks in recent months, her account is empty. The automatic payment bounces when the first payment comes due on November twenty-eighth.

"So how is she going to pay this money? How is she going to pay it without Russ Stager knowing about it?. . . So what does Mrs. Peterson do? My goodness, you loan somebody $10,000 and they miss their very first payment. She gets on the phone and Barbara says, 'That's okay. I'll get it paid. I'll get it paid.'

"So when does Barbara make that payment for November? She makes it on December twenty-eighth, the day the second payment becomes due. But at that time she still doesn't have any money in her account. So the December payment comes up insufficient funds and what does Mrs. Peterson do? She calls Barbara and Barbara seems upset and she says, 'Please don't call my husband; we're having family problems.' And she talks about another woman.

"Now does that sound similar to something you have heard in this case? Do you really believe there was another woman? I suggest to you there wasn't, never has been, never will be."

But Mrs. Peterson doesn't want to cause trouble, Evenson noted, and Barbara was able to hold her off from telling Russ and letting him learn of this new big debt.

The overdue payment for December is brought to the bank on January 6, 1988, and on the following day a check for $500 is drawn from Russ's account at the credit union, payable to Barbara.

"It's a forgery, according to Agent Matheny. Now, who do you think drew that particular document? He says he can't be sure, but he had a high degree of belief that it was her signature."

That check was deposited into her account on January 7. The third payment on Barbara's loan was due January 28. It, too, bounced. The very next day, a check for $1,500 was drawn against Russ's First Union checking account. Another check for $175 was drawn against his credit union account that day as well. That was, Evenson noted, the same day that Russ was voicing his concerns about Barbara into a tape player at his office. Both checks were written to Barbara, Evenson noted, and Matheny had found Russ's signature on each to be a forgery.

That brought Evenson to the morning of February 1, 1988, and again he turned to his charts to show times of events. The call to the dispatcher came at 6:08, he said. The first deputy arrived at 6:18. Barbara and the deputy had arrived at the Duke Medical Center emergency room at 6:53. At 7:00 the school secretary received a call from Barbara saying Russ wouldn't be at school because he was sick.

"Ms. Cagle thought it was a normal sick call. Now, is it unreasonable for me to imply that a normal person under those circumstances would be hysterical at Duke Hospital at that moment? And yet Ms. Cagle thought it was a normal call. . . . At that time, Doris Stager is waking up. The phone doesn't ring at her house. She leaves for work at seven-fifty. The phone never rings once. At eight-forty, who calls but the defendant's mother and says, 'Doris, you need to come out to Duke emergency room. Barbara wants you out here.' Not get out here quick, there has been an accident. Barbara wants you out here. Now, why would the defendant's mother say Barbara wants you out here? Is this something that she feels like the victim's mother needs to know, that Barbara needs her out there? Why is she saying that?"

Russ had died at 12:35 that day, Evenson reminded the jurors, and at 2:15, Barbara's father had the bedding. "So isn't it interesting that on that day when he's shot and killed that the Terry family thought it was sufficiently important when all they had to do was comfort their daughter and their grandsons, they thought it was important to go and wash those things on that particular day."

That same day, too, Evenson reminded the jurors, the bank manager had instructed an employee to call Russ and tell him about the missed payment on the loan Barbara had negotiated, but it was too late. Russ was already dead.

And on the following day, the statement from Russ's credit union checking account was mailed, showing that a $500 forged check made out to Barbara had been written against his account nearly a month earlier. The implication was clear. Within a day, Russ would have learned of the forged check and that would have led to his discovery of Barbara's secret loans and financial shenanigans and a certain confrontation, one that Barbara couldn't face.

Also on the morning of February 2, Barbara had deposited two checks for $1,500 and $175 in her account, both dated January 29, both with Russ's name forged, an obvious move to clear his accounts of all cash before they fell into his estate and the accounts were frozen. Yet at eleven that morning she was at the funeral home. " 'I don't know what to do. I just don't know what to do. Do you need my Social Security card? Can I draw a Social Security check on these two boys for this husband along with the first husband?'

"On February the third, Russ Stager is buried. On February the fourth, she calls Chris Wagner. 'Chris, can you come over and pick up all of Russ's clothing, just get it out of the house?'

"On February the fifth, she phones Doris Stager. 'Was Russ ever in the regular army? I have been to the VA and was told that Russ had to be in the regular service before he would have insurance and was told the form number I would have to fill out.' This was Friday. At one-forty-five, Barbara reenacts the shooting. I want to play that for you at this time. Now, keep in mind I'm going to play this thing, and then I want to come back and point out some things on this tape because you really can't look at this tape too many times, and you see things that kind of pop out at you."

The tape was started, but Evenson stopped it after Barbara, a flickering image, had begun demonstrating what happened.

"All right. When she stretches her hand underneath the pillow, she feels something. I want you to think about that just a little bit. How many times has she told you in this case that he and she have argued about him sleeping with guns under the pillow? Do you really believe when she feels something that she had a doubt about what that was that she felt? She knew exactly what that was if there was a gun under the pillow. There was no gun under the pillow."

The tape resumed, but Evenson quickly stopped it again.

"Okay. Right there she said, 'I stayed asleep.' Her initial story was that the alarm went off in Jason's room. She says she fell back asleep. I would contend to you what she's telling the investigators is because she's thinking about evidence at this point. She's saying Jason got up. She has to give him time to get in the

shower because I would contend to you that when this happened Jason was in the shower. The phone call went out at six-
oh-eight. If his alarm clock went off at six, that gives you eight
minutes, so she has to give him time before she reaches under
the pillow to get that gun to let him get in the shower and I will
tell you why in just a minute."

Another short portion of the tape was played.

"Okay. Did you see how her hand was when she said, 'I
started pulling it out'? Her hand is right behind his head below
the midline—*below* the midline. That's totally inconsistent with
the physical evidence, and look how close the gun is at this
point."

Again the tape.

"She says she has no idea how her hand was. There's only
one way for that gun to go off, and she knows her finger was in
the trigger pull. It was inside the trigger guard. There's only one
way. She says, 'I heard the awful noise.' "

The tape.

" 'Now, wait a minute,' " Evenson said, echoing Barbara. 'That
wasn't quite right.' She has seen the errors she's making and she's
seeing how inherently ridiculous this story is, so she's going to
have to reposition his body because she does know the angle of
that bullet."

Tape.

"She knows how she had it in her hand."

Tape.

"She's thinking angle."

Tape.

"Why is she doing that? In just a minute you will hear her say
that she's blind without her glasses. As you will recall, Doug Griffin says the house was dark when he went in. How does she
know how his body was positioned to the point she can tell the
detectives as she runs her hand down the contour of his back
and pulls his head back? She's thinking angles and evidence. The
reason she knows the position of the body is because she was
able to clearly see it when the gun went off, and the reason was
that the light was on in the room, I contend to you, and she had
a clear shot."

Tape.

"Do you notice the hand gesture she's making? She's like this.

She's pointing the gun at his head, and it's right behind his head and it's still below the midline. Still *below*. You know, his head is naturally facing forward at this point. Your body just naturally goes forward if it's limp. It's a limp body. He has been shot. There's no rigor. It's limp. His head is slightly forward in the pillow."

Tape.

"Okay. He has the gun if it would help her. 'Oh, no, don't give me the gun. I can't stand guns. I'm terrified.' Yet she has the gun right there on his waist crawling all over him."

Tape.

"Okay. She doesn't even know how it was in her hand. It doesn't even register. She's fuzzy about that, she says, but do you recall the reason she says she was pulling out the gun? Because she heard Jason's alarm go off and she was afraid that Russ might think it was burglars. Something is not right here. You can't have it both ways. You can't be fuzzy-headed about how the gun was and at the same time have a clear head about what you're doing pulling that thing out."

Tape.

"Couldn't figure out what it was. Do you believe that? The .25-caliber goes off right in front of you, and you say I sort of realized what it was, heard the awful sound."

Tape.

"All right. She turns over and gets her glasses. Where's the gun? Where's the gun when she now turns over and gets the glasses? She doesn't tell you that, does she?"

Tape.

"See that? Did you all see that, what I was pointing at? Do you know what it was? It was a phone. It was a telephone. And on that same table did you see the lamp?"

Tape.

"Now, she says, 'I might have even turned him over some, like that.' Do you remember the EMT said the body was in a semifetal position with one leg on top of the other? If she rolled that body back, as she said she did, you know what happens to the leg, don't you? It falls over. There is no rigor. It's a limp body. He has been shot, so how is it that leg got back on top when the EMTs got there? It's because she never rolled him. She never rolled him one time. Don't you think she might have done that?"

Tape.

" 'I turned the light on, told Jason to call 911.' "

Tape.

"Okay. Earlier in the tape she said that she got up, she went to the bathroom, turned the light on, came back and saw what happened, saw the pillow. She saw the blood. Later in the tape, she says, 'I heard the awful sound,' said, 'Jason, call 911,' and then came back. Why did she tell Jason to call 911 if she hadn't yet turned the light on to see what's on the pillow? Where is Jason when this happens?"

The tape played out.

"Ladies and gentlemen," Evenson said, "as you can see, things are not right on that reenactment, and have never been right, and one of the main reasons is that the angle is all wrong. She told Dr. Honkanen she was three to five feet, getting off the bed, and just basically sliding the gun off the bed, but in this particular film, the gun is right behind his head. If the gun was like that, the bullet would have come right here and gone up through his head. She has to start repositioning his body. . . .

"Just think about the probabilities of the angles of the bullet. If that gun really went off accidentally, don't you think the probabilities are greater that it would have maybe blown off his ear, or gone in his neck, or off the top of his skull, or in his shoulder or back? But look at where that bullet hit. I hate to say it, but it's a bulls-eye. It's perfect, and does that show accident? The angle says more about this being intentional. This is the very back of his head. It's a perfect shot. Isn't it amazing that the one accidental shot on that occasion was so perfect?"

Evenson turned to the report written by Doug Griffin, the first person on the scene on the morning of the shooting, reading from it how Griffin had entered the darkened house, banging on the walls as he approached the bedroom. The door was slightly ajar, then it opened and the lights came on.

"Why aren't the lights on?" Evenson asked. "They should be on. She's standing in the dark. Did Jason phone in the dark? Did she cut the bathroom lights off that Jason had? She should be sitting there, I would contend to you, holding him in her arms. It's her husband. She loves him. Rocking him, head in her lap. Wouldn't she have wrapped a towel or something around his head? The EMTs didn't notice any blood on her. I think it would be vivid in their minds."

He read from the report about Griffin noticing the pistol and Barbara saying she had already moved it.

"What does that mean? 'I've already moved it.' You wouldn't have said that. And then the chant begins. 'Why does he keep those things in here? He has been hearing sounds. He placed the pistol under his pillow the night before.' I thought she didn't know the pistol was under there. Now she says he did place it under there. Did she ever say was he going to be all right? Oh, I love him, please help him, is he breathing? Please, is he going to be okay? Was this a case where the grieving wife was terribly and vitally concerned about the welfare of her husband, or is this a person who is being defensive and trying to set the stage for what has really happened?

"You know, in nature the praying mantis is so careful when he catches a fly. He's kind of a bulky insect and he can do it with so much care and stealth that he can catch a fly, yet a fly has five thousand eyes, and I would suggest to you that she was so careful in the way she had this thing set up that she almost fooled a lot of eyes out there, and as a matter of fact, Detective Buchanan said, 'Well, it looks like an accident to me.' Because, you see, this thing had been thought out.

"Why didn't she call somebody? Isn't it natural that when someone, your loved one, is hurt, you want to immediately get help? Why did she ask Jason to call? Well, I would suggest to you, when she went into the bathroom to get Jason, she told him to call and she set that place up. She picked up the shell casing, put it under the pillow. She picked the gun up, set the stage and anybody coming in there would be duped. They would think, well, she looks like a normal person to me, a housewife, two kids. I would never think that she could commit a murder like this—she's acting like she's upset. . . . And, you know, it's probably the best thing that ever happened that Detective Buchanan said, 'Well, it's an accident,' because she kind of dropped her guard in a way. You know, she went down and took that forged will and she thought the five thousand eyes were off of her, but they weren't."

Evenson next went into detail about what a safety-conscious person Russ was. "Do you really believe that somebody with that kind of background would sleep with a loaded pistol under their pillow? . . . A person who was safe would have to make all the following mistakes for this to happen. Number one, he would have to put a gun under his pillow; he would secondly have to load it; third, he would have to cock it. He would have to cock it and he would have to have a round in the chamber and he would have to have the safety off, and don't you think that if he was that safety-conscious that he would not have made all of those mistakes? I mean, if you don't have any other evidence, common sense tells you that would never happen."

Next Evenson turned to the strategies and tricks of lawyers.

"Do you know what they do if they don't have a case, if they don't want you to put their client on trial? They put everybody else in the courtroom on trial. They put the DA on trial. We haven't tried to cover anything up."

They had brought in seventy-four witnesses from eight states, he reminded. Yet Cotter had tried to make it appear that he was the one who wanted the entire tape of Russ's voice played, and the state was trying to keep certain parts out.

"The DA's office has a responsibility not only to try the case but to do it in a clean fashion. We have got to do it that way."

He had played the parts pertinent to the case, Evenson pointed out, but Cotter had been aware that he was asking all the defense witnesses if they had based their judgment about the voice on the entire tape. He had seen that the state might play the whole tape on rebuttal.

"So what did he do? He stole the thunder, as they say. I will play it, and then it can look like the DA is trying to hide something."

Evenson then turned to Barbara's supposed fear of guns, taking the jury back through Carlton Stanford's testimony and through her telling Buchanan of going to the gun shop with Russ to buy the pistol that killed him, questioning whether she truly was afraid of guns and knew little about them. Sandra Biddle had testified that Russ was teaching Barbara how to use the pistol for protection in the fall of 1987, he reminded the jurors.

"That was when the bank notes were coming up. That was when she was deep in debt without him knowing it. . . . Do you think it's possible she might have been asking Russ, 'Will you show me how to use this gun?' "

Evenson then turned to inconsistencies in Barbara's story of the shooting, pointing them out one by one.

"What if Russ had lived?" he asked. "What would she do? She couldn't fire twice. She had to make it good. She can't see without her glasses. I could suggest she probably turned the bathroom light on. It shines on the back of his head. It's a perfect shot.

"She had to wait until Jason was in the shower, because she was standing up or on top of the bed and was like this," he said, holding out his arms as if he were about to fire a pistol with both hands, "pointing at him. If Jason was in the shower, he won't walk in on her. Jason was out of the way."

Barbara fires, he said. "She puts the gun where she thinks it should be. She puts the shell casing there to set the stage, and then she turns the light off. She gets her son to call and says it's an accident. She waits for the EMT and then she starts her story.

"She knew she couldn't afford to miss because then Russ would be able to say what really happened. I guess you might say he was the only real witness and he didn't live to tell it.

"But he did tell it, and she doesn't like it one bit. He told exactly what was going on. Is it not odd that the loving wife shoots the loving husband and then gives everything away and she's down there probating the will before they even shovel all of the dirt on his box?"

Evenson now turned his attention to the will, noting the forgery, the conflict in testimony about the time the will was notarized. Of Barbara's family's testimony on that subject, he said, "Take it with a grain of salt because it's not consistent and it's not believable, and I would suggest to you that perhaps the stories are not fitting together just right."

After touching on insurance policies and Barbara's failure to mention to officers the $50,000 policy that had been taken out just the year before, Evenson moved on to Larry Ford's death, offering the pictures of Larry's body sprawled on the bed.

"That is the most awkward position that you would ever want your loved one to be in. His back is like this. His feet are off the side of the bed. He's up here, as she says, gasping for breath. He's gurgling. He's bleeding. He's wanting to breathe. This is her husband. Don't you think maybe she could have lifted his legs and got him a towel? But while he is gasping, she picks up the phone and . . . she calls her mother long distance in Durham, and her mother says, 'Well, you better call the ambulance or the police.' He's back in the bedroom and she's talking to her mom."

Just as she had with Russ, Evenson suggested, Barbara had staged the scene. She had placed the gun aimed toward Larry, had put the clip in the bed, perhaps had even moved the body to make it all fit.

"If you're going to kill somebody, you shoot them in a strategic place. You shoot them in the heart or you shoot them in the head. Accidents, you could be shot anywhere on your entire body. These two men were accidentally shot in strategic places."

About Cotter's argument that it was the duty of the state to bring charges if Larry's death could be shown to be murder, even if it were ten years later, Evenson asked, "Is he talking about us? The district attorney of Durham County has absolutely no jurisdiction to do anything about this case. He says they haven't charged because they have no evidence. Well, you heard the evidence. Sounds pretty good. He didn't fire the gun. He didn't drop it. Her stories are inconsistent.

"I don't need to argue all of the similarities of these cases. Two husbands shot in bed with .25-caliber semiautomatic pistols during normal sleeping when she's the only one in the house in essence. She's the last one with each man. She's the first one to discover the bodies. She's the one that is the beneficiary on the insurance policies. She's the beneficiary on both wills. She's the one that shows lack of true remorse in both cases, and she's the one that disposes of his items right after it happens. I ask you, do you really detect in all of the evidence that has been presented a deep grieving love for her husbands?

"See, the plans were made, the explanations were made, the showers were taken, the funerals were attended, the clothes were packed and moved out, the evidence was washed, the insurance forms were applied for, the will was probated and after that, sorry, kids, the dog got run over, life moves on, we're just going to have to live with it. Where is the heart?

"No one ever knew the dark turmoil seething in her mind. Her deceptions had their endings, but the truth should win and that's your job."

To help them come to truth, Evenson said, they had the benefit of true revelation.

"You have got the documents and you have got the spoken word. And where does the spoken word come from? It comes from the best witness of all. It comes from Russ Stager.

"Ladies and gentlemen of the jury, you have a rare opportunity today to hear from the actual victim. You all know it's him, because it's just too much detail. They want you to believe that someone else made that tape. No one else is going to simulate that voice. Your reason and common sense tell you that was his voice. And you know he's talking to you from his cold, wet shroud six feet under the earth, and he's telling you what really happened.

"I don't know where that tape came from. Maybe an angel flew into Durham High School and put it there because heaven couldn't tolerate this."

Once more Evenson had the tape played for the jurors, this time straight through, and as the voice echoed through the silences of the courtroom, the jurors listened as intently as if they could see Russ talking to them from his cold, wet shroud.

When the tape was finished, Evenson briefly went over a few points that he wanted to stress. Russ had been given pills on Wednesday night. He awoke at five on Thursday morning, an hour earlier than Jason's alarm. The next night he was again given pills but he didn't take them, and he awoke to find Barbara looking on his side of the bed to see if he had hidden them.

"On Friday, she has concern. Did he take the pills? So now does she wonder, is he on to her? The next six o'clock alarm for Jason would be that Monday, and that's when he was shot. And I would suggest to you that you're hearing his voice and that's the best evidence that you could ever want, is somebody telling you exactly what's really going on underneath the appearance. But appearance is not always reality. This is reality, and I would ask you to return a verdict of first-degree murder in this case."

The courtroom remained quiet after Evenson sat down, awed perhaps by the clarity of his summation. Nobody seemed to notice that the closing arguments had gone well past the court's normal time for adjournment. Judge Allen broke the silence to dismiss the jurors for the day and give them another night to think about all that they had seen and heard.

# Chapter Thirty-five

The judge's instructions to the jury took less than a half hour on Wednesday morning, May 17. When the jurors departed for deliberation, Judge Allen turned to the lawyers, but he was addressing everybody in the courtroom.

"I can appreciate the emotions and strong feelings on behalf of the friends and family members. . . . I'm talking to the four lawyers now, but I'm talking loud enough so everybody can hear me.

"If and when this jury comes back with a verdict, I do not want to hear from anybody except one of you four lawyers. I do not want to have any outbursts in the courtroom in any way."

It had been 9:55 when the jury went out, and the judge now put the courtroom at ease until a verdict could be reached. The judge retired to chambers. Reporters, witnesses and family members sat chatting softly in the courtroom, or wandered in the broad hallways to smoke or seek refreshment.

The jury room was located directly behind the judge's bench. It was small and hexagon-shaped, without windows. A stout rectangular oak table, big enough to accommodate twelve cushioned chairs, commanded the center of the room. A Bible lay in the center of the table.

After all the jurors had taken their seats, the first chosen, Norman Watkins, volunteered to be foreman. Nobody objected.

None of the jurors had any idea what the others had been thinking of all the evidence they'd been presented, and Watkins's first suggestion was that they take a turn around the table expressing their feelings. By the time the last juror had spoken, they all realized that they had been thinking the same way.

At 10:39, just forty-four minutes after the jurors had left the courtroom, a small clear electric bulb suddenly flashed at the edge of the judge's bench.

A buzz went through the courtroom. Surely the jurors had a question, some in the courtroom thought. They had not been gone long enough to have reached a verdict.

Word went through the courthouse. Spectators and witnesses hurried back to their seats. Technicians took their places at the stationary TV camera that had been recording the trial. Reporters scurried for closer seats, leaning intently into their notebooks. The judge was quickly fetched from his chambers.

"All right," the judge said, after taking his seat at the bench, "I do not know whether it's a verdict, but again, I will remind anybody if you can't control your emotions, please leave the courtroom now."

The judge leaned over to the bailiff. "You go see if they have a verdict," he said. "Bring them all in. Mr. Sheriff, you bring in the alternates."

The courtroom was taut with tension as the jurors filed back into the box, all wearing unreadable expressions. On their front-row bench Barbara's parents, sons and brothers reached for one another's hands, until they were linked in a solid line of support behind her.

"All right," the judge intoned, "let the record show the twelve jurors are now present and the alternates are in the courtroom. Ladies and gentlemen of the jury, have you reached a verdict?"

"Yes, we have," said Watkins.

"Would you have the foreperson hand the verdict sheet to the bailiff? Hand it to me, Mr. Bailiff."

The bailiff delivered the slim file folder to the bench. The judge looked it over briefly and straightened in his chair.

"I will hand the verdict sheet to the clerk," he said, passing it to Cynthia Myers, "and ask the clerk to take the verdict."

Myers stood. "Members of the jury, would you please stand?"

she said in a nervous voice straining to be strong. With the jurors standing, Myers turned and looked straight at Barbara.

"Members of the jury, in the case of the State of North Carolina versus Barbara Stager, you have returned as your unanimous verdict guilty of first-degree murder."

Barbara gasped deeply and burst into sobs. Her lawyers reached to comfort her.

"Is this your verdict?" Myers continued. "So say all of you by raising your hand."

All twelve jurors raised their hands.

Barbara raised her own hand to her heart and turned to face her family, her face stunned with grief and disbelief.

"Barbara, we love you," her friend Sherry Sims called.

"Thank you," the judge told the jurors. "You may sit. Let the record show that the jury has advised the clerk that the jury has found the defendant guilty of first-degree murder, and that all of them have raised their hands indicating that is their verdict. Would you like to have them polled?" he asked Cotter.

"Yes, sir," Cotter said somberly.

One by one the jurors stood and said that, yes, this was their verdict.

The trial now would go into its second phase, the judge told the jurors, but that would not begin until the next day. They still were not to talk to anybody about any aspect of the case, he reminded them before dismissing them for the day.

Judge Allen then revoked Barbara's $250,000 bond. She would not be going to lunch with her family today, would not be returning to their home in Durham this night.

"Do you want to be heard?" the judge asked Cotter.

"No, sir."

"All right, Mr. Sheriff, she's in your custody. Everybody else remain seated at this time."

Two deputies moved to Barbara's side to escort her to the Lee County jail. She seemed heavy on her feet, almost unable to walk. Behind her, friends and family sat as if in shock, some suppressing sobs.

As Barbara neared the door that would take her from the courtroom, she suddenly turned. "Bryan, Jay!" she cried. "I love you!"

"All right," said the judge as she disappeared through the door. "We will be at ease."

The tension in the room broke, and for a long moment an eerie stillness set in. People seemed reluctant to move.

Doris and Henry Ford and Doris and Al Stager remained seated, side by side, on their front-row bench, across the aisle from Barbara's family. Now Bryan stood and faced the four people he had known as his grandparents.

"I hope y'all over there are happy now," he cried angrily.

Cotter remained at the defense table, his shoulders sagging as if all spirit had drained from him. He stood as Barbara's father approached, offering his hand.

"You did the best you could," James Terry said.

Outside the swinging doors of the courtroom, a crowd of reporters and photographers lined the steps leading downstairs, waiting for the two families to emerge. Bright TV lights flicked on as Barbara's family and friends came out.

"Get the hell out of the way!" Jason yelled at a cameraman.

As Malbert Smith and his wife, Virginia, drove Doris and Al home that evening, a van pulled alongside their car containing members of the Terry family. Angry shouts came from the van. At one point the van swerved toward Smith's car before speeding away.

When the Stagers finally arrived home, they found a message on their answering machine:

"Kill! Kill! Kill!"

They recognized the voice, and it broke their hearts.

# Chapter Thirty-six

On the morning after the jurors had found her guilty, Barbara returned to face them looking beaten and listless in the same blue turtleneck blouse and print skirt that she had worn the day before.

Judge Allen began court by sending out the jury. SBI agent Steve Myers had come to his chambers earlier that morning to tell him about the threatening actions toward the Stagers the day before, and he wanted to make it known that any more such actions would result in harsh measures.

"I want to make an announcement right now," he said sternly. "It has come to my attention that yesterday some harsh words and some actions were exhibited by some folks. I do not know who did it. I don't care to know who did it at this point.

"Again, I realize and can appreciate deep emotions and strong feelings from relatives and friends of both the defendant and the deceased. I am not personally accusing anyone of any wrongful conduct. However, I want to warn everyone that I will not tolerate any outbursts whatsoever, any disruptions whatsoever, nor will I tolerate any threatening or harassing actions by anyone toward other people in this courtroom or around this courtroom."

After the judge had spoken his piece, Cotter asked again that the case be dismissed. His request was quickly denied.

For the sentencing hearing, Evenson said, the state would rest on the evidence already presented. Cotter, however, had many witnesses eager to speak on Barbara's goodness.

To send a person to death for murder in North Carolina, the

state must prove one or more of eleven aggravating
circumstances—that the crime was committed for money, that it
was done in the commission of another felony, that it was particularly heinous and so on. Stephens and Evenson felt certain that
they had shown without doubt the single aggravating circumstance that applied in Barbara's case: She had killed Russ for
money.

Any number of mitigating circumstances might save her, however, and Cotter and his partner, Edward Falcone, knew that their
only chance was to show that Barbara was indeed the warm and
loving person that many of her friends and family thought her to
be, that she still might be of service to others. Falcone was in
charge of the sentencing phase of Barbara's defense, and he conducted the questioning of Barbara's witnesses.

Worth Colvard, an accountant who had known Russ and Barbara for eight years, was first on the stand. He told of visiting
often with Russ and Barbara, of going on trips with them, lifting
weights with Russ, working with both in his church's youth
program—and Russ and Barbara didn't even go to their church,
he noted.

"She would do most anything she could for you," he said of
Barbara.

Colvard's wife, Phyllis, spoke of Jason and Bryan. "There are
no better children."

Ann Hilliard, who often sat with Barbara in church, said that
Barbara was there every Sunday and was active in all areas of
Homestead Heights Baptist Church. "She is a very loving, warm,
friendly person. There's no greater friend. She would do anything
in the world for you. If you have a problem, she will run right
over and help you."

"Did Russ love those kids?" Evenson asked Hilliard, who also
had spoken highly of Bryan and Jason.

"Yes, he did."

"And they loved him?"

"Yes, they did."

Charles Root, who had been pastor of Rose of Sharon Baptist
Church during the years that Russ and Barbara had been members there, told how they had taught Sunday school classes and
had led the church's youth program. They had taken a special in-

terest in his own son, Les, he said, giving him a lot of encouragement at a time when he needed it.

"I think he became a more confident person, more confident
in his Christian endeavors through his association with them," he
said of his son.

Root's wife, Linda, not only had known Barbara at church,
but had worked with her at Duke. "Barbara is a good listener,"
she said. "Barbara is a supportive friend. There were times I
needed to confide in Barbara and she was there for me."

"Russ was a strong church member?" Evenson asked her.

"Yes, he was."

"And he was just a good guy, wasn't he?"

"Yes, I thought an awful lot of Barbara and Russ."

Barbara's cousin, Carol Belcher, called Bryan and Jason two
"fine young Christian men."

"They respect people and I would be very proud if they were
my sons."

Barbara always made certain that they were at church, she
said. "She took them to church and she just raised them in a fine
Christian home."

"Did you know their natural father?" Evenson asked.

"Yes, I did."

"He was a nice guy, wasn't he?"

"I did not know Larry that well."

"Would it be fair to say Russ spent probably as much time
with those two boys as she did?"

"I would think so."

Ginger Payne said she had become very close to Barbara
when Barbara taught her Sunday school class during her final
year in high school. "She would take special time out for me,"
she said. "I was going through a hard time during my senior year
in school, and she was always there. She would take me places
just to talk, very loving friend, caring."

Had Barbara remained her friend? Cotter asked.

"Yes."

"Still?"

"Most definitely."

Vivian Burch spoke of Bryan and Jason. "Her children and
my children have been in and out of each other's homes for the

past three years." Jason and her son Joshua were best friends, she said, and her daughter Greta was close to Bryan.

"I know Jason and Bryan very well," she said, "as well as I do my own almost. Aside from being normally rascally boys, they're the kind of children that you would be very proud of, well behaved, sensitive. You couldn't ask for better."

Asked if Barbara were her friend, she said, "Yes, she is a very good friend. Barbara is my prayer partner. My husband and I were privileged to put our house up as part of her bonding to help get her out of jail."

Greta Burch, now a student at Wake Forest University, called Barbara "the best friend you could have. . . . She has been like my second mom. She was there for me when I needed her. She always writes me and I can always get advice from her, stuff I'm scared to ask my mom. She's just wonderful."

With those words, Falcone brought his string of praise-filled witnesses to an end. Cotter offered a computer printout showing that Barbara had no criminal record, not even traffic violations.

"That's our evidence," he said.

"Defense rests?"

"Yes, sir."

"Evidence for the state?"

"None, Your Honor," said Evenson.

Judge Allen sent the jurors out while he and the lawyers agreed on the wording he would use to instruct the jury. When the jurors were brought back, Allen told them that he would dismiss them for lunch. After lunch, he said, the lawyers would offer their final arguments.


Ron Stephens led off the prosecution. "I'm not going to preach to you," he said, but he went on to do just that, quoting from the Bible, " 'I know not, Lord, am I my brother's keeper?' "

"We are all our brother's keeper," he said. "That's what gives us security in this life. That's what makes us the nation we are, responsible for each other, a common bond. If she is not the keeper of Russ Stager, then we all rise up and we are all his keepers."

Stephens stressed that Barbara had killed Russ for money.

"Money was something that totally controlled her, completely engulfed her, was one of the most important things in her life, the motivating factor in the death of her husband, a killing obsession, this greed for money."

Most family murders, Stephens noted, are the result of passion, an explosive moment. "That's not what happened here," he said. Barbara had represented her marriage as happy, not volatile. "Therein lies the deceit, the treachery with this killing. That sets this killing apart, treachery, betrayal."

Stephens brought up his days as a helicopter pilot in Vietnam and recalled two Vietnamese pilots he had known who had been assassinated. "Maybe 'assassin' is not a proper term for Barbara Stager," he said, "but she flat-out eliminated Russ Stager. And this was not a Saturday-night domestic situation.

"Don't forget the manner of the killing," he told the jurors, calling it "a cold, methodical elimination as he lay sleeping.

"And for what? For what? For money . . . the most important thing in her life.

"And she knew the ropes about this," he said, bringing up Larry Ford's death. "This greed was nothing new for Barbara Stager."

There were two sides to Barbara, Stephens said, a public and a private side. And while he was certain that all of the morning's witnesses were sincere, he said, they had seen only one of Barbara's faces, and it was a convincing face indeed. But the other face had been shown during the trial, he said.

"We have seen that Barbara Stager is a liar, that she is a person who schemes, that she is deceitful, that she is treacherous.

"Barbara Stager doesn't have to answer to me. She doesn't have to answer to the family of Russ Stager. She doesn't even have to answer to the court for the crime she committed, but she has to answer to each one of you for that crime. I trust and know that you will do what is appropriate. We ask that you do justice in this case."

Evenson began his last appearance before the jury in a slow ramble, talking about how the trial had unfolded almost as if it had been a melodrama on TV, something apart from normal life, an abstract thing, and how the most important fact was pushed to the background.

"You know what I'm talking about," he said. "I'm talking about the fact that a living, breathing, walking, talking human being named Russ Stager is gone forever.

"It's almost like it really didn't happen, that he's just a photograph. You see, this could be an intellectual exercise, but for God's sake, ladies and gentlemen," he said, fire building in his voice, "don't forget that on the first day of February, 1988, that Russ Stager wanted to live just as bad as any of the rest of us. On that morning, he was in his own bed asleep. He was totally defenseless and he was at her mercy and she showed none. Now when they get up here in just a moment and they dance on the head of a pin and talk about mercy . . ."

"Objection," Cotter called, breaking the mood Evenson was setting.

The judge reminded the jurors not to consider Evenson's rhetoric as evidence. "You may proceed," he said.

"He was an innocent human being," Evenson said of Russ, "and he lies out there in his box under the sod because of the criminal conduct of that defendant seated over there. You know, he will never pitch another baseball. He will never go over to his mom's house and eat Sunday lunch. He will never coach another team. He will never serve his country again.

"You know, it's the little things in life that make it worthwhile. It's not the exciting things. It's not the money you spend or where you go. It's the breeze on your face and the sun on your head. You think about that when you walk out the courthouse doors, that he will never again experience those things.

"Sometimes it's hard for the jury to think about those realities because it does become kind of an abstract game where the lawyers block this move and keep this evidence out and try to get this evidence in, but that's why we're here, because he is not."

Evenson picked up the .25 from the exhibit table.

"Russ Stager was dispatched to eternity at the business end of this gun," he said. "Warm blood and tissue is no defense for the rip-roaring piece of hot lead that comes blowing out the end of that thing when the trigger is pulled, and I'm talking about brain tissue, and don't you know she knows that? She's seen what it can do before."

Evenson went on to describe how Barbara had reached for Russ's hand at his parents' house the night before he was shot, an open display of affection designed to fool his parents, he maintained. "Not once did she think about anybody but herself as she's holding his hand and she's setting his own mother up." Doris Stager had no idea, Evenson said, that in the morning her daughter-in-law would be blowing her son's brains out.

"Now you think about that. At dawn I'm going to be doing it when the death bell sounds at six. His son's alarm is his death bell. The alarm goes off and that's it. It was so well planned, you see. It was perfect. All for cash.

"The Bible says that the love of money is the root of all evil, and, ladies and gentlemen, you were witnesses to one of the greatest evils you can ever see when a wife murders her own husband for money."

She had showed no mercy, Evenson said, but her lawyers soon would be asking mercy for her. "One of the lawyers might step up here and say imposing capital punishment is seeking revenge. He might say that vengeance is mine, saith the Lord. This case has nothing to do with revenge. What we're talking about is justice."

Barbara's rights had been protected, he said. "But what rights did Russ Stager have that morning? She was his judge, jury and executioner. There was no due process. There was no well-lighted courtroom. There was only this defendant and this wicked weapon standing behind him."

Evenson went on to quote liberally from the Old Testament about the fate of those who murder, before he launched into the mitigating factors that Barbara's lawyers would be arguing in her behalf.

That she had reared two fine sons, regularly attended church and was a good friend to many was no excuse for murder, he said.

Her lawyers might argue about the horrors of the gas chamber, Evenson said, but think of the horrors that Russ had gone through.

Even sentenced to death, Barbara would have one advantage that Russ never had, he said. "She has got time to make peace with her maker.

"The only appropriate punishment in this case is the ultimate punishment. Capital punishment is a thunderous statement by

you and by society that we will not tolerate the taking of innocent life and especially cold-blooded murder by anyone."

In deciding for death, Evenson said, the jurors would not be
making the judgment.

"The judgment was already made on February the first. She
knew the law. She wrote her own judgment."


Edward Falcone had come into Barbara's case too late to take
much of a role in her defense, but he had questioned that morning's witnesses, and now he pleaded with the jurors to spare Barbara's life as "the right thing to do."

He reminded the jurors that their responsibility was grave.
"You have more legal power right now as you sit there than any
human being. Each and every one of you is responsible."

Barbara, he said, maintained her innocence. "But I am not
going to argue that point with you here. We're not asking you to
excuse what you have found Barbara Stager to have done.
There's a world of difference between excusing and mitigating."

Witnesses had said that Barbara didn't even know how much
money she was going to get from Russ's death, he noted. "Somebody's out to kill somebody just for money, don't you think they
would know exactly how much insurance we're talking about?"

What's more, he said, the single and questionable aggravating
factor was not greater than all the good in Barbara that the witnesses had told them about. "Your job is not just to tally," he
said. "Your job is to feel. I ask you to temper vengeance with
mercy. It's natural to lash out. Russ Stager had a right to live.
There is nothing you can do to bring him back. I say to you that
based on what you heard about Barbara Stager, her life is worth
saving. I ask you to send her to prison for the rest of her life,
where she won't harm anyone and where she can make peace
with her maker before God takes her away, and I ask you to let
God take her away and not the State of North Carolina."

The love and mercy of the New Testament should supersede
the harsh dictates of the Old Testament that Evenson had quoted,
Falcone said. "If Barbara Stager is executed, I ask you, will the
world be a safer place? A more loving place? Will the world be a
better place?"

This decision would remain with them for the rest of their

lives, Falcone reminded the jurors. "Make sure it's yours and not others'."

Barbara, he said, was a person, too. "She's human. Barbara breathes. She hurts. She hungers. She loves just like the rest of us. What you have said she did is a bad thing. There's no getting around that, but there is a lot of good in Barbara Stager. What I'm asking you to do is not to vote to kill Barbara Stager. Give her an opportunity to share that good with the people she loves. She'll be behind bars. It won't be a pleasant life. She'll be caged. But give her an opportunity to see Bryan, who's twenty, finish college, see Jason, who's fourteen, grow from a fine young man into an adult. Don't make them see their mother die.

"Let her see the birthdays of her parents, Marva and James, her brothers, Steve and Al. I'm not asking you to set Barbara Stager free. I'm not asking you not to punish Barbara Stager. I'm asking you to put her in prison for life. There is reason to let her live, and I ask you to do so."

Bill Cotter looked as if the weight of the world rested on his slumped shoulders as he rose to fight his last, life-or-death round on Barbara's behalf.

He reminded the jurors of how he had questioned them about their feelings about the death penalty during jury selection. He had done that, he said, so the jury would be made up of people who understood that just because a person was convicted of first-degree murder, the law did not require death.

"You have found her guilty and that's a done deal," he said. "She is a murderer. I'm not going to quarrel with your decision. You heard the evidence. Some of the evidence I would have preferred you did not hear. Some of the evidence I didn't think was fair, but I was overruled. You have found her guilty beyond reasonable doubt, and you did so in overwhelming fashion.

"I'm afraid that you're going to go back there and vote to put her to death," he said, his voice breaking. "I really am afraid of that, and I would ask you not to."

One of the problems with the death penalty is that it is final, he said. "Then five years later, eight years later, they find out a certain tape was not really a tape of Russ Stager's voice, or they find out that some evidence was not proper, or that it was made up."

The system is not perfect, he noted, reminiscing about a recent TV show he had seen about the assassination of John F. Kennedy. No other murder had ever been the focus of such a massive investigation. All the greatest experts were called into it. "And after all these years, they have more questions than answers."

If the jurors sentenced Barbara to death, he reminded, a date would be set. It would be changed several times, but eventually she would be led down a hallway and killed. "And if anything comes up years later, it's too late. She's dead."

The death penalty should be reserved for cases that go beyond horrible, Cotter said, "reserved for people who are so wicked and evil and so inhuman that there's absolutely no reason that they should live." Cotter went on to cite horrible cases that would justify the death penalty, but this, he maintained, was not such a case. Barbara was not a worthless person.

"She is described as she might have two faces. Well, maybe she has two faces. We all have more than one. She has two sides. Even if she has two sides, even if there is something despicably wrong with her character, so twisted that because she is in such a bind about money, the only way she can reason to get out of that is to kill her husband, even if she has that character defect, that is not enough to kill Barbara Stager.

"I have to assume you're going to find that the murder was committed for pecuniary gain. I'm not a fool. You were out for forty-five minutes. I have to assume you believe most, if not every single bit, of the state's evidence, and at least a third was Barbara shifting money around and needing money."

That was but one aggravating factor, one of eleven possible to justify death, he pointed out, and the mitigating factors in Barbara's favor should outweigh it.

"I'm not saying, yeah, that makes murder okay, the fact that she raised two fine children, that she was a good friend. Nothing makes murder okay. . . . There's some good in Barbara Stager. There's some decency and humanity."

Barbara was not likely to kill anybody in prison, he said. Nor was she apt to escape from prison and kill somebody. She had been out of jail for a year, he pointed out, without harming a soul. She was not aggressive. "She's a rather peaceful, quiet, meek, scared, trembling forty-year-old woman right now who has a serious character defect."

Pecuniary gain was one of the least of the aggravating circumstances that could send somebody to death, Cotter maintained, going on to cite many of the good things Barbara had done for others. In prison, Barbara would still have a chance to do things for others, he said, especially family.

"These people have a lot to work out. They may have some explaining to do to each other. They have some soul-searching they have to do." He gestured toward Barbara's two sons. "Their two fathers are dead. What purpose would it serve to kill their mother? It doesn't bring Russ Stager back. It doesn't bring Larry Ford back. It takes from those two young boys their mother." But Larry's death, he hastened to add, was not an issue here and they shouldn't consider it.

"Excuse me a minute before I sit," he said, his voice impassioned, his face grave as he turned to the defense table to examine his notes. "I'm scared to death. I don't want to sit down and then drive home tonight to Durham and say, 'Well, why didn't I mention this? You wrote it down and why didn't you say this?' If I can think of anything, if I knew what to say or do to convince you not to kill this lady, I would do it. I would say it, because I firmly believe that you should not vote to have her killed. The Old Testament is not the law. The law is not if you kill someone, you die. It's not a death-penalty case. It's a case where she should get the second worst punishment that is available. I would ask you to please bring back a decision for life in prison."

Barbara's fate was now up to the jurors, and Judge Allen released them, as he had once before, to go home and think about it overnight.


As Barbara was led back into the courtroom for the denouement of her trial Friday morning, she still bore the pale, stunned look of disbelief that had swept over her at her conviction two days earlier. She also still wore the same turtleneck blouse and print skirt.

Judge Allen briskly set about the day's business, taking only thirty minutes to instruct the jurors in their duties. Looks of nervous dread filled the jurors' faces as they shuffled back to the jury room at 10:04. Under North Carolina law, only they could decide whether Barbara lived or died. Their decision would be binding on the judge.

When they were gone, the judge ordered Barbara returned to a holding cell, then put the courtroom at ease and returned to his chambers. The trial's participants and observers settled in for what they anticipated would be a long wait.

Throughout the courtroom and in the hallways outside, people formed in small clumps to speculate about the jurors' decision. Some thought that they would never choose death for a middle-class white mother whose friends proclaimed her to be a loving person and a strong Christian. After all, the jurors had looked daily at her two sons, had heard the lawyers' impassioned appeals in their behalf. "They've already lost two fathers, don't kill their mother, too." Others pointed out how quickly the jurors had convicted Barbara, how conservative they seemed to be.

After taking their seats in the jury room, one juror suggested that they begin by seeking guidance from the Bible. Melanie West, a nursing instructor, picked up the Bible from the center of the big table and read aloud the Twenty-third Psalm.

As he had done before, the foreman, Norman Watkins, suggested that they take a turn around the table to allow everybody to speak their feelings. It quickly became apparent that this time there was no unanimity, and there would be no quick decision. The first vote was split, six for death, six for life.

When the light on the judge's bench flashed before eleven, the court quickly and nervously reassembled, wondering if the jurors could have reached a decision so quickly. But the bailiff delivered a note to the judge instead. The jurors requested five Cokes, four Diet Cokes, two Dr Peppers and a 7-Up. The judge ordered that the state buy them and deliver them to the jury room.

The jurors sent out a second note at 11:48, this time a question: "Does life imprisonment actually mean that you will be in prison until the day you die?"

It was now noon, and Judge Allen brought the jurors back and told them that the meaning of life imprisonment was not for them to consider and they should eliminate it from their minds. Then he sent the jurors to lunch in a group, accompanied by the bailiffs, telling them to be back by one-thirty.

When the jurors had returned to their deliberations, the courtroom settled again to waiting. Lawyers, law enforcement officers and others from the prosecution side were relaxed, chatting in groups, sometimes joking and laughing.

Barbara's family and friends huddled together for support, tense and worried. Cotter sat alone much of the time in a dark mood. When a reporter, Libby Lewis, approached to ask where he might be later in case she needed a comment for her story, he looked up with a little smile.

"Drunk," he said.


In the jury room, some jurors sat looking inward, saying nothing for long periods. Others cried and read the Bible. But each vote was changing now, one or two votes swinging after each period of deliberation.

After the judge brought the jurors out for a fifteen-minute recess at three, they returned for a new round of talking. Only two jurors remained to be swayed. This time when Watkins asked for a new vote, all twelve hands went up, some of them slowly.


The light on the judge's bench flashed again at 3:55, and the court quickly reassembled.

"All right," said the judge. "There's a light on indicating that the jury wants to come out. I do not know if they have a verdict or not, but again I will remind everybody that if you cannot control your emotions, please leave the courtroom now." He turned to the bailiff. "All right, Mr. Tolliver, go see if they've got a verdict."

The jury did.

"All right," said the judge, "tell them to put all of their twelve copies in one sheet. Tell the foreman to be sure it is signed and dated and put the original in the other envelope and hold that until they come in here."

As the jurors filed back in, an anxious courtroom strained to read their faces.

"Mr. Foreman, have you reached a verdict?" the judge asked.

"Yes, sir, we have."

"Would you hand first all of the twelve sheets to the bailiff and keep the verdict? Mr. Tolliver, give this to the clerk. I will ask the clerk to take the verdict."

The verdict was passed to Cynthia Myers.

"Mr. Foreman," she said, "will you please stand?"

Watkins stood.

"You have returned as your verdict on the issues, issue one, aggravating circumstances, yes."

The jury had agreed that Barbara had killed Russ for money.

But as the clerk continued to read, it became clear that the jurors had agreed to all the mitigating factors as well.

Barbara's life would rest on whether or not they had found the four mitigating circumstances—that she had reared two fine children, that she was an active and helpful church member, that she had been a friend to many people, and she had no significant criminal record—to outweigh the single aggravating factor.

"You have returned as your recommendation that the jury unanimously recommends that the defendant, Barbara T. Stager, be sentenced to death," Myers read, her voice quavering.

A gasp swept through the side of the courtroom where Barbara's family and supporters sat. Barbara collapsed in her chair, sobbing.

"Is this your verdict?" Cynthia Myers was asking.

"Yes, ma'am."

"Is this still your verdict?"

"Yes, ma'am."

"Do you want the jury polled?" the judge asked a morose William Cotter.

"Yes, sir."

As each juror stood, confirming the verdict, Barbara turned to her family with a look of agony and silently mouthed, "I love you."

"Let the record show that the court accepts the recommendation of the jury and orders that it be recorded," the judge intoned. "Everybody remain seated and no one leaves this courtroom until I tell you you can."

He thanked the jurors and told them they were free to go. After the jurors had filed out, he turned to Barbara and her lawyers.

"All right, Mr. Cotter, do you and Mr. Falcone, or does the defendant wish to be heard?"

"No, sir," said Cotter.

"You don't?"

"No, sir."

"Take this down. The prisoner, Barbara T. Stager, having been convicted of murder in the first degree by unanimous verdict of the jury duly returned at the term of the Superior Court of Lee County, North Carolina, and the jury having unanimously recommended the punishment of death, it is therefore ordered, adjudged and decreed that the same Barbara T. Stager be and she is hereby sentenced to death, and the sheriff of Lee County, in whose custody the said defendant now is, shall forthwith deliver the said prisoner to the warden of the state penitentiary at Raleigh, who the said warden on the twenty-eighth day of July 1989, shall cause the said prisoner, Barbara T. Stager, to be put to death as by law provided. May God have mercy on her soul.

"Mr. Sheriff, I will ask that everyone else remain seated and you may escort Mrs. Stager out of the courtroom."

After Barbara was led away by bailiffs and court was adjourned, reporters crowded around her family.

"Just go away," Bryan told them.

Across the aisle, the mothers of Russ Stager and Larry Ford met in silent embrace.

Before the trial, Doris Stager had promised God that if He would allow Barbara to be convicted, she would not ask Him for the death penalty, and she had kept her word. But she was grateful now that He had seen fit to grant that, too. "I've been in agony, deep depression and mourning, day and night, ever since my son's death," she told the reporters who clustered around the Stagers and Fords. "The only thing that has kept me going is that I know that my son Russell had Christ as his Lord and Savior, and therefore his spirit went immediately to heaven when he died. . . . Justice has been done."

"It'll never be over for us," said Russ's sister, Cindy, "because Russell's dead."

"Our lives have been shattered," Henry Ford said. "It has

taken eleven years . . . to give us the unanswered questions in our hearts.

"God is a God of miracles, and He certainly proved it in this case. Our prayer was that His will be done in every respect of this trial and give us faith to accept the truth. We feel He has done so, and we thank Him."

When the reporters turned to Eric Evenson for his comments, he expressed sympathy for Barbara's two sons. "They may not grasp what has happened here," he said, "but they are the ones who have ultimately suffered with the Stagers and the Fords."

# Chapter Thirty-seven

Barbara refused meals at first after being taken to the North Carolina Correctional Institute for Women in Raleigh. She was too upset and depressed to eat, she said. But an outpouring of support from family, friends and church members caused her to rally and begin taking meals.

Family and friends clung to Barbara's innocence, unable to accept that the dark specter that had been revealed in her trial could be real. Instead, they trusted the brighter face that she always had presented to them: dutiful daughter, loving sister, faithful wife, devoted mother, good friend, devout Christian, upstanding citizen.

Some friends wrote letters to newspapers decrying her conviction and sentence. Carol Galloway chastised the jury for failing to consider the evidence carefully. "As a result," she wrote, "an innocent woman is facing death, two sons are without a mother, two fine people are without a daughter, two fine young men are without a sister, a lot of people are without a true friend, and the world is without a wonderful person. This is truly sad."

Sherry Sims wrote of her pride in having a person so good as Barbara for a friend. "I wish everyone could know her as I do; then there wouldn't be any doubt in anyone's mind that Barbara could never hurt anyone willfully or intentionally. She is just not that type of person. I admire Barbara, too, for holding on to her faith in God through this terrible ordeal."

The faith that Barbara's friends had in her was understandable. If the secret side of Barbara shown at the trial was true, then they had been duped, and they did not want to acknowledge that. Some never even questioned whether Barbara could have committed the acts of which she was accused, saying that as Christians they were not to pry or judge, only to love her. For them, it simply was impossible to believe that a person of Barbara's background could do such things, because to do so would threaten all that they held true and precious. She had been taught Christian values and morals and continued to voice them. She had been saved and baptized. If dark forces could overwhelm that and take control of her against her professed will, they could snatch anybody.

"To me, it is so devastating that I feel like that could be my daughter," said a friend of Barbara's mother.

For Barbara's family and friends, accepting her innocence was far easier than facing the monstrous possibilities that her guilt implied. They had to believe that the Barbara they knew was the only Barbara.

"Barbara has been done a big injustice," her mother told a reporter from Raleigh's *News and Observer* in the only public statement she would make after the trial. "She has always been a good child, a good person. I can't understand how the circumstances can be as they are."

"It's broken their hearts totally," a close friend of Marva's said of the family, "but it's drawn them even closer together, because they're working for the same thing, and that's to save Barbara."

Barbara's family knew that she would not be executed in July as Judge Allen had ordered. All death sentences are automatically appealed in North Carolina, and ten years or more could pass before such a sentence would be carried out. Also, they knew that Barbara had an excellent chance of winning a new trial. Even Judge Allen acknowledged in a newspaper interview that the chances were good that his rulings could be overturned by higher courts.

The trial intrigued legal scholars because of the unusual combination of issues that it raised. The first, and most important, was that Larry's death, for which no one ever was charged, had been allowed into evidence. Although the United States Supreme Court had made it easier in recent years for evidence of unproven crimes to be introduced, nobody was sure just how far that could be taken and whether it would stand in Barbara's case.

Vital to this were the similarities in the two deaths, which Eric

Evenson had gone to great lengths to show, and the evidence that Larry's death had indeed been something other than accident or suicide, which the investigators had spent weeks trying to prove. But the conviction also could stand or fall on the reason the evidence had been allowed. In this case, it had been admitted to show that Russ's death had not been an accident.

The second issue was the tape of Russ's voice. Was it authentic? Was it relevant? Had it turned up too late? Should the jurors have been allowed to hear it?

Those two issues would be the heart of Barbara's appeal, and the legal community would be watching closely as this case crept through the appeals process.

Because Barbara was indigent, that process was initiated by Gordon Widenhouse of the state appellate defender's office in Raleigh. Young and energetic, with a reputation as a superb appeals lawyer, Widenhouse was looking forward to arguing Barbara's case. But a month after Barbara's conviction, Widenhouse was informed that it was being taken from him. Led by her brother Alton, who recently had filed for legal custody of Jason, Barbara's family once again was coming to her defense. They had hired a prestigious, politically powerful and expensive law firm in Raleigh, that of brothers Wade and Roger Smith, to conduct Barbara's appeal. Wade Smith had been one of the lawyers who represented Dr. Jeffrey MacDonald in his famous murder trial. Roger Smith would handle Barbara's case. Her family was determined to save her, even if it cost them everything they had earned in a lifetime of hard work.

Only one other woman was on death row when Barbara went to prison. Before the North Carolina Supreme Court would hear her case nearly two years later, two others would join them. They lived in cells seven feet square, where they took all their meals. They were allowed out once a day to shower, once a day to walk in a small exercise yard. Once a week, on Saturday mornings, Barbara was allowed a two-hour visit with any three of fifteen people she put on her visitor list, most of whom were family members.

Barbara quickly became a model prisoner. She joined a Bible study group and attended religious services faithfully. She took up needlepoint, knitting and other crafts. She began showering friends and family with gifts of needlepoint Bible verses, afghans, stuffed toys. She read a lot, and spent many hours answering the great volumes of mail she received.

"Keep praying for me," she kept writing to her devoted supporters.

Roger Smith argued Barbara's case to the state Supreme Court on May 6, 1991, nearly two years after her trial. As expected, he emphasized the evidence of Larry's death, arguing that it never should have been allowed. When it came to the similarities between the deaths of Russ and Larry, Smith pointed out that similarities weren't always relevant.

As an example, he cited a famous list of incidental similarities between the assassinations of Presidents Abraham Lincoln and John F. Kennedy. But three justices interrupted to point out that nobody had tried to claim that those killings were accidents.

Wasn't it relevant, asked Justice Burley Mitchell, that a person charged with murder in a death that she claims to be an accident is discovered to have had a similar incident in the past? "After a while," noted the justice, "you begin to smell a rat."

The reaction of the justices to Smith's arguments heartened District Attorney Ron Stephens, who thought that the court was leaning toward upholding Barbara's conviction. He had far less hope, however, that her death sentence would stand.

More than a year earlier, the U.S. Supreme Court had issued an order that voided an instruction routinely given to jurors in capital cases in North Carolina. Previously, jurors had been told that they had to agree unanimously on mitigating factors. Not so, said the court, and the ruling was expected to affect at least seventy of the state's eighty-five death row prisoners, including Barbara. All likely would get new sentencing hearings as their individual cases came before the state's Supreme Court.

On August 14, that court ruled just as Stephens had expected. The justices clearly believed that Barbara was a murderer, and her conviction was upheld. But she was granted a new sentencing hearing because of the judge's instruction on mitigating factors.

Stephens was pleased. "A major concern to us obviously was to convict Barbara Stager of first-degree murder," he told a reporter. "We are happy and excited that the Supreme Court upheld the conviction. Now we'll just have to prepare for resentencing."

"If you had a son who was shot and killed in his sleep, how would you feel?" Doris Stager said to a reporter who called to ask for her reaction. "I've turned the whole thing over to God and ask that His will be done. That's what I have to depend on."

Barbara had been so confident that she would be granted a new trial that she lapsed into depression upon hearing the news and was unable to sleep. A psychiatrist consulted with her six days after the ruling and prescribed an antidepressant, doxepin, to help her sleep, but Barbara had a bad reaction to the drug. When Benadryl was prescribed, she began sleeping again and soon was responding once more to the encouragement of family and friends, who, while disappointed that her conviction had been upheld, were heartened that at least she had been granted another chance to save her life.

To lead that fight, her family turned to another lawyer. At one time Arthur Vann had been Durham's best-known criminal lawyer. "If you're guilty," it was said in Durham, "get Art Vann." Other criminal lawyers in Durham still considered Vann to be "a true warrior," as one of them put it, but he was past seventy now, and many thought that he was well past his prime. But Edward Falcone, the quiet young lawyer who had handled the sentencing phase of Barbara's trial, was an associate of Vann's, and he was well versed in Barbara's case. They would handle the resentencing hearing together.

The hearing would in essence be a second trial. New jurors would have to be chosen. All the evidence would have to be presented. The primary difference would be that the jurors would be deciding only whether Barbara should live or die.

As Cotter had done before him, Vann began filing motions to get the sentencing hearing moved, to keep the jurors from being told about Larry's death or hearing the tape of Russ's voice. He succeeded only in getting the hearing moved, this time to Pittsboro in rural Chatham County. But Chatham adjoined populous Orange County, and Pittsboro was only fifteen miles from Chapel Hill, the home of the University of North Carolina and the state's seat of liberalism. For years Chapel Hill had been spilling over into Chatham County, and Barbara's chances of finding a juror there who would not go along with the death penalty were far better than they had been in Lee County.

With the hearing set to begin on August 16, 1993, Vann took

a step that Cotter had not. He hired a psychologist to prepare a psychological evaluation of Barbara. Dr. William Scarborough of Durham met with Barbara early in May. He administered two exams, the Minnesota Multiphasic Personality Inventory—2 and the Rorschach Ink Blot Test. He conducted a long interview with Barbara and a telephone interview with her parents.

Both Barbara and her parents portrayed her childhood as normal, without "significant psychological or physical trauma," as Scarborough later would write. Barbara denied any physical, emotional or sexual abuse in her youth. Indeed, the only problem she could claim was that she was "overprotected."

The tests showed that Barbara had no major personality disorder, that she functioned much like other people. At the same time, she was socially isolated, immature, excessively introspective and prone to focus on her negative features. She did not have strong needs for emotional closeness, which she probably viewed as "threatening and dangerous," and her relationships were apt to be superficial because she had "little real interest in others."

"She may attempt to escape into unrealistic views of herself as a means of avoiding what she perceives to be unresolvable stresses," Dr. Scarborough wrote. "There is a conflict between the person that she projects herself to be around others and the person that she truly sees herself as. When this public self is challenged, she may experience significant distress resulting in loss of thinking ability."

Scarborough's findings had similarities with a pop psychology test Barbara had administered to herself just seven months prior to Russ's death from a book titled *Please Understand Me: Character & Temperament Types* by David Keirsey and Marilyn Bates, which had been found during the raid on her house.

In the answers she had given, Barbara had revealed herself to be, in her judgment, realistic, careful, punctual, practical, orderly, structured, objective, serious and determined, a person who favored the routine over the whimsical.

It bothered her to have things incomplete. She wanted matters to be settled and decided, and she was always more comfortable after a decision had been made than before. She thought herself to be more hardheaded than softhearted, more reserved than approachable. The option to buy gave her more pleasure than having bought. She was more comfortable making logical judgments than value judgments. She would wish for herself clarity of reason over strength of compassion. And she was swayed more by circumstances than by laws.

The test results had revealed Barbara to have a primary drive to serve, a need to be needed. She did things the established way and became annoyed with those who did not. She was neat and meticulous and often turned her irritation inward, creating tension and fatigue.

During her interview with Dr. Scarborough, Barbara revealed that after she married Russ she was always striving for his love and attention. She and Russ had tried to present "a certain image," she said, and she was always buying things for him and letting him spend money the way he wanted because she was "afraid he wouldn't love her" if she didn't.

Russ didn't like the way she dressed, she said, and would buy her clothes trying to get her to dress differently, making her feel that she "wasn't pretty enough, good enough for him." She didn't tell him about these feelings, she said, because she "was always afraid that he would leave."

"I was insecure a lot," she added.

When Scarborough brought up Russ's death, Barbara became tearful. She had been doing a lot of thinking about that, she said, but she couldn't tell him exactly what had happened that morning.

"It was not planned," she said, "not an intentional act."

She was not aware of doing anything to make the gun go off, she said, yet she acknowledged that "I was aware of what I was doing at some level."

She had been wondering lately, she said, if she had acted subconsciously. "Did I know what I was doing, yet would not admit it to myself?" she asked, adding, "I would not consciously do something like that." She loved Russ, she said, crying, missed him and wished it never had happened.

"Maybe I'm better off now," she said, recovering her composure. "There's no pressure to be someone that I am not."

Scarborough thought that Barbara was genuinely remorseful about Russ's death. She was, he concluded, "a hard-working, church-attending, caring mother whose purpose in life was to please her parents, family, husband and children. Her efforts apparently were based on a very deep need for acceptance and approval."

Although Barbara was very good at maintaining the appearance of a well-adjusted person, she was filled with serious self-doubts and fears of rejection and abandonment, Scarborough decided, although he was unable to pinpoint the causes of such powerful insecurities.

"The struggle between the two views of herself may have been sufficiently powerful that her psychological defenses against her impulses may have been overwhelmed, leading her to bring about the death of her husband," he wrote in his report. "She cannot allow herself to think that she could have committed such an act. It follows that she may not have consciously planned to kill her husband but did so unconsciously out of a reaction to the stress placed on her by maintaining a facade of respectability and prosperity."

So it was the struggle to be middle-class and the strain of living up to an image Russ supposedly had imposed on her that had turned Barbara into an unwitting killer. The implication, in essence, was that Barbara was the true victim, and Russ, with his expectations, had brought about his own death. The question was whether a jury, more apt than not to be middle-class and to understand the stress that being middle-class brings, would accept that reasoning and spare her life.

# Chapter Thirty-eight

The scene of Barbara's resentencing hearing was in opulent contrast to the stark courtroom in which she had been convicted four years and three months earlier.

The two-story red brick Chatham County Courthouse occupied the center of the small town of Pittsboro, set on a tiny circular grass island that straddled the intersection of two busy U.S. highways, 64 and 15–501. Built in 1882, the courthouse had been recently renovated and was now a national historic site. Its copper-sheathed, cupola-topped roof gleamed in the sunlight. At its main entrance, facing north, a bronze Confederate soldier stood silent sentry against the possible advance of any hostile hordes from Chapel Hill.

The courtroom had an air of majesty about it. Nine huge gold-rimmed, bowl-shaped white glass chandeliers hung by gold chains from the twenty-foot ceiling. On the sides facing north and south, twelve-foot windows with white shutters lined plastered walls painted the blue of a robin's egg. The polished mahogany pews were padded and upholstered to match the plush, patterned aqua carpet. On the wall behind the bench, which was paneled in thick, lustrous mahogany, was a huge portrait of the man for whom both county and town had been named, William Pitt, the first Earl of Chatham, resplendent in silk, lace and powdered wig.

As the final week of August 1993 began, a bespectacled, soft-spoken, genteel man of fifty-two, Judge Craig Ellis of Laurinburg in Scotland County, occupied the imposing bench beneath the portrait. A self-professed "country lawyer," Ellis was a graduate of the University of Virginia and the University of North Carolina School of Law. He had served as a district court judge before being elected to the superior court bench nearly ten years earlier.

Barbara entered the courtroom that morning smiling broadly at the circle of family and friends who had come to support her. She wore the same hairstyle and the same big glasses that she had worn at her trial, and she appeared little changed by her years in prison. She sat now at the defense table beside Edward Falcone, the quiet, studious, pinstripe-suited young lawyer who had led the fight for her life at her trial. In this encounter Falcone would defer to his far more outgoing and flamboyant law partner, Art Vann.

At seventy-one, Vann was lean and tanned with a full shock of white hair. A native of Sampson County in eastern North Carolina, he had practiced in Durham since 1951, and he claimed to have tried more than two hundred murder cases. He still wore seersucker suits and white straw hats on blistering summer days, and he had the affected courtliness of an Old South lawyer. But while he could be solicitous and appealing one moment, he could be irritable and snappish the next, and he would offend as many jurors as he charmed before this hearing was over.

At the prosecutors' table sat Ron Stephens, still the district attorney of Durham County, the new judgeship he had hoped to win having failed to materialize. Beside him was William Farrell, a native of Pittsboro, the head of the criminal division of the State Attorney General's Office. Farrell had argued the state's case against Barbara before the Supreme Court and was well acquainted with all of its intricacies. Sitting inside the bar, directly behind the prosecutors was Rick Buchanan, no longer a detective. A new sheriff had been appointed in Durham County, and only a few weeks earlier he had dismissed Buchanan and several other officers in a political move. Buchanan, who was planning to run for sheriff himself, was now in private security work, but he had taken off to see his biggest case to its conclusion.

Eric Evenson, now an assistant U.S. district attorney in Raleigh and no longer involved in the case that had occupied so much of his time and energy, sat in the front row in the audience, behind the prosecution table, next to Doris Stager, surrogate for her missing husband, Al. Al had suffered immense stress from Russ's death and the anxiety of Barbara's trial. Six months after her conviction, his heart condition had worsened and he had been hospitalized. He would need more surgery, the doctors had determined, but in preparing for it, they had discovered another problem: multiple myeloma, a malignancy of the bone marrow. He had lived with it for two and a half years and died just five months earlier, in March, leaving Doris even more devastated. Family members believed that it was Russ's murder that actually had killed Al, and now they worried about Doris as well. She was hardly eating, and she looked pale, tiny and drawn, her eyes haunted by the blows that life had dealt her. At her other side sat Doris and Henry Ford, looking fit and at peace. Since Barbara's trial they had moved to the mountains of Virginia, where they continued to hike and helped to maintain a long stretch of the Appalachian Trail.

To the left of the prosecutors sat the jury, which the lawyers had taken a week to pick. Its members were mostly middle-class and young to middle age, evenly divided between males and females.

William Farrell rose before them to give the opening statement for the state. He was precise, succinct and well organized. Vann, on the other hand, was rambling and disorganized when his turn came, starting sentences and dropping them, moving on to other thoughts, his voice occasionally rising with passion— "These lawyers want her to go to the gas chamber! You understand that?"—then falling so low that he barely could be heard. More than once the judge admonished him that the purpose of an opening statement was to preview the evidence, not to argue his case.

Eventually, though, Vann's strategy became clear. Having failed to sway the judge to eliminate any testimony about Larry's death, he would attempt to convince the jurors that it had indeed been an accident, that therefore Russ's death could have been an accident, too. And Barbara, a woman guilty only of exceptionally bad luck, sat convicted before them, her life in their hands. If that failed, he would overwhelm the jurors with Barbara's goodness. Cotter and Falcone had used only four mitigating circumstances at Barbara's trial. Vann already had a list of fifteen that he planned to present, and the list would grow as the hearing continued.

Ron Stephens knew that he was at a disadvantage, that

chances were good that Barbara would not again be sentenced to death. Jurors rarely chose death when there was only one aggravating circumstance, particularly if that circumstance was pecuniary gain. And they usually were reluctant to give the ultimate penalty to women. Only three had been executed by the state since 1910, the most recent, Velma Barfield, in 1984. Moreover, Stephens had to convince all twelve jurors to pick death. Vann needed to win only one. If the jury could not reach a unanimous decision, Barbara automatically would receive a life sentence.

Beyond that, Stephens would be presenting a truncated version of the evidence he had offered at the trial, using only about half the number of witnesses. This was partly in the interest of time, partly to cut expenses, partly because the jurors wouldn't need as much information to sentence Barbara as to convict her.

Stephens would take only three days to present his case, and as witnesses began to come and go, one problem with the courtroom became apparent. The constant rumble of big trucks negotiating the tiny traffic circle just beyond the courtroom's walls penetrated the "soundproof" windows and made hearing difficult even for the attorneys and jurors, much less for those in the audience. At times, testimony had to be momentarily halted, and witnesses constantly had to be reminded to speak louder.

Barbara dabbed at her eyes as her videotaped reenactment was played during Buchanan's testimony.

"Do you know that the Randolph County medical examiner calls Larry Ford's death an accidental shooting?" Vann bellowed at Buchanan afterward, waving the report before him, as he would do for all the state's witnesses who testified about Larry's death.

"I know it's what that document says," Buchanan replied.

When Vann cross-examined Doris Stager on the second day of testimony, he tried to get her to admit that Russ had been a heavy spender during his marriage to Jo Lynn.

"Isn't that the reason she left him?" Vann asked.

"In my opinion, the reason she left him was that they were like two mules, each pulling in their own way," Doris said firmly.

Jo Lynn was not there to hear Doris's comment. She had attended most of Barbara's trial and had married for the third time shortly thereafter, this time happily. She and her husband now operated a business in Raleigh. Russ's death had caused her to form a new and lasting bond with her former in-laws and she wanted to be with Doris throughout the hearing, but her own mother was in the hospital gravely ill, and she would get to come only twice to support Doris.

Vann now got Doris to describe some of the cars Russ and Barbara had bought both before and after the financial crisis she had testified about earlier.

"And they bought each other Rolex watches?" he said.

"They sure did," Doris agreed.

"When they had that conversation with you, it didn't do much good, did it?" Vann said, referring to the financial crisis that Doris had sought to alleviate.

"I wish I could say yes," Doris added.

Later, as the tape of Russ's voice was played, Doris and her daughter Cindy sat sobbing and comforting one another while Barbara stared stoically ahead.

Barbara's defense would take two days, and Vann planned to present twenty-seven witnesses, nearly twice as many as had appeared on her behalf at her trial. He began with the psychologist he had paid to examine her, then followed with a prison social worker who reported that Barbara was a model prisoner and identified some of the crafts that she had made. Vann took the crafts from a big paper bag behind his chair and paraded them before the jurors before submitting them into evidence. There were two framed works of needlepoint, one of them a verse from Joshua—"As for me and my house, we will serve the Lord" (which, Doris Stager noted, was the same verse that had always hung by her own kitchen door). There also were two stuffed animals, a cat and a mouse. Whether or not there were psychological implications, some in the courtroom noted that Barbara's mouse was six times bigger than her cat.

An education coordinator for the prison told of the classes Barbara had been taking: art and creative writing. She also had begun a correspondence program through the University of North Carolina to complete her degree in sociology, he said, and after getting it, she hoped to be able to teach inmates who could not read or write.

By Thursday afternoon, the courtroom had taken on the air of a tent revival, as preachers and prison missionaries took the stand one after another to testify about Barbara's religious fervor, her dedication to prison religious services and Bible study classes.

"We count on her," said Sam Roane, a deep-voiced eighty-four-year-old lay minister. "She's such an intelligent, bright person and just keeps growing deeper in the word of God as time goes by. The main reason I think she had grown so much in her faith in these past four years is because she is interested in what we are studying. Right now we're studying Paul. Praise the Lord for Paul!"

Outside, thunder rumbled from an approaching storm.

"That's the Lord talking now," said Vann.

"Yes, sir, that's Him," said Roane.

Roane's enthusiastic wife, Gales, raised fits of laughter from Barbara's friends and family after Vann got her to describe the prison ministry she and her husband had maintained for thirty-two years. "How'd the Lord get you to do that?"

"I don't know," she responded with a big smile, "I've been waiting for my parole."

She got more approving chuckles when she told Vann that she had been praying for him, then turned pointedly to the prosecutors and said, "and for YOU, and for the judge and the jury."

"We thank her for her prayers," Stephens said when his turn for cross-examination came, "and we have no questions."

A parade of Barbara's friends and former fellow church members followed to endorse her good points, and family members took the stand to once again cast doubt on the validity of Russ's voice on the audiotape, to try to make Russ's and Barbara's relationship seem fine and to attempt to paint Russ as the bigger spender of the two.

Both of Barbara's sons testified this time. Bryan, now twenty-four, had finished college and was living in Wrightsville Beach, where he worked in a restaurant. Jason had undergone some troubled times after his mother's conviction and had been sent to a military school, from which he had graduated. Now nineteen, he was living in Charlottesville, Virginia, with Barbara's brother Steve and his wife, Astrid, and also working in a restaurant.

Barbara's father, who had not testified at her trial, was the only family member who did not testify at the hearing.

Barbara's mother was the final witness Friday afternoon. She had retired from her job at Duke eight months earlier, and she and James, also retired, now had their house on the market. They had bought a farm in the mountains of Virginia, not far from where the Fords lived, and planned to move there, away from Durham, the only home they had ever known, where so many people knew about Barbara's case. She took the stand carrying a sheet of notes and wearing an expression of self-assurance. Guided by Vann, she expressed pride in her three children and described Barbara as "a super child."

"She was excellent, made excellent grades. . . . Her brother had a horrible time trying to do the same kind of grades she did."

She told of Barbara winning a scholarship, going off to college, meeting Larry and getting married.

"Barbara dropped out of school. With our help, we got Larry through."

Doris and Henry Ford looked at one another and shook their heads sadly.

When Vann asked how Barbara had adjusted to prison, Marva said, "She has amazed me, she really has. I don't know that I could have gone every week to see her if she had not had the attitude she's had."

"It takes a lot of guts to do that," Vann put in.

"It certainly does. I love her very much. I would rather be there myself than to have her there."

"She, of course, loves you," Vann offered as Barbara cried two seats away.

Marva fought back her own tears and quickly regained her composure as Vann once again brought out Barbara's needlepoint, her stuffed animals and a brightly colored afghan she had made.

"She's done some other beautiful things, too," Marva said, then offered a tight smile and added, "I'm going to open up a store."

After she departed the stand, the defense rested, and court was recessed for the weekend.


A lectern had been set before the jury box when court reconvened Monday morning. Barbara, who had made no public statement since her arrest, wanted to address the jury. Vann took her by the hand and led her to the lectern. The whole courtroom leaned forward, listening intently as Barbara began to speak in a tiny, nervous voice.

"Ladies and gentlemen, you know that my name is Barbara Stager. You know that many times in our lives we have a chance to look back and reflect on the way our lives have been. I have had a chance to do that in these past several years.

"I have made a lot of mistakes in my life. I've done a lot of things that I knew were wrong. I have disappointed a lot of people that love me and that I love. I've done things that were against my nature. I've done things that were against the values that my parents instilled in me. But nevertheless, I know that I—that my life does have some meaning, and that I can be of help to other people at some point in my life.

"I'm not perfect. I don't know of a single human being alive that is perfect. There are many things about the past that I wish I could change. I wish I could, and I know that I can't.

"I've been convicted of taking the life of Russell Stager. I'm sorry about that. I'm sorry for his family, for the loss and the pain that they have had to suffer. I wish I could take it back. I wish I could take all of that away from them."

As Barbara spoke, Doris Stager sat leaning forward, straining for every word, her hands tightly gripping the seat at her sides, her eyes fixed intently on Barbara's face only a few feet away, but Barbara never glanced in her direction.

"My parents, my family, my sons, my brothers, they have had to suffer, too. I wish I could take that away from them, too.

"You've heard a lot of testimony, and you've seen an awful lot of evidence. And even though intent is not an issue at this point, whether or not I intentionally took his life, I'm still responsible. That's a terrible, terrible burden to bear. But I am aware of it, and I've accepted that responsibility.

"I realize the hurt and the pain and the anger that it's caused his family, people that love him, my family, and people that love me. I just wish I could take that away. I wish I could turn the clock back and change things. But I know I can't.

"One of my deepest regrets is the injustice that's been done to Larry Ford. His memory has been misused because of me. I'm sorry to his family for that. I know this has been terrible for them, too, and I'm terribly sorry for that. I hate it for them, and for his sons.

"Like I said, I have been convicted of taking Russell Stager's life. I'm really, really sorry for that. Russ and I had a roller-coaster marriage. We had really good times and we had really bad times. Not unlike many and most marriages.

"I feel bad that my actions and my mistakes led to his death. I regret that. Most of all, I regret that. I wish I could turn the clock back. I wish I could change all of it.

"In spite of the circumstances and reasons for my being here today, I realize, too, that I'm very fortunate in many ways. I have a loving and supportive family who has continued to stand by me no matter what. And I'll never forget them, and I thank them from the bottom of my heart. And I have a large circle of friends who have supported me though this, and continue to. And I'll never forget them, either.

"But most of all, I know that I have the Lord on my side and in my heart. I thank God for the ultimate sacrifice He made of His son to give me forgiveness and salvation, that I can stand up to this and endure with peace, with strength, with courage. And I know that whatever decision you people make, I know that I'll be with the Lord. I know that. I don't have any doubts about it.

"And I also know that God and I are the only ones who know the absolute truth. That gives me an awful lot of peace.

"You have heard that I have a goal. Since I've been in prison I've been trying to further my education so that I can help people less fortunate than I am while I'm in prison. I would like to have the chance to be able to see that goal come to an end. I would like to be able to finish that education and help whoever I can while I'm there.

"I hope that every one of you will consider everything that you have seen and heard, everything. And I hope you will decide to give me another chance."

As she turned and walked quickly back to her seat, Doris Stager's anger-filled eyes followed her every step.


"Barbara Stager stands up here and talks about intent, still not able to accept that in cold blood she murdered her husband," Ron Stephens told the jury in his closing argument, which was much longer and more impassioned than his closing at the trial.

"I'm not mad," he said. "I'm enraged. I make no apologies about it. *You* should be enraged."

The defense had made a special effort to show that Barbara was not a dangerous person, and Stephens now countered that with a simple question. "How dangerous is Barbara Stager? You tell me. Would you want your son or your brother to marry her and share her bed?"

William Farrell had taken note of Vann's theatrics with Barbara's needlepoint and stuffed toys, and stepped before the jury holding the gun that had killed Russ.

"Russ Stager is gone, gone forever, dispatched to eternity by the business end of a .25-caliber pistol," he said, holding up the small gun. He turned and picked up the toy cat that Barbara had made. "Dispatched to eternity by the hand that could make this. The hand that made this also could use this." He placed the cat and the gun on the railing before the jury box, where they would be in plain sight throughout the rest of his argument.

"Did she really say she was sorry for killing Russ Stager?" Farrell said of Barbara's plea to the jury. "Or did she tell you she was sorry for getting convicted?"

There were two Barbaras, he pointed out, and her family didn't truly know her because they couldn't accept what a monstrous person she really was.

"If the facts of this case do not justify capital punishment, please tell me what would," he pleaded with the jurors. "What more would you require? How many more bodies?"

"People who commit first-degree murder come from all walks of life. Some don't have a chance. Some of them do. If we are not going to impose the ultimate sanction on people who've had Christian training, how can we impose it on the others? I ask you to ensure—*ensure*—that she never has the opportunity to do this again."

Edward Falcone led for the defense, reading the same speech he had delivered at the sentencing phase of Barbara's trial, altering it to include the expanded list of mitigating circumstances, now numbering twenty-one. Among them were that Barbara had led a Christian life, was a model prisoner, was remorseful and had shown no propensity for violence "other than to her husband."

The fire and thunder were left to Art Vann, and he began by

reading from the Bible, in Luke: " 'Wherefore I say unto thee. Her sins, which are many, are forgiven; for she loved much: but to whom little is forgiven, the same loveth little.

"And he said unto her, Thy sins are forgiven. . . . Thy faith hath saved thee; go in peace.' "

Vann's closing argument was even more disorganized and disjointed than his opening statement, and he fell back on old lawyer tricks, employing theatrics, dropping the gun to the floor, misrepresenting the evidence to confuse the jurors, even figuratively waving the flag in Barbara's behalf.

One of his favorite phrases was "the King's English," and he had employed it often throughout the hearing. He held Larry's death certificate high in the air for all to see. "It says right here in the King's English," he said, his voice rising dramatically, "accident—it's not Hebrew or Icelandic, it's English. Accident means *accident.*"

At one point, apparently forgetting that Barbara already had been convicted and that this was a sentencing hearing, he lapsed into an old refrain that he had used at many a trial. "In this great land, you are presumed to be innocent. That presumption of innocence sits with this woman. She is an innocent person. Not guilty! Innocent!"

Vann went on to punch at the validity of the tape of Russ's voice, although he called it the videotape. "Whatever you get out of that tape, you'll just have to decide," he ended up saying. He took a swipe at the forged will, noting that the house was all that Barbara and Russ really owned, and under North Carolina law the house automatically went to the surviving spouse. "I don't know why there was such a fuss about that," he said of the will. "That ain't no big deal. That ain't the end of the world. So whatever you gather out of that, you just gather."

He went on to attack Russ's spending—"Just to run another rabbit with you," he said by way of introducing it—then noted Barbara's industry. "This lady—and she is a lady, she's not a murderer—she worked. I don't think there's any question in anybody's mind about that."

He held up a sheaf of papers, school records, the Bible study certificates Barbara had earned in prison. "Y'all've seen these things," he said, trying to get the jury involved on his side. "Have you seen 'em? Just shake your head up and down. Here's her

criminal record, nothing on it. She's not of a vicious nature. Nobody has said anything ugly about her, because there's nothing
ugly to be said."

In closing, Vann thanked the jurors. "I hope you'll find it in
your hearts not to put this woman in the gas chamber. She has
the gift of patience with people, of understanding of people, and
she has made a tremendous influence in the lives of these people
she's involved with now.

"Don't slam the door on her mother and father, her two sons,
her brothers. Don't slam the door in the face of her friends who
love her and care for her. I ask you a question. What is the value
of taking her life? Who's going to gain anything by that?

"You heard what she told you. She's at peace with her Lord.
That I believe and that I hope you'll believe. Don't forget what
Luke said about it. Here was a woman, I take it she was a pros-
titute. She washed our Lord's feet and dried it off with her hair,
and He said she was forgiven. Your sins are forgiven."

Vann finished at 3:45, too late, the judge decided, to charge
the jury and let them begin deliberations this day. They could
start fresh in the morning.


Only seven minutes after the jury went to deliberate at 10:13
Tuesday morning, August 31, the foreman sent back a question:
"With a sentence of life imprisonment, is there a possibility of be-
ing released prior to death?"

The judge brought the jury out to tell them that they should
not be concerned about that, then sent them back to deliberate
until lunch. After lunch, the jury returned to the spacious jury
room on the northeastern corner of the courthouse with its long
mahogany table, comfortable upholstered armchairs and views of
the outside traffic.

At 3:20, the courtroom quickly reassembled, but the jurors
only had another question: "If the jury cannot unanimously decide for death or life, what happens?"

That, too, was not their concern, the judge informed them,
but the question clearly disheartened the prosecutors, who could
win only with unanimity.

Only eighteen minutes later, the jury returned again.

"Without telling me the outcome," Judge Ellis said to foreman

Leon McCormick, "have you reached a unanimous verdict in this case?"

"We have."

The verdict was passed to the judge, who read it and turned it over to the court clerk, Debra Jones, who stood to read it.

The jury had answered yes to the question of whether Barbara had acted for pecuniary gain. The suspense dragged on as the clerk waded through the jury's answers to each mitigating factor, yes to the first twenty, no to the final one, a catchall that they could fill in for themselves. Were the mitigating factors insufficient to override the aggravating? Yes. Only one more question remained. Was the sole aggravating factor sufficient to recommend death?

"No," read the clerk, but only the lawyers and the reporters seemed to grasp that this was the verdict, that Barbara's life had been saved. No gasp of relief or indignation came from the rest of the audience until Debra Jones made it clear: "We, the jury, unanimously recommend that the defendant, Barbara T. Stager, be sentenced to life in prison."

Barbara turned and flashed a big smile at her relieved family. Doris Stager broke into tears of disbelief. The prosecutors slumped in their chairs. Art Vann turned and thrust a fist of victory into the air at Barbara's father, who returned the gesture with a big smile.

When the jury was polled, it became clear that there had been confusion in the jury room. The eldest member, a seventy-five-year-old man who was hard of hearing, answered no when asked if this were his verdict, then changed his mind after the question was read to him again. "I didn't hear," he said. Another male member of the jury raised his hand when his turn came. "I've got a question," he said. "Does it have to be unanimous either way?" After an explanation from the judge, he, too, agreed that this had been his verdict.

Barbara was instructed to rise.

"Anything else that you'd like to say?" the judge asked.

She shook her head, and he quickly sentenced her to prison "for the term of her natural life."

"She'll be in the custody of the sheriff," the judge intoned, and the bailiffs quickly ushered her from the courtroom, she turning and waving with a smile to her family and friends as she left.

The judge thanked the jurors and dismissed them, then adjourned court.

As the jurors were leaving the jury box, two women stopped and bent over to say something to Doris Stager, who sat in the front row in stunned disbelief, but they hurried away when she flared at them and was restrained by her daughter. One juror walked past the Fords and Doris Stager without acknowledgment and went to the other side of the courtroom, where she embraced the Terrys, who quickly had formed a congratulatory circle around Barbara's attorneys.

Reporters chased after the jurors to find out what had happened.

"I think they had a pretty strong case," the foreman told one reporter. "It simply didn't warrant the death penalty."

Others said that the jury had been split eight for death, four against. One juror, another said, had announced soon after entering the room that she was opposed to the death penalty and never would vote for it, although she had told the prosecutors under oath that she could choose death if the circumstances warranted it. The eight had finally gone over to the side of the four, this juror said, because everybody was tired and wanted to go home.

"I think she killed them both," a female juror told another reporter. "She'll get off in twenty years and she'll get her another one and pop him off."

Actually, Barbara could become eligible for parole in only twelve years, and that disgusted the sole black male on the jury, DeVaughn Jordan. "I feel as if this lady should never get no kind of parole, nothing," he said. "In all fairness, she should have got the death penalty."

The reason she didn't, he said, was that some jurors, when faced with the reality of it, just couldn't bring themselves to vote for it. "It's like bungee jumping," he said. "You get up there and you just decide that you can't jump."

He shook his head. "Crime's too high. People don't value life. Your life ain't worth five cents out here. But some people don't want to do what it takes to stop it. Killing's just too easy, too easy."

Barbara's family wouldn't respond to reporters' requests for comments, but when the reporters clustered around Doris Stager, she said, "Okay, I've got a statement, just one." Her voice rose as she spoke until she was fairly shouting. "I have learned to live with the fact that Barbara Stager blew my son's brains out with a gun while he slept in his own bed. If I can learn to live with that, I guess I can learn to live with the fact that she is in prison. The first time she gets a chance for parole, she'll put on another act." She paused, her anger surging, thrust a finger in the air and shouted loud enough to be certain that the Terrys could hear her. "Correction, cold-bloodedly shot my son's brains out!"

"I want to add," said Cindy, "that an opportunity was not given to my brother to live a minute past February first, 1988, but a great opportunity has been given to allow Barbara to continue living. How can justice be served?"

Then she put her arm around her mother and started to lead her away. "I'm sorry," she told the reporters, "she's already gone through enough pain." Rick Buchanan hurried to take Doris's arm and escort her through a side door to drive her home.

While the reporters had been gathered around Doris, the Terrys and their friends had hurried from the courtroom. As Doris and Henry Ford were leaving behind them, a reporter stopped them.

"In a sense, I am disappointed, but I still know God makes no mistakes," Doris said. "Maybe in time we'll understand."

To a friend she said, "How can I be so sad when God knows why He's allowed this? I'm not going to be bitter and sad."

Soon the courtroom was empty except for a small group of reporters comparing notes. Suddenly, a rear door burst open and a jubilant Arthur Vann came striding back into the courtroom as if he had forgotten something.

"I want you to put this in the paper," he told the reporters. "Mr. Vann said, quote, 'This is a righteous verdict.'"

"Is that the King's English, Mr. Vann?" one reporter asked.

"That's the King's English."

# Epilogue

On the day that Barbara's lawyers had begun presenting her case during the resentencing hearing, Doris and Henry Ford had returned to the courtroom early after lunch, and there, sitting all alone, was Bryan, their first grandson, who had been gone from them for more than fifteen years now. He was just five years younger than his father had been when he was killed, and he was the very picture of Larry. He was so much of their blood, yet so alien to them; so physically close, yet so far away. He looked so forlorn and lonely that they both burst into tears.

"It hurts," Henry said. "It hurts."

The Fords knew that Barbara had poisoned Bryan and Jason against them, but for years they had held out hope that their grandsons might want to find out the truth for themselves someday. They were convinced that Barbara held her sons in a psychological bond as tightly as her own mother had held her, yet they had no idea how to break through that. Bryan in particular had to have questions about all that had happened, they thought, and they hoped that someday he might find the strength to raise them and confront the truth at last. Only by doing that, they were convinced, could he and Jason ever break the bonds of the lies that skewed their visions of life. Only by doing that could they face the future with any realistic hope. Only by doing that could they restore their heritage and accept the love that their grandparents ached to give them.

On the following day, the Fords arrived at the courthouse and saw Bryan sitting on a bench in the hallway amid a group of Barbara's family and friends, all soon to be witnesses in her behalf. Doris couldn't resist her instincts. She walked straight up to her grandson and hugged him, feeling the rigidness of the tension in his body. "Bryan," she said, "we love you."

He continued to sit stiffly erect, saying nothing, and did not return her embrace. "But he didn't push me away," Doris said later, clinging to any sign of hope.

Barbara avoided looking at the Fords during her hearing, but they had no problem facing her. They had forgiven her, but they doubted that she ever could forgive herself. That, they knew, would require her to acknowledge that she was indeed a murderer twice over. That would cost her the faith of her sons and make them her victims, too. It might also cost her all else that she had left: the undying loyalty of the family and friends who trusted so fervently in her innocence and avowed Christianity. Yet failing to face her sins, the Fords believed, would be at the price of her soul.

"You cannot serve two masters," Doris said.

The Fords did not doubt the good in Barbara. They had become convinced that there were two Barbaras, one good, the other bad, and the good Barbara simply could not acknowledge the other. They thought that her mother was at the root of her problems, but whatever their source, the problems and their mysteries clearly were tightly entwined with religion. Every time the bad Barbara did something wrong, the good Barbara always sought sanctuary in church, the Bible and prayer. Deep within her subconscious, the Fords thought, the good side of Barbara wanted the bad side to pay for what she had done. Her guilt over Larry's murder had pushed her to kill Russ in the same way, leaving a trail of evidence that was almost certain to assure that she would be caught and punished. Once the bad Barbara had been exposed, though, she had been banished, and only the good Barbara remained, steadfastly proclaiming her innocence.

"To this day I think of her as the little girl that something terrible made her into what she is," Doris Ford had said not long before Barbara's new sentencing hearing. "I don't hate her. I feel a deep sorrow. How can you hate somebody who's got one foot in hell itself?"

* * *

Doris Stager did not see Barbara in such complex terms. To her, Barbara was simply evil. She had chosen wickedness and become a consummate actress and pathological liar to cloak herself in piety so that she could disguise that she truly was an agent of Satan.

"Satan is the ruler of this world, and God has given him that power until Christ comes again," she said. "He tries to get everybody in his group and those he can he does and those he can't he keeps on trying. Satan has power, power, power on this earth."

Only by facing the murders, admitting her sins and truly accepting Christ did Barbara have any hope for salvation, Doris believed, and, like the Fords, she thought that never would happen.

After the sentencing hearing, Doris fell into another deep depression over the realization that in a relatively few years Barbara would be free again, perhaps to find another unwitting husband, some other mother's son.

Although she had filled her house with photos of happy family times (Barbara's image had been carefully snipped from every picture in which she had appeared), her home was not happy any longer, and at times it seemed as dark and icy as a tomb. A month after the resentencing hearing, Doris put the house up for sale. She planned to move to Tennessee to be near her daughter.

One night soon after fall had arrived, she sat at her kitchen table talking about the terrible and lasting impact Barbara had had on the lives of so many people who had been close to her.

"Can you ever forgive her?" she was asked.

Doris paused, deep in thought, and remained silent. The silence stretched on and on, as she stared back in time and into herself. Finally she spoke in a soft voice.

"God really is the only one who can forgive," she said.